Contents

Page

USEFUL INFORMATION **2**
Your guide to hospitals, banks,
tourist information centres and much more.....

DETAILED ROAD MAPS **3-5**

GAZETTEER by Liz Luck **6-25**
In depth focus on 100 towns and villages.
Historical facts, important people and points of interest.

IMAGES OF CORNWALL **26**
Photography by Mark Norton.

SARDINA PILCHARDUS by Nick Howell **27**
The importance of the humble pilchard
in the nineteenth century.

TATE ST. IVES by Mark Norton **28-29**
A look at Cornwall's most important art gallery.

BEACHES **30-49**
A review of 100 Cornish beaches.
Full directions and facilities included.

THE NATIONAL TRUST IN CORNWALL by Liz Luck **50-51**
The crucial work undertaken by the National Trust
to ensure protection of the landscape and
important buildings in Cornwall.

IMAGES OF CORNWALL **52-53**
Photography by W. Hocking/National Trust.

POWERHOUSE HAYLE by Bret Guthrie **54**
How a small village in the west of Cornwall
was at the centre of an industrial revolution.

CORNISH PUBS **55-57**
A selection of friendly pubs from St. Austell Brewery.

WALKING AREAS AND VIEWPOINTS **58-83**
75 of Cornwall's best places to walk.
Detailed maps and directions included.

IMAGES OF CORNWALL **84-85**
Two evocative images from specialist monochrome
photographer Clive Vincent.

CORNISH LIFEBOATS by Sue Denny **86**
A look at the crucial work of the R.N.L.I. in Cornwall.

AIR AMBULANCE! by Richard Taylor **87**
Cornwall's flying emergency service.

ANCIENT CORNWALL by Mark Norton **88**
Chamber tombs, standing stones and stone circles......

CLASSIC CORNISH FISHING VILLAGES by Mark Norton **89**
Ten classic fishing villages to explore.

IT'S FREE! **90-101**
70 things to see and do in Cornwall that won't break the bank!

LITERARY CORNWALL by Liz Luck **102-103**
How Cornwall has inspired authors and writers over the years.

CORNISH ENGINE HOUSES by Mark Norton **104-105**
Those evocative mine buildings and their place in Cornish history.

A DIRECTOR'S PARADISE by Sue Craig **106-107**
How the Cornish landscape has captivated film and TV directors.

IMAGES OF CORNWALL **108-109**
Photography by W Hocking/National Trust and Tim Guthrie.

CYCLING **110**
Where to get some two wheeled exercise....

ATTRACTIONS **111-135**
138 quality attractions. Theme parks to museums, historic houses and
gardens to steam railways. Includes opening hours and directions.

LEISURE CENTRES **136**
Where to swim, play badminton and squash....

COARSE FISHING **137**
Where to cast that line....

GOLF IN CORNWALL **138-139**
32 golf courses with directions and yardage details.

RIDING IN CORNWALL **140**
Detailed stable list and contact numbers.

OPINION PAGE AND FREE DRAW **141**
Help us to improve and receive an exclusive car sticker
(not available elsewhere!). All replies entered for our free draw.

CLASSIC WALKS: CORNWALL **142**
How to order Cornwall's most popular walks book.

INDEX **143-144**

Dairyland. Page 125.

Coronation Boating Lake and Gardens. Page 93.

Charlestown. Page 9.

Publishers:
Norton Publishing Limited, PO Box 12, Perranporth,
Cornwall. TR6 0YE. (07000) 782688

Designers:
Design and Print (01736) 753638

Printers:
Millenium Web Offset plc (01326) 376666

Distribution in Cornwall:
SEYMAC (01209) 313212

USEFUL INFORMATION

SUPERSTORES

ASDA
Cromwell Road, St Austell (01726) 66616

Co Op LEO'S
Ponshardon, Falmouth (01326) 319976
Copper Terrace, Hayle (01736) 756832
Newport Ind Est, Launceston (01566) 776350
Oakley Terrace, Newquay (01637) 874321
Moorland Road, St Austell (01726) 65601

Daniel's
Fore Street, Hayle (01736) 753174

Safeway
Priory Road, Bodmin (01208) 78763
Stuckley Road, Bude (01288) 355546
Plymouth Road, Liskeard (01579) 340873
Treloggan Road, Newquay (01637) 851328
Long Rock, Penzance (01736) 351231
Illogan Highway, Pool,
Redruth (01209) 212121

Sainsbury
Station Road, Truro (01872) 260881

Somerfield
Dennison Road, Bodmin (01208) 78297
Fore Street, Newquay (01637) 876006
Tamar View Ind Est, Saltash (01752) 848874
West Hill, Wadebridge (01208) 815587

Tesco
Wesley Street, Camborne (01209) 711272
Clodgey Lane, Helston (01326) 573834
Hurdon Road, Launceston (01566) 776947
Garras Wharf, Truro (01872) 75222

BANKS

Given the changing nature of the banking industry, it may be advisable to ring first to be certain of the branch's opening arrangements.

Barclays
Bodmin (01208) 77022
Bude (01288) 353755
Callington (01579) 382205
Camborne (01872) 78341
Camelford (01726) 72444
Carbis Bay (01736) 796270
East Looe (01503) 263827
Falmouth (01872) 78341
Fowey (01726) 72444
Hayle (01736) 362271
Helston (01736) 362271
Launceston (01566) 775116
Liskeard (01579) 342130
Lostwithiel (01208) 872343
Mawnan Smith (01326) 220530
Mullion (01326) 240531
Newquay (01872) 78341
Penzance (01736) 362271
Penryn (01872) 78341
Polperro (01503) 72235
Portscatho (01872) 580337
Redruth *Pool* (01872) 78341
Redruth *Penryn Street* (01872) 78341
Saltash (01572) 843626
St Agnes (01872) 552742
St Austell *Church Street* (01726) 72444
St Austell *Mount Charles* (01726) 72444
St Columb (01726) 72444
St Dennis (01726) 822512
St Ives (01736) 362271

St Mawes (01326) 270453
Tintagel (01840) 770649
Torpoint (01572) 812465
Truro *King Street* (01872) 78341
Truro *Lemon Street* (01872) 78341
Wadebridge (01726) 72444

LLOYDS
Bodmin (01208) 812348
Bude (01288) 353771
Callington (01579) 343409
Camborne (01209) 213601
Camelford (01208) 812348
Carbis Bay (01736) 752125
Falmouth *Church Street* (01326) 212600
Fowey (01726) 73504
Gunnislake (01822) 832061
Hayle (01736) 752125
Helston (01326) 563311
Illogan (01209) 213601
Launceston (01566) 773691
Liskeard (01579) 343409
Looe (01579) 343409
Lostwithiel (01726) 73504
Mawnan Smith (01326) 212600
Mevagissey (01726) 73504
Mullion (01326) 240766
Newlyn (01736) 361484
Newquay *Central Square* (01637) 871323
Newquay *Chester Road* (01637) 871323
Padstow (01208) 812348
Penryn (01326) 212600
Penzance (01736) 361484
Perranporth (01872) 77411
Pool (01209) 213601
Porthleven (01326) 574049
Redruth (01209) 213601
Rock (01208) 812348
Saltash (01752) 266897
St Agnes (01872) 77411
St Austell *High Cross Street* (01726) 67685
St Austell *Mount Charles* (01726) 73504
St Blazey (01726) 73504
St Columb (01637) 871323
St Ives (01736) 752125
St Mawes (01326) 212600
St Mawgan (01637) 874249
St Just (01736) 361484
St Blazey (01726) 73504
Tintagel (01208) 812348
Torpoint (01752) 266897
Truro *Treyew Road* (01872) 77411
Truro *Boscawen Street* (01872) 77411
Wadebridge (01208) 812348

Midland
Bodmin (01208) 72859
Camborne (01209) 719116
Falmouth (01326) 312073
Fowey (01726) 833344
Helston (01326) 573323
Launceston (01566) 772624
Liskeard (01579) 342274
Looe (01503) 263881
Newquay *Bank Street* (01637) 873821
Newquay *Henver Road* (01637) 876679
Padstow (01841) 532315
Penzance (01736) 364277
Polperro (01503) 72440
Redruth (01209) 215434
Saltash (01752) 221471
St Austell (01726) 64491
St Ives (01736) 796168
Truro (01872) 74451

Wadebridge (01208) 814646

NATIONAL WESTMINSTER BANK
Bodmin (01208) 78256
Bude (01288) 354517
Callington (01752) 226226
Camborne (01209) 715522
Camelford (01840) 212323
Falmouth (01326) 212020
Helston (01326) 563464
Launceston (01566) 772473
Liskeard (01752) 226226
Newquay (01637) 875166
Penzance (01736) 365574
Redruth (01209) 215267
Saltash (01752) 226226
St Austell (01726) 75911
St Ives (01736) 797367
Truro (01872) 73559
Wadebridge (01208) 813591

TSB
Bude (01288) 352066
Bodmin (01208) 72595
Camborne (01209) 612422
Falmouth (01326) 212488
Helston (01326) 565131
Launceston (01566) 776565
Penzance (01736) 360633
Redruth (01209) 313548
Saltash (01752) 842789
St Austell (01726) 69696
Truro (01872) 260757
Wadebridge (01208) 812439

TOURIST INFORMATION OFFICES

Bodmin
Shire House, Mount Folly Square.
(01208) 76616

Boscastle Visitor Centre
Cobweb Car Park (01840) 250010

Bude
The Crescent Car Park. (01288) 354240

Camelford*
North Cornwall Museum, The Clease.
(01840) 212954

Falmouth
28 Killigrew Street (01326) 312300

Fowey
The Post Office, 4 Custom House Hill.
(01726) 833616

Hayle*
Lethlean Lane. (01736) 754399

Helston
79 Meneage Street. (01326) 565431

Isles of Scilly
Town Hall, St. Mary's. (01720) 422536

Launceston
Market House Arcade, Market Street.
(01566) 772321

Looe*
The Guildhall, Fore Street, East Looe.
(01503) 262072

Lostwithiel
Lostwithiel Community Centre, Liddicoat Rd.
(01208) 872207

Mevagissey
8 Tregony Hill. (01726) 842266

Newquay
Municipal Buildings, Marcus Hill.
(01637) 871345

Padstow
Red Brick Building, North Quay.
(01841) 533449

Penzance
Station Road. (01736) 362207

Perranporth
The Seiners Arms. (01872) 573368

Polzeath*
Coronation Gardens. (01208) 862488

St. Austell*
By Pass Service Station, Southbourne Road.
(01726) 76333

St. Ives
The Guildhall, Street an Pol. (01736) 796297

Truro
Municipal Buildings, Boscawen Street.
(01872) 74555

Wadebridge*
Town Hall. (01208) 813725
* Denotes Seasonal.

CORNWALL TOURIST BOARD
Daniell Road Centre, Lander Building,
Daniell Road, Truro TR1 2DA (01872) 74057

PUBLIC TRANSPORT

Cornwall Public Transport Timetable
available at £1.60 from: Passenger Transport
Unit, County Hall, Truro, Cornwall TR1 3AY
Western National Bus Services
(01209) 719988
(01208) 79898
Truronian Travel (01872) 73453

CINEMAS

Looe The Cinema, Higher Market Street.
(01503) 262709.
Newquay Camelot Cinema, The Crescent.
(01637) 874222.
Padstow Capitol Cinema, Middle Street.
(01841) 532344.
Penzance Savoy Cinema, Causeway Head.
(01736) 363330.
Redruth Regal Cinema, Fore Street.
(01209) 216278.
St. Austell Film Centre, Chandos Place.
(01726) 73750.
St. Ives Royal Cinema, Chapel Street.
(01736) 796843.
Truro Plaza Cinema, Lemon Street.
(01872) 72894.
Wadebridge Regal Cinema, The Platt.
(01208) 812791.

RADIO FREQUENCIES

BBC Radio Cornwall
Mid & West Cornwall 103.9
North & East Cornwall 95.2
Isles of Scilly 96.0
Pirate FM
East Cornwall 102.2
West Cornwall 102.8

HOSPITALS

Casualty services available at
Treliske Hospital Truro. (Well signed)
West Cornwall Hospital Penzance
(Well signed)
If in north Cornwall, it would probably be more convenient to head for
North Devon District Hospital Barnstaple.

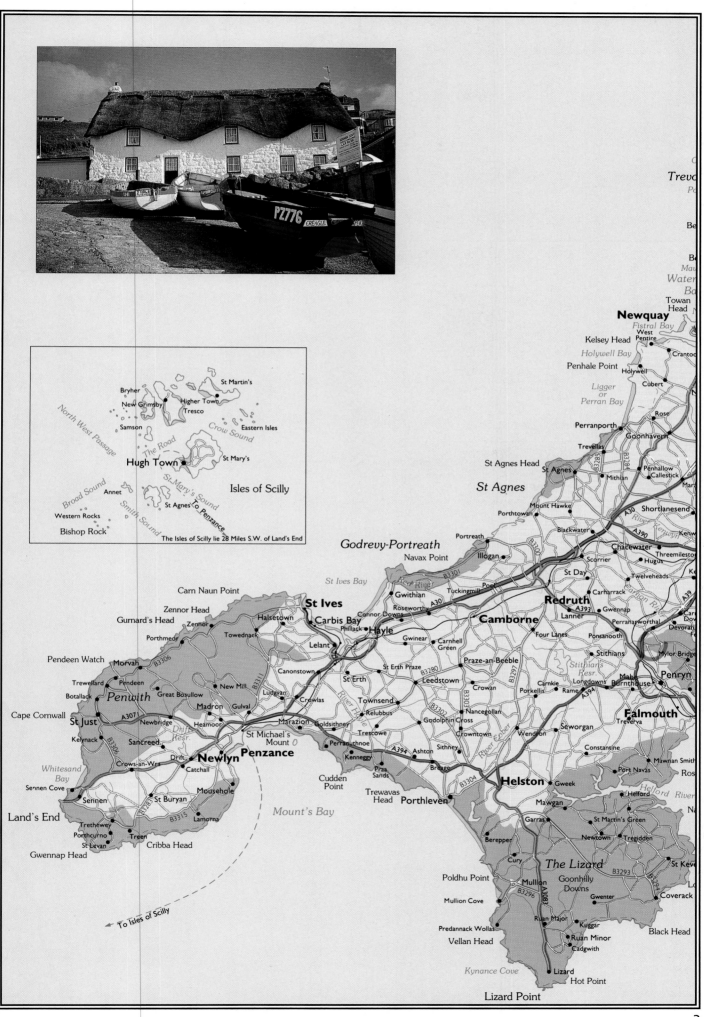

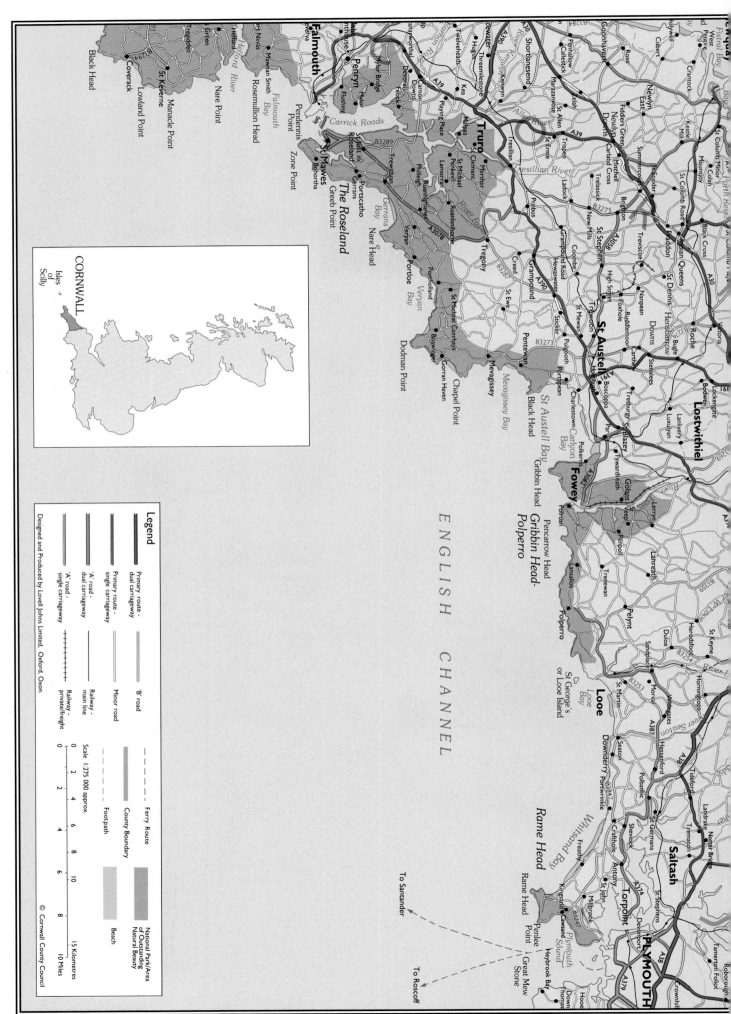

ENGLISH CHANNEL

Falmouth

Pendennis Point
Zone Point

Black Head

Lowland Point

Manacle Point
St Keverne
Coverack

Nare Point

Helford River

Rosemullion Head

Mawnan Smith
Bay
Falmouth Bay

Black Head

Trefusis Green
Trefusis
Flushing

Penryn

Mylor
Mylor Bridge
Restronguet
Feock
Devoran

Carrick Roads

St Mawes
Bohortha
Greeb Point

St Just in Roseland
Portscatho
Gerrans
The Roseland
Gerrans Bay
Nare Head

Trewithian
Philleigh
Ruanlanihorne
Ruanhighlanes
Veryan
Portloe
Veryan Bay
Portholland
St Michael Caerhays
Boswinger
Gorran Haven
Chapel Point
Dodman Point

Mevagissey
Mevagissey Bay
Black Head

St Austell Bay
Gribbin Head
Gribbin Head-Polperro

Pencarrow Head

Fowey
Golant
Lerryn
Penpoll

Lanreath
Lansallos
Trelawne
Polperro

Pelynt

St George's or Looe Island
Looe Bay
Looe

Rame Head
Rame Head

To Santander
To Roscoff

Truro
St Clement
Merther
St Michael Penkevil
Lamorran

Kea
Malpas
Playing Place

St Austell

Lostwithiel

Saltash

PLYMOUTH

Torpoint

CORNWALL
Isles of Scilly

Legend

Primary route - dual carriageway

Primary route - single carriageway

'A' road - dual carriageway

'A' road - single carriageway

'B' road

Minor road

Railway - main line

Railway - private/freight

Ferry Route

County Boundary

Footpath

National Park/Area of Outstanding Natural Beauty

Beach

Scale 1:275 000 approx.

0 2 4 6 8 10 15 Kilometres

0 2 4 6 8 10 Miles

Designed and Produced by Lovell Johns Limited, Oxford, Oxon.

© Cornwall County Council

4

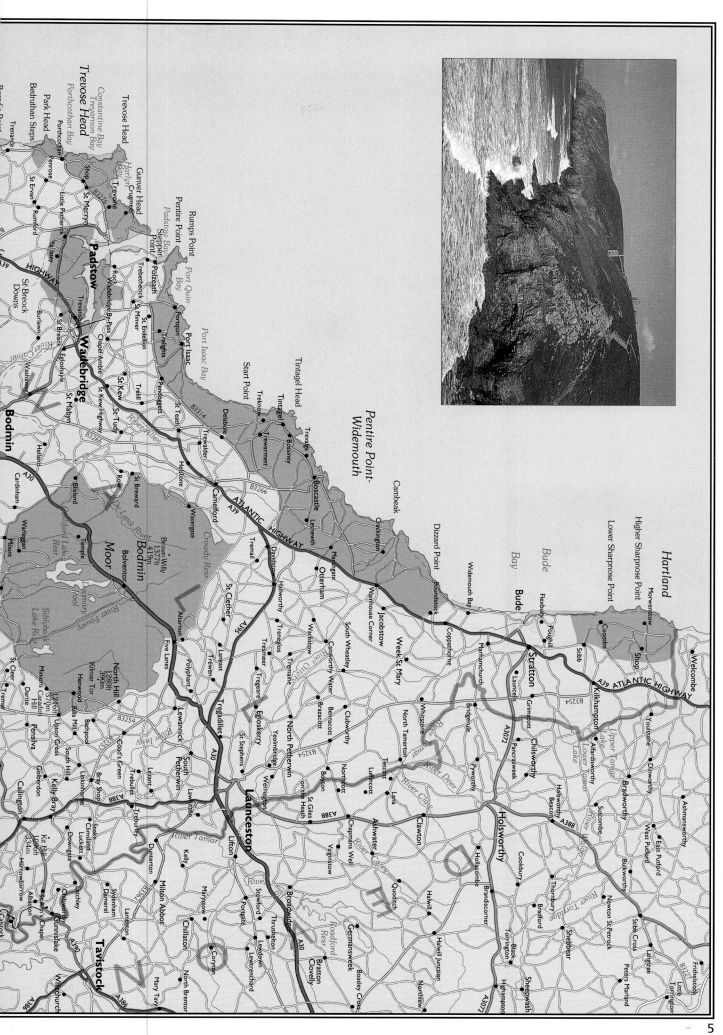

Gazetteer

Liz Luck works for the National Trust and has written a number of books, leaflets and articles on Cornish subjects, including *South Cornish Harbours* (Fowey Rare Books 1995, first pub. 1988). She was born in Golant, read history at Pembroke College, Oxford, and lives in Tregrehan, near Par, with her son Bevil.

Altarnun

Sheltering in a wooded cleft just below the windswept heights of Bodmin Moor, Altarnun is a lovely village with a fine fifteenth-century church dedicated to St Nonna. Sometimes known as the Cathedral of the Moors, the church has one of the tallest towers in Cornwall. Inside there are some splendid sixteenth-century bench ends by the carver Robert Daye, including one of a man playing the bagpipes.

The old bridge below the church, with a roadway just 7ft wide, is probably fifteenth-century; beside it is a much older ford across the lesser Inney. The great Cornish historian Charles Henderson believed that '*no prettier picture can be found in Cornwall than Altarnun Bridge with the tall grey church and swelling churchyard behind it.*'.

Look out for the early Wesleyan meeting house with a relief portrait of John Wesley carved over the doorway by the gifted local sculptor Neville Northey Burnard (who was born in the adjoining house, went on to become celebrated throughout the country but died penniless in Redruth Workhouse in 1878).

Altarnun. Cornwall Tourist Board.

Blisland

A village green in Cornwall is a rare bird indeed, and here at Blisland – riding high on the western edge of Bodmin Moor – is the finest of the few that exist. Dotted with tall trees and fringed with granite cottages (and, as you would expect, the village pub – the Royal Oak), it gives the place a spacious and timeless air.

Below its southern slope is the church of St Protus and St. Hyacinth, a particular favourite of John Betjeman. It was, he wrote in 1948, '*the first really beautiful work of man which my boyhood vividly remembers... it looks over the tree tops of a deep and elmy valley and away to the west where, like a silver shield, the Atlantic shines...*'.

A mile to the north, near the hamlet of Pendrift, stands Jubilee Rock. Having dined at Pendrift in October of 1810, a certain Lieutenant John Rogers and his recruiting party of the 65th Regiment carved Britannia and the royal and other arms, including those of the Rogers family of Blisland, upon this moorland rock in celebration of the Golden Jubilee of George lll.

Bodmin

Cornwall's old county town, finally eclipsed only in this century by Truro, is strewn with grand buildings, some of them now ruinous, which tell of its important past. Bodmin's history began in the sixth century when Cornwall's chief patron saint, St Petroc, arrived here from Padstow and founded his famous priory. By the time of Domesday Book in 1086 a town had grown up around the priory, the only one in the county recorded as having a market.

Nothing remains today of the priory, but the fifteenth-century church which probably occupies the same site is the largest in Cornwall. In the churchyard are the ruins of the earlier Chantry Chapel of St Thomas Becket.

The Assizes have been moved to the County Court in Truro, but the splendid neoclassical granite court building still dominates Mount Folly at the lower end of the town.

The mid-Victorian prison – Bodmin Jail – is now a dramatic semi-ruin, although parts of it are open to the public.

High on Bodmin Beacon, dominating the scene for miles around, is the 144ft Gilbert monument, erected as a tribute to a famous son of Bodmin – Sir Walter Raleigh Gilbert – who was a general in the British army in India.

Bodmin Moor

The 100 square miles of Bodmin Moor, designated an Area of Outstanding Natural Beauty, is perhaps the last remaining piece of Cornwall (of any significant size) that is truly remote. The main route west – now the A30 – goes right over this great granite upland as it has done since man first came to this peninsula, but this only serves to speed travellers on their way and to accentuate the wilderness.

During the Bronze Age (2500-600BC) Bodmin Moor was densely populated and there are numerous remains to be seen of prehistoric farms as well as ritual and burial sites, including stone circles, standing stones, barrows and cairns.

Until 1813 and what seems to have been a mistake or a blatant invention by the Ordnance Survey, it was known as Fowey Moor: moorland of the River Fowey, which rises in it (compare Exmoor and Dartmoor, both named in the same way). The source of the Fowey is near Brown Willy which, at 1,377ft is Cornwall's highest point. Roughtor, nearby, is slightly lower (1,300ft) but more dramatically rocky – a good road from Camelford and a car park also mean that it is more accessible.

There are two large reservoirs on the moor – Colliford and Siblyback – and one small natural lake called Dozmary Pool. Due to its ancient reputation for being bottomless (having ridden through it on a horse as a child, I can attest that it is quite shallow – but the rumours persist that it has bottomless holes within it...), it became associated with the Arthurian legend as the final resting place of Excalibur. Nearby at Bolventor is Jamaica Inn, made famous by Daphne du Maurier's novel of smuggling and skulduggery.

Boscastle. Andrew Besley/National Trust.

Boscastle

Boscastle harbour, despite being a narrow and tortuous inlet, is one of the few natural harbours for refuge and trade to be found along Cornwall's forbidding north coast, and as such it has had a long and busy history. Until the 1890s there was a regular import trade in coal, limestone, ironwork and general merchandise, with 200 ships calling in one year and cargoes of timber coming directly to Boscastle from Canada. Local slate, china clay and oats were the main exports. Today the National Trust owns the harbour and much of the dramatic coastline to either side; it remains one of Cornwall's most fascinating and picturesque places. Look out for the famous blowhole, known as the Devil's Bellows, below Penally Point - it is active for about an hour on either side of low water.

The village which struggles up the hill behind the harbour is still, as Betjeman described it in the 1960s, '*neither artified nor self-conscious*'; it has a real community, some genuinely unspoilt old buildings and splendid pubs – a rare combination.

Two miles up the wooded Valency Valley is the church of St Juliot which Thomas Hardy came to restore in 1870; here he met Emma Gifford, his future wife. Boscastle and its environs feature largely in his novel *A Pair of Blue Eyes* and in several poems.

Gazetteer

Botallack

Half a mile west of the old mining hamlet of Botallack is one of Cornwall's most famous mines. The two Crowns engine houses of Botallack Mine, restored in 1985 by the Carn Brea Mining Society, are perched precariously on rocky ledges just feet above high water mark; miners who worked the deep levels which ran out under the sea could hear the sound of waves pounding the cliffs and boulders grinding on the sea-bed far above their heads. Wilkie Collins included a hair-raising description of his descent of Botallack in 1850 in his *Rambles Beyond Railways*. Most work had ceased here by 1895 due to low tin prices.

South of the Crowns engine houses, this extraordinary old mining landscape continues around Kenidjack Head to Cape Cornwall. The imposing engine houses of West Wheal Owles and Wheal Edward, which were on the point of collapse, have recently been repaired by the National Trust. In 1893, this section of West Wheal Owles mine was the scene of one of Cornwall's worst mining disasters: nineteen men and a boy were drowned when the old flooded workings of neighbouring Wheal Drea were holed. Their bodies were never recovered.

Crowns Engine Houses. MDN.

Breage

Pronounced to rhyme with 'Haig', and sometimes to rhyme with 'league' the village of Breage is renowned above all for the mediaeval wall paintings in its sturdy granite church. Soon after its completion in 1466, the church's limewashed walls and window splays were painted with a series of figures, including St Christopher and Christ of the Trades, which today loom vaguely at you out of the gloom in softly dappled colours. They are thought to be the work of monks who travelled the country decorating churches in this way as a form of religious education. Somehow they have survived being painted over countless times since the Reformation, the final coat of emulsion having been applied as late as 1950. Tregonning Hill, nearby, was where William Cookworthy discovered china clay in the mid-1740s. However, the deposits here were very limited, compared to those he subsequently found further east, and workings never developed beyond the small-scale.

Bude. MDN

Bude

Isolated from the rest of Cornwall, and indeed from everywhere else, Bude developed in the last century as an agricultural trading port, serving the large, remote, rural area around it, and, in late-Victorian and Edwardian times, as a genteel holiday resort. The infant port was linked to the inland farming communities by the 35 miles of the Bude Canal, built between 1819 and 1826. One of the unusual aspects of the canal is that incline planes, instead of locks, linked the different levels and the barges – fitted with wheels – were hauled up on rails, powered by counterbalancing water-filled buckets in deep shafts. The incline from Helebridge up to Marhamchurch rises nearly 100ft. The original intention of the canal builders was to create a navigable link with the upper Tamar, so joining the English and Bristol Channels (and making Cornwall an island), but it never made it that far and once the railway arrived in this area the canal was largely abandoned. Only a mile or so now survives (a walk along this section is described on p.82), but much of its route further inland can still be traced.

Today Bude is a popular family resort and surfing centre, famed for its beaches. The Bude Surf Life Saving Club, formed in 1953, was the first of its kind in the country. Sir Goldsworthy Gurney, inventor of the earliest steam road-locomotive amongst other extraordinary things, built the small castle by the canal entrance which is now council offices.

Cadgwith

One of Cornwall's loveliest villages, Cadgwith is crammed with cottages built of rough lumps of serpentine – the gloriously variegated local stone – and roofed in thatch. Such a concentration of thatched roofs is a rarity in this county where slate has been in general use for so long, but down here on the Lizard we are a long way from ready supplies of good slate. Look out for the chains which are used to hold down the eaves of some of the roofs

Cadgwith has a long history of pilchard fishing, crabbing and smuggling, and a lifeboat was stationed here until 1961. The bright-painted boats on the beach, the wires, chains, blocks and winches and the tell-tale smell of fish about the place are reminders that there is still a small fishery here, catching mostly crabs and lobsters.

Just to the south is the awesome Devil's Frying Pan, a 200ft deep hole in the cliffs formed long ago by the collapse of a sea cave. A mile to the north is rocky Carleon Cove with the substantial ruins of an old serpentine factory.

Callington

This small market town, which once stood at the gateway to one of the richest copper mining districts in the world and an area of intense industrial activity in the second half of the last century, is much quieter today although there is an air of growth about it. Behind the town, and dominating the scene for miles around, is the mighty swell of Kit Hill – a wonderful 1000ft hill crowned by an 80ft-high stack built in 1858 for the winding and stamping engine of Kithill Consols mine. Rumour has it that every known mineral in the world may be found on, or under, Kit Hill. Prince Charles, the Duke of Cornwall, gave the hill to the county in 1985 and it is now a country park.

Dupath holy well, a mile from the town, is enclosed in a fine granite building of 1510. The water in the basin was believed to cure whooping cough.

Cadgwith. MDN

Calstock

An important river port since Saxon times, the village of Calstock with its tall white houses clings to the steep Cornish bank of the Tamar fourteen miles upriver from Plymouth Sound. The scene is dominated by the splendid viaduct of 1908 which carries the branch line from Plymouth to Gunnislake. Calstock's zenith as a port came in the last century when it served an area of intense industrial and mining activity, of which many remains still exist, and a rural parish renowned for its cultivation of fruit and flowers.

A mile downriver by footpath lies the enchanting mediaeval house and estate of Cotehele, owned by the National Trust since 1947, together with its river quay, watermill, estate workshops and glorious woodland walks.

South Crofty. Tim Guthrie.

Camelford

This small, attractive town on the north-western edge of Bodmin Moor takes its name from the River Camel (probably 'crooked one' in Cornish). Thanks to the proximity of Tintagel (and to the unfortunate identification of Camelford with Camelot), spurious Arthurian associations abound in the area, particularly at nearby Slaughterbridge which is said to be the site of Arthur's last battle. Tennyson came here twice to visit the seventh-century inscribed stone which was incorrectly believed to refer to King Arthur.

There is a good museum and art gallery in Camelford, and Roughtor, Cornwall's second highest peak, is just a couple of miles away at the end of a rather thrilling roller-coaster of a road. Down by the ford beyond the car park you will find the stark and lonely memorial to Charlotte Dymond, murdered here by her lover in 1844.

Trevithick Statue, Camborne. David Hastilow/Kerrier Tourism Office.

of metalliferous mining in the country, which includes a fine geological museum. South Crofty, between Pool and Tuckingmill, is the last working tin mine in Cornwall.

Camborne is particularly associated with a number of great engineers and inventors who helped to transform the industry and economy of the county and made Cornish mining engineering famous throughout the world. Richard Trevithick, responsible for the high pressure boiler and the first true Cornish beam engine amongst many other things, was born here in 1771. There is a fine statue of him outside the public library, the cottage in nearby Penponds in which he spent his early years is owned by the National Trust, and his birthday on April 26th is celebrated in fine style every year as Trevithick Day.

Cape Cornwall

This dramatic headland, crowned by a handsome stack, is the only one in the country to be known as a cape (i.e. a promontory that marks the meeting-place of two oceans or channels). As far as mediaeval navigators were concerned, this was the true Land's End, the most westerly point of Britain and the point where the English Channel met St. George's Channel. Although it is now known that the two channels actually divide at Gwennap Head (known as the Fisherman's Land's End) eight miles to the south, Cape Cornwall keeps its proud appellation nonetheless and is still, to many Cornish people, the true Land's End.

The Cape was bought for the nation by H.J. Heinz Ltd. in 1987 and given to the National Trust. It now forms the central point in a four-mile stretch of magnificent Trust-owned coastline, rich in archaeological and mining remains.

Camborne

Camborne was just a village until transformed by the mining boom which began in the late eighteenth century and saw the Camborne and Redruth district become the richest mining area in the world. Although a considerable number of ruinous stacks and engine houses remain, they cannot begin to convey the scenes of 150 years ago when scores of mines transfigured the landscape. Most famous of these was Dolcoath ('old ground' in Cornish) which was known as the Queen of Cornish Mines. Dolcoath was the deepest (550 fathoms – 3,300ft), most productive (first in copper and then tin) and longest lived of all the mines in the county. Today there is little to be seen, but enthusiasts can still visit the site of Dolcoath and identify the few remains with the help of *Exploring Cornish Mines* by Kenneth Brown and Bob Acton (Landfall Publications, 1994).

Two engine houses of the East Pool and Agar Mine are preserved by the National Trust at Pool; nearby is the renowned Camborne School of Mines, the only school

Cape Cornwall. Andrew Besley/National Trust.

Cardinham

This small village and its surrounding parish on the southern edge of Bodmin Moor, where steep wooded valleys plunge down from the moorland heights, is unusually rich in relics of the past. The lovely church has two of Cornwall's finest Celtic crosses in the churchyard, one of which is well over 8ft tall and beautifully decorated. Nearby is the privately-owned site of the important early-mediaeval Cardinham Castle; a little further away is a Romano-British inscribed stone.

The Forestry Commission provides a series of forest trails in Cardinham Woods to the south of the village.

Cawsand/ Kingsand

The two villages of Cawsand and Kingsand on the Rame peninsula may seem like one settlement today, but a tiny stream behind the Halfway House Inn was, until the 1840s, the boundary between Devon and Cornwall; further back in history this sliver of water in effect separated Celtic Cornwall from Saxon England.

The deep water of Cawsand Bay was the chief anchorage for ships in Plymouth Sound until the breakwater was built in 1841 and many great expeditions, led by such figures as Gilbert, Drake and Hawkins, gathered here before setting off for distant lands.

Pilchard fishing and smuggling were the main occupations of the villagers until the mid-nineteenth century and there is a string of old pilchard cellars along the water's edge beyond Kingsand.

The Rame peninsula is one of Cornwall's very special corners. This is splendid walking country; the landscape is littered with massive fortresses, mostly dating from the 1860s in response to a perceived threat of invasion from France; Rame Head has an early-mediaeval chapel on its summit; Rame Church is wonderful and Mount Edgcumbe Country Park has miles of footpaths, a deer park and a Grade 1 listed historic garden.

Charlestown

The harbour village of Charlestown was a Georgian 'new town', a port development planned by local landowner Charles Rashleigh (after whom it was named) and built between 1790 and 1810 for the export of copper and china clay. Throughout the nineteenth century the little dock was packed with ships and the harbourside sheds and warehouses thronged with complementary businesses: boatbuilding, ropemaking, brickworks, lime burning, net houses, bark houses and pilchard curing.

Today there are two remarkable things about Charlestown. One is that, against all the odds, it has survived as a working port and a small amount of china clay is still exported in an average of 30-40 ships a year, and this saves the place from becoming a cosy caricature of itself with plenty of 'heritage appeal' but no real life. The second is that – again, against all the odds – it has largely escaped 'development' and remains one of the finest and most fascinating places on the Cornish coast. Perhaps the words 'so far' should be added to these two observations, for who knows what will happen to Charlestown in the future? At the time of writing, the harbour is the home port for a famous collection of old ships which are employed in film projects all over the world – they have brought work and life to the quays and harbour buildings and are a particular draw for visitors.

Coverack

This lovely village on the east coast of the Lizard, with its tiny harbour wall of 1724 made from local hornblende and serpentine, seems a peaceful and sheltered place on a sunny summer's afternoon – but the photographs in the bar of the Paris Hotel show just how devastating a storm here can be. The hotel is named after an American passenger liner which ran aground off Lowland Point in 1899. There was no loss of life on that occasion, but only a year before that the steamship *Mohegan* was wrecked on the dreaded Manacle Rocks beyond Lowland Point and 106 people were

Charlestown. MDN.

drowned. Soon after that a lifeboat was stationed at Coverack (and the stout lifeboat house built just by the harbour) because, as was said at the time, '*the fishermen at this village are familiar with the Manacles and the boat could be launched in all waters*'.

Crackington Haven

Sheer cliffs tower above the beach at Crackington; this is a remote coastline of dramatic scenery and extraordinary geology, with the horizontally-layered strata bent and contorted by ancient earth movements. Coastal vessels used to run up on the beach here to land limestone and coal and load slate from the local quarries – a hazardous undertaking in any weather on this exposed coast but the one to which the hamlet of Crackington Haven owes its existence.

A mile to the south High Cliff rears up above Strangles Beach – at 731ft it is the tallest cliff in Cornwall. Just inland is the lovely old farmhouse of Trevigue, owned by the National Trust, which has a shop, café and information centre open during the summer season.

Crantock

Separated from Newquay by the heavily silted-up estuary of the Gannel, the ancient churchtown of Crantock has been swollen by postwar suburban housing. The church of St Carantocus is unusual and, in the view of Sir John Betjeman, one of the most attractive in Cornwall.

Crantock Beach, which occupies much of the old mouth of the estuary, is a broad expanse of sand; a cave in the deep cleft of Piper's Hole on the south side of the beach contains carvings of a woman and a horse with some lines of verse, the work of a local man called Joseph Prater in the early 1900s. West of the village is the enchanting beach of Polly Joke, sheltering between the headlands of Pentire Point West and Kelsey Head. The grazed cliffs here provide glorious carpets of wild flowers in the spring and early summer.

Coverack. MDN.

Delabole

Within the place-name of Delabole is evidence that the great slate quarry for which the village is famed is over 700 years old. The Cornish word *poll*, meaning 'pit', was attached to the name Deli as early as 1284. Delabole slate is the best in Cornwall and its quality as a roofing material is easily distinguishable by the untrained eye from the cheaper Spanish alternative, let alone from the artificial asbestos 'slate' that has become so prevalent in recent years.

The quarry itself is over 500ft deep with a circumference of 1.5 miles; although still very much a working concern, there is a viewing platform for the public and a showroom selling gifts.

Nearby, at Deli Farm, is Britain's first commercial wind farm which has a visitor centre on site.

Devoran

Devoran had a short but glorious career as one of Cornwall's busiest ports, thanks to the Redruth and Chasewater Railway which linked its docks and quays on Restronguet Creek to the greatest copper mining district in the county, around St. Day and Gwennap. Ironically, the same mines which brought such riches also helped to cause the heavy silting of the Carnon river, which drains the mining area, and Restronguet Creek into which it flows.

Today Devoran is a pleasant village, but down on the water's edge there are still plenty of reminders to be seen – wharves, ore bins, massive granite bollards – of its origins as a substantial riverside port.

Duloe

The name Duloe means 'two pools' or, more specifically in this instance, 'two Looes', the parish being situated on high ground between the East Looe and West Looe rivers. The village is noted for its stone circle of eight large quartz stones, one of which has fallen; it is the smallest of Cornwall's stone

circles which date from the late Neolithic and early Bronze Age (c.2500-1400 BC). The parish church has a massively-built thirteenth-century tower topped by a Victorian pyramidal roof and, inside, the splendid carved tomb of Sir John Colshull (who, in 1450, was the second richest man in Cornwall).

Falmouth

Falmouth Harbour and Carrick Roads form one of the finest natural havens in the world, and the third largest after Sydney and Rio. The estuary with all its many creeks covers a total shoreline of nearly 70 miles. Falmouth is a mecca for boat-lovers of all kinds, and even the most steadfast inland soul could not fail to enjoy a trip upriver or down to the Helford in a sturdy river cruiser.

Until the late sixteenth century, Falmouth was little more than a fishing hamlet known as Smithick or Pennycomequick. Penryn and Truro were the main ports on the estuary because, being further inland, they were more easily defended against seaborne attacks from the Spanish and French. The development of Falmouth was orchestrated by the Killigrew family, and its success ensured by being chosen, in 1688, as a packet station for the Post Office. For 160 years, Falmouth's packet ships delivered mail to Spain, Portugal, the West Indies, North America and Brazil. Ancillary trades attracted by the packet business, particularly ship repair, enabled the port to survive and grow after it lost the contract in 1851. Falmouth Docks, founded in 1860, today handle ships of up to 90,000 tonnes and have a worldwide reputation for yacht building. Castle Drive, which leads up to the sixteenth-century Pendennis Castle, forms a gallery above the docks providing a fascinating view; John Betjeman called it '*one of the most beautiful scenic roads in Britain*'.

The town has plenty of pubs and restaurants, with beaches and hotels to the south on Falmouth Bay. The maritime

museum, housed next door to the old packet office, is well worth a visit. Public access from the main street to the waterfront, with its glorious views, is not all that it could be, but there is a real sense of fun and vitality about the place and it is not hard to see why it is such a popular holiday resort.

Look out for the fleet of Falmouth working boats, lovely gaff cutters which race regularly throughout the year. A working core of these boats still dredges the oyster beds in the northern part of Carrick Roads and is the last working sailing fleet in Western Europe.

Flushing

Facing Falmouth across the Penryn River, Flushing is a handsome village and still almost entirely unspoilt. In the seventeenth century, local landowner Francis Trefusis transformed the hamlet of Nankersey into the flourishing little town of Flushing with the help of engineers from Flessinghe in Holland (hence the name) who supervised the draining of low-lying marshland and the building of the fine dry-stone sea walls and quays.

With the coming of the packet service to Falmouth, Flushing became the chosen home of packet captains and naval officers; a place of high fashion and gentility where, we are told by James Silk Buckingham who was born here in 1786, ' *dinners, balls and evening parties were held at some one or other of the Captain's houses every evening...*'.

Fowey

The mouth of the Fowey River, with the town of Fowey on one side of the deep-water estuary and the village of Polruan on the other, is breathtakingly beautiful. Even the modern developments on the skyline above old Polruan cannot mar the glory of the scene. Fowey was one of the foremost ports of mediaeval England, famed for its piratical seamen and its shipbuilding, and it is still a busy harbour today. Yachts and dinghies crowd the estuary in the summer and from the docks, which lie upriver, over one million tonnes of china clay are exported each year making Fowey the eleventh busiest port in the country. To see something of the beauty of the river, it is well worth taking a boat trip on the high tide from Town Quay up past the docks to Golant, or beyond as far as Lerryn. The castle on St. Catherine's Point at the harbour mouth was built between 1538 and 1542 as part of a chain of castles along the south coast of England commissioned by Henry VlII to protect his most valued ports. The blockhouse on the Polruan side is older, late 15th century, and built as one of a pair with a chain being slung between them during times of threat. The Fowey blockhouse is in a much more ruinous state, but still just discernible.

Fowey was the home town of Daphne du Maurier – she lived first at Ferryside in Bodinnick on the other side of the river (here she wrote her first novel *The Loving Spirit*), then at Menabilly a mile or so to the west – and of Sir Arthur Quiller-Couch,

Gyllyngvase Gardens, Falmouth. MDN.

known as 'Q', a great Cornishman and scholar whose memorial overlooks the harbour on Penleath Point between the main river and the creek called Pont Pill. Should you find your way to this monument by foot, across the Bodinnick ferry and up the hill, taking the footpath on the right signed to Polruan, you will have discovered perhaps the greatest historic walk in Cornwall. The first section of path, from Bodinnick to Penleath Point, is known as Hall Walk and was described in detail as early as 1585. King Charles l narrowly escaped being shot whilst walking here in 1644. Thereafter, the path which continues via the head of Pont Pill to Polruan may not have such a grand history but provides a glorious circular walk, returning to Fowey on the foot ferry from Polruan.

Looking down Pont Pill to the Fowey Estuary. MDN.

Godrevy. Kerrier Tourism Office.

Virginia Woolf's novel *To the Lighthouse* was partly inspired by her lengthy childhood holidays spent in St. Ives, with the view of Godrevy Lighthouse across the bay: '*For the great plateful of blue water was before her; the hoary lighthouse, distant, austere, in the midst; and on the right, as far as the eye could see, fading and falling, in soft low pleats, the green sand dunes with the wild flowing grasses on them...*'.

Golant

Picturesquely situated on the banks of the Fowey river, the village of Golant was once famed for its cider orchards, remnants of which can still be seen here and there, and today supports two thriving vineyards – how times have changed! There is a popular pub here and a fine walk across the high downs to Bodmin Pill, home of the successful Sawmills recording studio. The old Lostwithiel to Fowey railway runs alongside the river all the way but is now a goods line only, serving the china clay docks at Fowey.

Grampound

Named after the French for 'great bridge', the attractive village of Grampound grew up around an important bridging-point over the Fal. A classic 'rotten borough', Grampound once sent two members to Parliament but this right was extinguished even before the 1832 Reform Bill. The village is home to Croggon's tannery, a fascinating survival of an ancient and once commonplace industry.

Gerrans Bay

Lying between St. Anthony Head to the west and Nare Head to the east, this gentle bay backed by the lush farmland of the Roseland peninsula, provides several good beaches and some excellent walks. Local tradition relates that King Gerent (or Gerrenius) of Cornwall was buried in Carne Beacon, a huge Bronze Age barrow inland from Carne Beach, in about AD590. His body was supposedly carried across Gerrans Bay from Dingerein Castle, an earthwork above Treluggan Cliff, in a golden boat rowed with silver oars which were interred with his body. An excavation of the barrow in 1855 failed to corroborate this story, but a stone burial chest was found to contain ashes and charcoal.

Godrevy

Just off the coast at Godrevy Head, the lighthouse on Godrevy Island was built in 1859 in response to a public outcry over the number of lives lost in ships wrecked on a submerged reef just beyond the island. The Light is no longer manned, but the garden plots of the three keepers who used to live there can still be seen from the mainland.

Tulip fields near Portscatho. MDN.

Gunnislake

Until the construction of the Tamar road bridge at Saltash in 1962, Gunnislake New Bridge, built in the early 16th century, was the lowest bridging-point on the Tamar and one of the main routes of entry into Cornwall. The village which sprawls on the steep valley side owes its development more to the dramatic explosion of industrial and mining activity in the mid-nineteenth century, a period when the Tamar valley became the richest copper-mining centre in Europe. There is much still to be seen here for anyone interested in industrial history and its archaeological remains.

Gunwalloe

One of the more curiously-sited of Cornwall's old churches, the church of St Winwaloe at Gunwalloe is separated from the sea only by the rocky hump of Castle Mound, whilst its detached bell tower is actually dug into the cliff side. It is a precarious position which has frequently, over the centuries, had to be reinforced by the tipping of vast quantities of granite into the gap between the church and Dollar Cove to break the force of the waves. There was a major settlement here between the ninth and eleventh centuries, hence the siting of the church in such a seemingly isolated place. Today there is just church, farm and sandy beach – an idyllic spot, except in a storm. To the north is Halzephron Cliff, scene of many shipwrecks; the name comes from the Cornish *als* and *yfarn*, meaning 'Hell's cliff'. Nearby there is good food to be had at the Halzephron Inn.

Gweek

Lying at the head of the Helford River, nearly six miles inland and thus well-protected from threats of raids and piracy, Gweek was in the perfect position for a port in ancient times. It grew up serving the tin-mining district of 'Kirrier' and later took on the role as the harbour for Helston, once that

Bluebells near Helford. MDN.

old port had been cut off from the sea as Loe Bar began to form across the mouth of the Cober in the 13th century. Despite the silting of the river, there are still plenty of boats here, and busy quays and yards; but today Gweek is perhaps best known for its famous seal sanctuary.

Gwennap

Although once famed for yielding more mineral wealth in tin and copper from its acreage than any other place in the old world (and, at the same time, being the most populous parish in Cornwall), the parish of Gwennap is today better known for Gwennap Pit, a great green amphitheatre formed originally by subsidence but given formal terracing in 1806. Drawn by its natural acoustics and the shelter it gave from high winds, John Wesley, the founder of Methodism, came to preach here eighteen times between 1762 and 1789. It has been estimated that between twenty and thirty thousand people used to crowd into the hollow to hear him speak; it must have been an extraordinary experience. Gwennap Pit is still a powerful place of Methodist pilgrimage and worship today.

Hayle

Named from the Cornish *heyl*, 'estuary', Hayle is one of only very few sheltered estuaries on Cornwall's north coast and, as such, has been a port from the very earliest times. However, the harbour entrance has never been easy and dredging has long been needed to counteract the silting up of the river. The boom time for the harbour and, effectively, the birth of the town came in the first half of the nineteenth century when the name of Hayle became synonymous with mining-related industries such as tin and copper smelting, and the foundries of Copperhouse and, above all, Harvey's. Today there is not much left to be seen of the great Carnsew foundry of Harvey & Co., but for a time it was the most important in Cornwall, employing 1000 men and exporting Cornish beam engines and other mining equipment all over the world – to Australia, South Africa and the Americas.

Helford

'*Helford River, Helford River, Blessed may ye be!*' wrote Q (Sir Arthur Quiller-Couch), and it seems today as though it has indeed been blessed. Despite (or perhaps because of?) being something of a playground for the rich, the Helford has been saved from the worst excesses of tawdry development, and this estuary and its wooded banks retain an air of mystery and an irresistible enticement to explore. The village of Helford on the south side, which once supported a Customs House for the estuary, is idyllic. Just upriver is Frenchman's Creek, inspiration for Daphne du Maurier's novel. Porth Navas, on a northern creek, is home to the Duchy Oyster Farm.

Gweek. Cornwall Tourist Board.

Crowned Crane, Paradise Park, Hayle. Tim Guthrie.

Coronation Boating Lake, Helston. MDN.

Loe Pool, Helston. MDN.

Helston

Helston was one of the ancient coinage towns, where tin ingots were weighed to assess the duty to be paid to the Duke of Cornwall and a corner, or coign, struck off to be assayed (tested for quality). The main thoroughfare of the town is called Coinagehall Street (much admired by John Betjeman: '*it takes a beautiful curve, like the Oxford "High", and is well terminated at either end*') and there is still the dignified atmosphere here of an ancient borough, proud of its history. The Helston Furry Dance, held on the 8th May, is a celebratory day of dancing and spectacle with its roots in pre-Christian spring festivals. There is a very fine little museum in the old butter market, well worth seeking out, and in Coinagehall Street you will find the birthplace of 'Battling' Bob Fitzsimmons, Britain's first world heavyweight boxing champion (who won the title by knocking out 'Gentlemen' Jim Corbett with his bare fists). Nearby is the Blue Anchor, a fine pub made infamous by its home-made brew 'Spingo'.

In earliest times Helston was a port at the head of the estuary of the river Cober, but the great shingle bank of Loe Bar began to form across the estuary mouth from the thirteenth century onwards, eventually cutting off the port from the sea, and Helston's merchants turned instead to Gweek at the head of the Helford. The old estuary became The Loe, the largest freshwater lake in Cornwall, now part of the National Trust's Penrose estate and a glorious place for walking with five miles of path running right the way around the shore. RNAS Culdrose, southwest of the town, is the largest military helicopter base in Europe, and the centre for air-sea rescue activities around Cornwall. There is a public viewing enclosure alongside the base.

Kilkhampton

The fine old village of Kilkhampton stands at the head of the wooded Coombe valley, which reaches the sea at Duckpool on the bleak and impressive coast north of Bude. This is Grenville country, ancestral home of the family which spawned more than its fair share of heroes – notably Roger, who went down with his ship the *Mary Rose*, Sir Richard of *The Revenge* who died fighting the Spanish off the Azores in 1591, and Sir Bevil who led the Cornish army in the Civil War and died in the battle of Lansdowne in 1643. There are elaborate monuments to the family in Kilkhampton church. Their seat was at Stowe on the edge of the Coombe valley, where there is now a fine eighteenth-century farmhouse.

Kynance Cove

One of the most famous of Cornwall's coastal beauty spots, Kynance has been a mecca for excursionists since the eighteenth century. Brilliant turquoise water and white sand, with islands, caves and unexpected views are still a powerful draw today. The rock here is serpentine, so named because of its gloriously variegated colours, particularly when wet, which resemble the skin of a snake. There is a National Trust car park on the downs above, and the surrounding area is noted for its botanical rarities.

Lamorna

The tiny harbour in wild Lamorna Cove, at the seaward end of a bosky, tumbling valley, was built to serve the granite quarries which flourished here in the last century. The harbour suffered badly from its exposure to heavy seas and, more often than not, the granite had to be laboriously transported overland to Penzance for shipment. The old quarries and their dumps are eerily overgrown now, but the high-quality stone from here once went to build many great public buildings in London as well as the Bishop Rock, Wolf Rock and Longships lighthouses. The valley attracted a famous colony of artists in the early years of this century, notably Harold and Laura Knight, A.J. Munnings and Samuel John Birch, who was better known by his soubriquet 'Lamorna' Birch and whose radiant pictures may be seen in the gallery in Penlee Park in Penzance.

Helston Flora Day. Tim Guthrie.

Granite outcrop, Lamorna. MDN.

Gazetteer

Land's End

The most westerly point in England, 870 miles from John O'Groats, Land's End is one of the most celebrated places in the country. The coastline is dramatic, and features some curious names such as the Armed Knight, Kettle's Bottom and Dr. Syntax's Head. The rock known as Dr. Johnson's Head was looked on askance by Wilkie Collins when he came to Land's End in 1850; he could see nothing of Johnson in it but instead found, *'in violent exaggeration, the worst physiognomical peculiarities of Nero and Henry the Eighth, combined in one face!'* The present lighthouse on the Longships rocks, 1.25 miles west of Land's End, was built between 1870 and 1873; the Wolf Rock lighthouse, 8 miles away, should also be visible and on a clear day it is possible to see the Isles of Scilly, some 28 miles distant.

Land's End. Tim Guthrie.

Lanlivery

With its lofty church tower a landmark for miles around, the village of Lanlivery stands tall upon a windy hilltop. Here is the renowned Churchtown Farm Field Studies Centre, which offers environmental studies and outdoor adventures for people of all ages with a wide variety of disabilities. To the north is the mysterious, powerful landscape of Redmoor and Breney Common, part of which is protected as a nature reserve, with the great granite mass of Helman Tor isolated in its midst. To the south is the Luxulyan valley, full of rushing water and industrial remains and spanned by the monumental Treffry viaduct/aqueduct built in 1839.

Launceston

Betjeman called it *'the most rewarding inland town of Cornwall'*, and Launceston is still a fine looking place, dominated by the Norman castle of Dunheved and by the extraordinary church of St Mary Magdalene. The castle became the seat of the Earls of Cornwall and the mediaeval town crowding beneath it was enclosed by walls, the South Gate of which survives. Launceston was the capital of Cornwall until 1835 when that honour went west to Bodmin. The church of St Mary Magdalene, originally the town chapel, was rebuilt in the sixteenth century (the tower is 200 years older) out of moorland granite and given the most amazing display of decorative carving to be found anywhere in the county. Considering how hard a stone they had to work with, the skills of the masons can only be marvelled at; it is, as Betjeman had it, *'a mediaeval triumph of Cornwall'*.

Lelant

Lelant had its day as a port on the Hayle estuary in early mediaeval times, but it suffered badly from the silting of the river and lost its trade to St Ives. The silting helped to form the expanse of estuary marshland known as the saltings which is now an RSPB reserve. There is a station at Lelant on the scenic branch railway line to St Ives.

Lerryn

At the head of an unspoilt creek of the Fowey estuary, the village of Lerryn once had a significant role to play as a river port serving a large farming community. Today it is a peaceful spot which still maintains a vital village spirit. On spring tides, visitors and locals alike come up from Fowey and Golant by boat to enjoy a picnic by the river or a drink at the Ship Inn. There is a fine little sixteenth-century bridge across the river and a beautiful walk alongside the creek through the National Trust's Ethy Wood. An extension to this walk will take you to the near-perfect settlement of St Winnow on the main Fowey river - church, farm and vicarage gathered above an old river quay.

Liskeard

Liskeard was one of the ancient coinage towns for the tin industry (see Helston), and later flourished with the discovery of rich deposits of copper to the north, around Caradon Hill, in the nineteenth century. Many fine town houses survive from this boom time and Liskeard still has the life and vigour of a busy market town. There is a lovely branch line which runs from here down to Looe through the wooded East Looe valley, whilst the main line crosses the valley on the mighty Moorswater viaduct with the old stone piers of Brunel's original alongside.

Lizard

The name comes from the Cornish for 'court on a height' and refers to the whole peninsula as well as to the village near its tip and the point itself, which is Britain's most southerly place. Lizard Point, and most of the land around it, is owned by the National Trust and has benefited from a major programme of landscape improvements including the undergrounding of overhead wires and the creation of a new footpath from the village. The splendid Lizard light is the oldest mainland lighthouse in Cornwall. The twin towers date back to 1752, although a light was established here as early as 1619. Nearby is the alarming Lion's Den, a crater in the cliffs which was formed by the roof of a cave collapsing. Inland, rising out of a great expanse of heathland amidst the rare plants and ancient tumuli, are the vast dishes of the Goonhilly Earth Satellite Tracking Station.

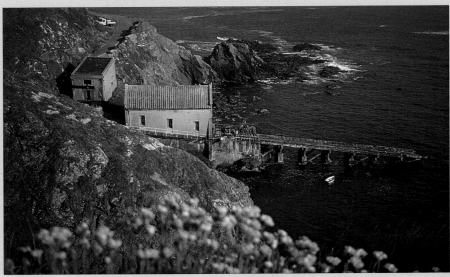

Old Lizard lifeboat house. MDN.

14

Looe

There are two Looes - East and West - just as there are two Looe rivers which converge upstream of the road bridge. West Looe is the smaller, quieter settlement whilst its eastern neighbour's streets are crammed and bustling. Huge amounts of copper and granite were shipped from the riverside quays in the last century and there is still life here today as Looe is a busy commercial fishing port and shark-fishing centre. Looe Island lies just offshore, home of the redoubtable Atkins sisters whose remarkable story is told in *We Bought an Island* and *Tales from our Cornish Island*. There are fine walks to be had up the West Looe valley and a splendid railway journey up the East Looe valley to Liskeard.

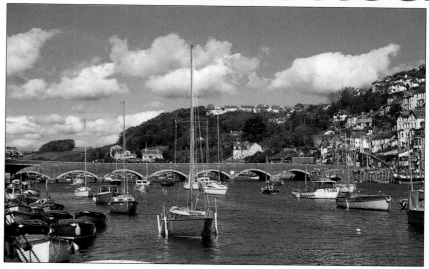

Looe. Cornwall Tourist Board.

Ding Dong Mine, near Madron. MDN.

Lostwithiel

An unassuming town with a fascinating past, Lostwithiel lies in a bowl of hills at the lowest bridging point on the Fowey river, where fresh water first mingles with the salt. The fine old five-arched bridge dates from the fifteenth century, but this would have been an important crossing from earliest times. The town is dominated by the lovely spire of St Bartholomew's Church and the impressive twelfth-century shell keep of Restormel Castle on a hill behind. It would be hard to guess that Lostwithiel was once the administrative capital of the county, under the patronage of the Earls, and subsequently Dukes, of Cornwall, or that for a time it was the sole port for Cornish tin, its foreign trade greater than that of all the Cinque Ports put together, giving it second place on the south coast after Southampton. There are still some remains to be seen of the massive 'Duchy Palace', but scarcely a hint of the once-thriving port; by 1400 the silting of the Fowey River from tin-streaming works upriver meant that Lostwithiel had lost nearly all of its trade to Fowey.

Madron

The church of St Madernus in this granite village overlooking Mount's Bay used to be the mother church of Penzance. A mile to the north is the celebrated Madron Well, a very early Christian site with the restored ruins of a chapel alongside. This has long been a popular place of pilgrimage and visitors still tie votive rags to bushes in the belief that once the rags have rotted their ailments will be cured. The water is supposed to cure rickets and to assist in divination. The parish is rich in early archaeological remains, including the impressive Romano-British courtyard village of Chysauster, and the massive chamber tomb of Lanyon Quoit which dates from the fourth millennium BC.

Marazion

An ancient town, formed as early as the twelfth century, Marazion catered for the pilgrims to St Michael's Mount throughout the Middle Ages, and still performs a similar function today. The Mount is joined to the shore here by a causeway which is only passable at low water; once the tide has risen there are ferries to take today's pilgrims across. With a long and fascinating history encompassing ancient harbour, monastery, shrine, fortress, castle and home, the towering half-island of St Michael's Mount is justly one of Cornwall's most popular attractions.

Mevagissey

Fishing still dominates the harbour of Mevagissey, but only just. This is an extremely popular destination for visitors in the summer, when it is sometimes hard to appreciate its undeniable charms for the press of people and traffic. The large inner and outer harbours are thronged with boats and, despite the many setbacks which the industry has had to face, there remains a thriving fishing community here as there has been since at least the fifteenth century when Mevagissey's first stone pier was built. To the south, beyond the cove of Portmellon, is the low promontory of Chapel Point with its distinctive white houses designed in the 1930s by the architect J.A. Campbell.

Mevagissey. Cornwall Tourist Board.

Minions

The exposed moorland village of Minions is in the centre of an area rich in mining and much older archaeological remains. A rich copper lode was discovered on the southern slopes of Caradon Hill in 1836 and by 1856 there were more than twenty active mines in the immediate vicinity; there are still many ruinous engine houses to be seen here today. To the north of the village is the extraordinary rock formation of the Cheesewring ('*If a man dreamt of a great pile of stones in a nightmare,*' wrote Wilkie Collins in his delightful *Rambles Beyond Railways, 'he would dream of such a pile as the Cheese-Wring*'). Nearby are the ancient stone circles called the Hurlers in the midst of a 'sacred area' littered with standing stones, burial cairns and Bronze Age settlements.

Cheesewring near Minions. MDN.

Morwenstow

In the wild far north of Cornwall, with its bleakly beautiful cliffs and wind-blasted settlements, the parish of Morwenstow feels like the edge of the known world. The poet Robert Stephen Hawker was the vicar here from 1834 to 1875; he is renowned for giving Christian burials to shipwrecked sailors and reviving the Harvest Festival, as well as for his poetry which he wrote in a driftwood hut on the cliff edge, now owned by the National Trust. His Gothic vicarage (with its chimneys modelled on the towers of his favourite churches) stands alongside the church of St Morwenna and St John in which there survives much fine Norman work.

16

Mousehole

Perhaps the fairest of all Cornish harbour villages, the yellow-lichened houses of Mousehole, built of fine-grained Lamorna granite, huddle around its sturdy curving harbour on the western shore of Mount's Bay and there is barely a jarring element to be seen. What is probably the oldest pier in Cornwall, dating from 1390 or thereabouts, is now incorporated into South Quay yet is still easily identifiable with its massive irregular blocks of stone. This was then the most important fishing port in Mount's Bay and a market was granted here, proof of its prominence, as early as 1266. In 1595 two hundred Spaniards landed at Mousehole and burned most of the village before moving on to torch Paul, Newlyn and Penzance; there is still scorched stone to be seen in Paul church and in some of the older buildings in Penzance. Dylan Thomas lived here in the 1930s ('...*really the loveliest village in England*') and was often to be found in the Ship Inn; today this pub is one of the least 'improved' in Cornwall, which makes it a rare and precious place. The story of Tom Bawcock, a fisherman who saved the village from starvation, is memorably celebrated on December 23rd – Tom Bawcock's Eve – and is now more widely known through its retelling in the children's book *The Mousehole Cat*.

Mullion

The tiny embattled harbour at Mullion Cove on the forbidding western flank of the Lizard was not built until 1895, giving protection to the pilchard fishery which had developed here against all the odds. The two piers are in almost constant need of rebuilding and repair due to their frequent exposure to storms; this task now falls to the National Trust which has owned and cared for the harbour since 1945. This is a most dramatic place even on a calm day, with great black cliffs towering all around and casting dark shadows on the turquoise water; in a westerly gale it is truly terrifying. On Angrouse Cliff , between the coves of Polurrian and Poldhu and just to the west of

Hawkers Hut. R. Rowling/National Trust

Mousehole. MDN.

Repairing the harbour wall at Mullion. MDN.

Mullion village, a memorial marks the site of Guglielmo Marconi's first high-power wireless transmitting station. From here in 1901 was sent the first wireless message across the Atlantic – a simple morse signal 'S,S,S'.

Mylor

Mylor Creek is a surprisingly peaceful, sequestered inlet off the Carrick Roads with the partly handsome village of Mylor Bridge at its head. At its mouth is the substantial harbour, thronged with yachts and dinghies, and the parish church of St Melorus with a wonderful Norman doorway and, outside the south porch, the largest cross in Cornwall – nearly half of which lies underground. The harbour, with its massive quays, was built as an Admiralty dockyard at the start of the nineteenth century to supply naval vessels with stores and ordnance and, later, to serve the training ship *HMS Ganges*, moored across the Roads in St. Just Pool from 1866 to 1899. In the last war it was used as a base by the Free French resistance fighters preparing to sail across the Channel, and by the US Navy for the fitting out of Seebees landing craft immediately prior to D-Day. The author Howard Spring lived here, in the churchtown, from 1939 to 1947 and Katherine Mansfield spent the summer of 1916 in a cottage on Church Road.

Padstow

Another popular resort on Cornwall's north coast, Padstow's development could not, however, have been more different from that of Newquay. It had the railway – the London & South West arrived here from Wadebridge in 1899 (now part of the Camel Trail cycle track) but it did not have the exceptional beaches quite so close at hand. There are lovely beaches nearby, but this is an estuary town and a fishing port more than it will ever be a seaside resort. The fatefully-named Doom Bar across the mouth of the Camel estuary makes for a treacherous entrance, but shelter on the north coast is hard to come by and Padstow has been an important harbour of refuge for centuries. The estuaries of the Camel and the Fowey mark either end of an ancient cross-county trading route, avoiding the passage around Land's End, which was also used by Celtic Christian missionaries travelling between Brittany and Ireland and Wales. St Petroc, Cornwall's chief saint, established a monastery at Padstow in the 6th century and gave his name to the infant settlement (Padstow comes from the English for 'holy place of St Petroc'). The harbour's first pier was built in the sixteenth century and Padstow went on to develop as a busy fishing and trading port as well as a centre for shipowning and shipbuilding. Today there are still plenty of fishing boats in Padstow, and the town has achieved new fame through Rick Stein's fabulous Seafood Restaurant and his recent television series which was enthusiastically received by lovers of Cornwall everywhere. Padstow has somehow avoided being swamped by its popularity, and this is never more apparent than on May Day each year when the whole town gives itself over to a festival which feels much older than St Petroc and is still, in essence, almost entirely impenetrable to outsiders.

Newlyn. MDN.

Newlyn

One of the top fishing ports in the country, Newlyn's large harbour is packed with boats and, despite the frequent setbacks which the industry has to face, there is an atmosphere here of activity and vigour. It is extraordinary to compare the grand 43-acre harbour of today, which largely dates from farsighted works undertaken between 1866 and 1888, with the first tiny pier of the mediaeval port which lies deep and nearly lost within its belly.

The name of Newlyn is synonymous with one of the great movements in English art which flourished in the late nineteenth century, but why this particular harbour village should have become such an inspiration and a focus it is hard to say. Even Stanhope Forbes, the 'father' of the Newlyn School (although by no means the first to arrive here) could not fully explain its curious magnetism: '*What lodestone of artistic metal the place contains I know not, but its effects were strongly felt in the studios of Paris and Antwerp, particularly, by a number of young English painters studying there who just about then, by some common impulse, seemed drawn towards this corner of their native land*'. The far west of Cornwall is still a great draw and stimulus for artists of all kinds, and their work can be seen at galleries in Newlyn, St Ives and Penzance.

Newquay

Cornwall's most popular holiday resort owes its development to the glories of the coastline (its spectacularly lovely beaches, in particular) and to the coming of the railway. The Par-Newquay line was originally intended to transport copper ore and china clay from south and mid-Cornwall to the newly-developed and enlarged harbour at Newquay. However, by the time of its completion in 1875 copper mining was in decline and Cornwall was beginning to discover a new wealth; the trains soon brought Victorian tourists rather than minerals, hotels and boarding-houses were built along the cliffs and a new era was born. Up on the cliff road near the Atlantic Hotel is one of the few reminders of old Newquay: the curious little huer's house where a watchman was stationed during the pilchard season to spot the approaching pilchard shoals and alert the fishermen with cries of 'Hevva, hevva!' The town today may have the reputation of being young and loud and brash, but there is such a refreshingly honest vitality here that it would be hard not to have fun; thank heavens no-one could ever accuse Newquay of being precious.

Padstow. MDN.

Par

The harbour at Par is owned by English China Clays and entirely given over now to the drying and export of china clay. It was built by the fascinating entrepreneur Joseph Thomas Treffry from the 1820s onwards as an outlet for his rich copper mines and granite quarries inland and in due course many industries were established around the harbourside, including smelting, brickmaking, shipbuilding, limeburning and pilchard curing. Much of the Par area was once a tidal estuary which flowed up to St. Blazey but had become heavily silted-up by Treffry's time and a sandbank had formed across its mouth. This is now Par Beach, and the old estuary bed has been almost entirely built over. Daphne du Maurier's novel *The House on the Strand* contains uncannily clear descriptions of this lost estuarine landscape.

Pendeen

The centre of what was a rich tin and copper mining area in the nineteenth century, the village of Pendeen with its rows of old miners' cottages' is on the spectacular coast road from St Ives to St Just. The last working mine in the far west, Geevor, closed in 1991 and is now being developed as a museum. Just along the coast at Levant, volunteers from the Trevithick Society maintain and run under steam the oldest beam engine in Cornwall in its stout little engine house on the cliff edge, now owned by the National Trust. The handsome lighthouse on the headland to the northeast known as Pendeen Watch was built in 1900.

Penryn

A far older port and settlement than neighbouring Falmouth, Penryn was established in the early thirteenth century by the bishops of Exeter and owed its growth and prosperity principally to maritime trade. In addition, the College of Glasney was founded here in 1265 and became a centre of ecclesiastical learning famed throughout Europe. Its magnificent buildings, including a church, gatehouse, canons' houses and three granite towers, were gradually demolished after the college's dissolution in 1549 and all that remains today is the odd bit of dressed Caen stone or gargoyle incorporated into newer buildings and garden walls. Today, Penryn is an exceptionally handsome town, thanks to a policy of careful restoration of its old buildings which was instituted in 1975. Most of the houses are built of granite from local quarries and it was this trade – the quarrying, dressing and shipping of this fine building stone – above all else which helped to keep Penryn alive after Falmouth developed as a superior port.

Pentewan

Tucked away at the far end of a large and popular beach, the old harbour of Pentewan is a strange place today: a dock basin filled with water and bearded with reeds that is separated from the sea by 400 yards of dry land. This dock was built between 1818 and 1826, on the site of a harbour that had been in use for hundreds of years, by Sir Christopher Hawkins, a local mine-owner who wanted an outlet for his mines and, in particular, his china clay pits. A stone can still be seen in the breakwater, now half buried in sand, bearing his initials and the Hawkins family arms.

Pentewan never overcame the problem it had had for centuries of silting from tin streaming sites further upriver and, by the time the dock was built, much more seriously from china clay works. Although the harbour was fairly busy, it was never popular with the clay magnates nor with ship owners and captains; in February 1862, for instance, sixteen ships were detained in the dock for five weeks because of sand blocking the channel. The last trading ship called at Pentewan in 1940; for another twenty years or so it was possible for a rowing boat to enter the harbour, but now the channel is part of the beach – dry land at even the highest tide.

The village grouped behind the harbour is attractive, particularly the elegant little Regency terrace half way up the hill. On the cliffs to the east, a quarry at Polrudden once produced *'the best free stone that Cornwall yieldeth'* (Norden, writing in 1584) which went to build many of Cornwall's finest churches and great houses.

Penzance

The town owes its name ('holy headland' from the Cornish *pen* and *sans*) to the small rocky headland to the south of the harbour and the chapel which once stood just inland (on or close to the site of the present church). The settlement of Penzance would have been not a great deal more than this for much of its history until the sixteenth century, Mousehole being the principal harbour on Mount's Bay before then. Following its burning by the Spanish in 1565 (see Mousehole), much of the infant town had to be rebuilt and it was not long before it was incorporated as a borough. In 1663 Charles II made Penzance a new coinage town for the tin industry (see Helston), removing this privilege from Bodmin and Lostwithiel at the same time and thus marking the westward movement of mining activity. From then on Penzance did not look back: its maritime trade became increasingly varied and vigorous and the town developed as a market for the whole of West Cornwall. Today Penzance is undeniably one of Cornwall's most attractive towns, both in terms of its architecture and position and, perhaps more importantly, its spirit. This is a place of great vitality and originality with much of interest to see and do: the Penzance and District Museum and Art Gallery in Penlee Park has a fascinating collection of paintings by the Newlyn School and the Lamorna group of artists; the statue of Sir Humphry Davy in Market Jew Street commemorates one of the greatest chemists this country has ever produced ('the *Cornishman of genius* par excellence', as A.L. Rowse has called him); and Trinity House's national lighthouse museum is down by the harbour. The *Scillonian III* operates from Lighthouse Pier with a daily service to and from St Mary's on the Isles of Scilly; there are also regular helicopter flights to the islands from the heliport on the eastern edge of the town.

Levant, near Pendeen. MDN.

Perranporth

It is no exaggeration to say that the history and development of Perranporth have been quite unusually dominated by sand. Perranporth today has become a popular holiday resort thanks to its three-mile stretch of golden beach, but the effects have not always been so positive. In the extensive dune system just inland, two ancient religious sites have been lost to the encroaching sands. The old oratory of St Piran, an important early Celtic monastery which became one of the foremost places of pilgrimage in mediaeval Cornwall (the shrine contained the relics of St Piran along with the teeth of St Brendan and St Martin), became overwhelmed by sand sometime before 1500. Following its excavation in the last century, it had to be reburied in 1981 to protect the structure and the site is now marked by a memorial stone. Nearby are the ruined walls of the Norman parish church (built c.1150) which in its turn had to be abandoned to the sand in 1804. Beside it is a fine cross which may be the one recorded as a boundary point in a tenth-century charter.

Polperro

The words 'Polperro' and 'picturesque' seem to go together hand in hand, so often are they seen in each other's company, but there is more to this dramatic harbour and village than its famed quaintness. Its position is truly breathtaking, crammed into a narrow gash in the cliffs, and there has been a fishing community here (at times, in the past, bolstered by a healthy smuggling trade) for around seven hundred years. The coastline to the west, towards Lansallos and Polruan, is particularly glorious and well worth the effort demanded by the switchback coast path.

Perranporth. MDN.

Polzeath

With its glorious position at the mouth of the Camel estuary and the long sandy Hayle Bay famed for its surfing, it is hardly surprising that Polzeath has become so developed in recent years. Only the National Trust's ownership of Pentire Point and The Rumps (with its magnificent Iron Age cliff castle) has halted the spread of housing and allowed this part of the north Cornwall coast to remain breathtaking. It is hard to believe that in 1936, when people locally and throughout the country raised the money to buy Pentire and present it to the Trust, the entire headland had been divided into building plots and put up for sale.

This is Betjeman country, and the late Poet Laureate is buried at St Enodoc Church between Trebetherick, where he spent so much of his life, and the great green swell of Brea Hill on the banks of the Camel.

Porthcurno

The beach at Porthcurno is arguably the most beautiful in Cornwall, with its white sand and improbably turquoise water in the bay backed by the striking granite ridges of Treen Cliff, but the steeply shelving beach and violent undertow means that it is not the safest place to swim – appearances can be deceiving. Until 1993 the village in the valley was home to the Cable and Wireless training college, continuing a relationship that dated back to 1870 when the beach was chosen as the landing-place for an all-undersea telegraph cable link between England and India. As hard as it is to imagine today, Porthcurno became the home of the largest submarine telegraph station in the world. This fascinating story is told in a museum housed in the station's wartime protection tunnels.

Cut into the cliffs to the south of the beach is the renowned open-air Minack Theatre; any performance seen here, with the unsurpassed backdrop of the sea and the dark, jagged promontory of Treryn Dinas with its famed Logan Rock, is surely one of the greatest experiences that Cornwall has to offer.

Porthcurno. Tim Guthrie.

Porthleven

It is rare to find a Cornish harbour which faces southwest, directly into the prevailing winds, and Porthleven's development as a port was always hampered by its orientation. Doubtless, Porthleven would have remained a small fishing inlet to this day had not there been an overriding need, in the early nineteenth century, for a harbour of refuge along this forbidding lee shore to which ships could run in times of distress. The construction of the harbour, which was completed in 1825, had been hugely problematical and, although a large drifter fleet was soon engaged in the mackerel and pilchard fisheries, Porthleven remained a dangerous and difficult harbour. Major improvements were carried out in the 1850s, after the port was taken over by Harvey & Co. of Hayle, and the handsome, massively-built harbour that we see today dates from this time. Porthleven went on to be famed for its boatbuilding and shipowning, but it never fully overcame its original, intrinsic problem; you only have to visit the place during one of the frequent sou'westerly gales that beset Cornwall through the winter to see why.

Trengwainton Gardens, near Penzance. MDN.

Porthleven. MDN.

Port Isaac

On Cornwall's spectacular but hostile north coast, where every possible inlet was exploited as a harbour, Port Isaac developed a pilchard fishery from mediaeval times and then, in the last century, a small coasting trade grew up around the shipping of slate from Delabole. Undeniably one of Cornwall's most attractive villages, it is apt to be overrun in the summer but offers fine walking on the cliffs to east and west. The neighbouring settlements of Port Quin and Port Gaverne also have their roots in fishing and the shipping of ores and slate, but both suffered severe declines in the last century with the capriciousness of the pilchard season, the failure of local mines and the coming of the railway to Delabole. Port Quin, in particular, is now a tiny silent place of a few cottages, whereas in 1841 it supported a community of 23 houses and 94 people.

Portloe

Like Port Isaac, Portloe must rate as one of Cornwall's most attractive coastal villages, largely because it has escaped the horrors of unwise development and remains truly unspoilt. Its situation is cramped and dramatic, squeezed in below the echoing, dark cliffs on the western flank of Veryan Bay, and it is hard to imagine when looking at the harbour entrance how any successful fishery could be run from here. Portloe did once support a small drift fleet and a seine fishery, however, whilst trading ketches landed and loaded goods on the beach; and some fishing still goes on today, and lobster and crab potting, to keep the place alive and real.

Portreath

No more than a small fishing port for much of its history, Portreath was developed as a harbour from the eighteenth century under the patronage of the wealthy mine-owning Basset family. Many works were undertaken during the next hundred years, including the construction of an inner basin and the first tramway to be built in Cornwall, linking the harbour to the richest centre of the mining industry around Camborne and Redruth. From here copper ore was exported to South Wales for smelting, the ships returning with loads of coal and timber for the mines. The harbour entrance was said to be particularly hazardous – ships had to squeeze between the pier and the cliff face then negotiate the length of the channel up to the inner basin, no mean feat without an engine – and no large vessel has entered Portreath harbour since about 1960. Tehidy Country Park, to the southwest, offers nine miles of woodland and riverside walks, linking to the coast at Basset's Cove, in what was the Basset family's Tehidy estate in the eighteenth and nineteenth centuries.

Probus

An ancient religious site (there was a monastery here before the Norman Conquest), Probus today is famed for the tower of its largely fifteenth-century church which, at 125ft, is the tallest in the county. The village is much quieter since the recent completion of its bypass; on its eastern edge is the County Demonstration Garden which explains many aspects of gardening through displays, layouts and designs.

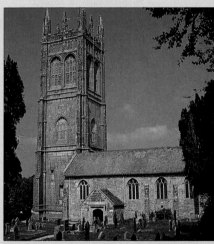

Probus Church. MDN.

Prussia Cove

Just to the east of Cudden Point lie the two rocky inlets of Bessy's Cove and Prussia Cove, described by Betjeman as *'a lesser version of the splendours of Kynance.'* Renowned today as the home of the International Musicians Seminar founded by Sandor Vegh, Prussia Cove was made infamous two hundred years ago by the smuggling activities of the Carter family and, in particular, the eldest son John who was known as the King of Prussia.

Engine house near Redruth. MDN.

Redruth

Mediaeval pilgrims used to stop at a chapel in the main street of Redruth on their way to St Michael's Mount, but there was never much of a town here until the mining boom which began in the late eighteenth century and most of the buildings date from then onwards. Along with its close neighbour and arch-rival Camborne, Redruth was at the centre of the richest mining area in the county. Surprisingly little evidence remains of the intense mining activity at the foot of Carn Brea, where old photographs show scores of smoking chimney stacks. Redruth's most famous resident was William Murdock who made the first gas engine as well as inventing gas lighting and using it to light his house here (at the back of Druid's Hall) in 1792.

The hill of Carn Brea, which looms so impressively over the town, has had a very long history, beginning with enclosures and defences from the Neolithic period (4000-2500BC). The small mediaeval castle, now a restaurant, was possibly the hunting lodge of the Basset family who went on to build a fortune from their mining interests. The monument on the summit was erected in 1836 to the memory of Francis Basset, Lord de Dunstanville, who was a patron of science, landscape gardening and painting.

Portreath. MDN.

Roche

The village of Roche on the northern fringes of clay country takes its name from the French for 'rock' although it is pronounced as a very English 'roach'. The rock itself, a remarkable granite outcrop just to the east of the village, is now known as Roche Rock. Rearing up out of the granite in a most dramatic fashion is the ruined chapel of St Michael, built in 1409, with a priest's room below it hewn out of the natural stone.

Stippy Stappy, St Agnes. Cornwall Tourist Board.

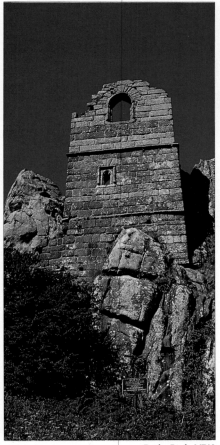

Roche Rock. MDN.

Sennen

The most westerly village in England has been an important lifeboat station since 1853 and its fine beach is popular with visitors. The pilchard fishery is no more but there is still crab and lobster potting from the cove. To the south, between the cove and Land's End, is Mayon Cliff which was given to the National Trust in 1935 by an anonymous group of society ladies known as Ferguson's Gang. To celebrate the occasion they composed a song which begins: *'Up on the cliffs by Mayon Castle, What 'as you seen to make a fuss? Up on the cliffs by Mayon Castle, There I seen the Octopus. What was the Octopus a-doing, East of the Longships as you go? E'd some bricks and a load o' concrete, For to start a bungalow. Scarlet bricks and rubbery tiling, Bright red boxes all in a row, Tin kiosk for the teas and petrol, Parkin' place for the cars to go.'*

St Agnes

The 629ft St Agnes Beacon swells up to the west of the village, commanding panoramic views across Cornwall. St Agnes itself is a village transformed by mining, with countless ruinous stacks and engine houses in the surrounding area. There have been five attempts to construct an artificial harbour at St Agnes from 1632 onwards, all of which succumbed sooner or later to the Atlantic storms. The last harbour was built at the foot of the cliffs in Trevaunance Cove in 1793, for the shipping of ore from the mines, with wooden staging high up on the cliffs for loading platforms and cargoes being lifted and lowered from there by horse windlass. It lasted until the 1920s and since then most of it has been washed away by the relentless sea. To the south of St Agnes Head is the popular National Trust beach of Chapel Porth and, on the cliffs above, the dramatically-sited engine houses of Wheal Coates.

Saltash

This is an ancient settlement, the foremost seaport between Dartmouth and Fowey at a time when Plymouth barely existed, and one of the main old crossing-points into Cornwall via the Ashe-Torre ferry over the Tamar. Today it is, inevitably, rather overlooked as cars stream into Cornwall across the 1961 road bridge and then through a tunnel under the town. Since 1859 the scene has been mightily dominated by Isambard Kingdom Brunel's magnificent wrought iron railway bridge, his last and arguably his greatest engineering feat, which the Admiralty specified had to span the river at 100ft above the high water mark with no more than one pier. Close to death, Brunel was unable to attend the official opening of his bridge by Prince Albert (after whom it is named) on May 2nd 1859, but later that month he was drawn slowly across it lying on a couch upon a flat truck.

In Culver Street stands the old cottage that was the birthplace of Mary Newman, Sir Francis Drake's first wife and the mayoress of Plymouth.

Sennen. Tim Guthrie.

St Austell

Little more than a small cluster of houses around a fine church for much of its history, St Austell was utterly transformed by the discovery in the mid-eighteenth century, by the chemist William Cookworthy, of huge reserves of china clay to the north and west of the village. Put simply, china clay is decomposed granite, but the process is not common to all granite areas – it is, in fact, found in very few places in the world which made the deposits found in Cornwall and Devon particularly valuable. By the 1850s, some 7,000 men, women and children were employed in the St Austell clay district in the extraction, processing, transportation and export of the clay, and heavy wagons constantly rumbled through the streets of St Austell on their way to the ports of Charlestown, Pentewan and Par. The town grew and prospered out of all recognition. There are some fine buildings from this period to be seen today, the White Hart Hotel for instance, and the Market House, but much of the town centre seems to have lost its way. The parish church is still the glory of St Austell, with its beautifully-carved tower of Pentewan stone. Today, although production methods have changed considerably, English China Clays, the company which now operates most of the pits, is still one of Cornwall's biggest employers. The uses of the clay have changed, too, and diversified; papermaking is the principal market, but it is also used in the manufacture of paints, medicines, porcelain, dyes and cosmetics and is exported all over the world. Readers keen to learn more about the industry and its history should visit the excellent Wheal Martyn Museum, north of St Austell, or read *Cornwall's China Clay Heritage* by the Cornwall Archaeological Unit (published by Twelveheads Press).

China Clay mounds, St Austell. MDN.

St Buryan. Tim Guthrie.

St Buryan

'The parish is richer in antiquities than any in Cornwall', wrote the great Cornish historian Charles Henderson in 1925, *'and we may note the large number of Celtic crosses marking the ancient roads which converge upon the church'.* The church is a stately fifteenth-century building, set in its windswept granite churchtown, on an old holy site. The dedication is to St Beriana, and the place is still correctly pronounced 'Berrian'. Of the countless Bronze and Iron Age relics to be found in the parish, the most famous are the stone circle of Boscawen Un (Nine Maidens) north of the village, and the Pipers standing stones and the Merry Maidens stone circle to the southeast, in an area with an astonishing range of ancient ritual and burial monuments.

St Cleer

Like nearby Minions, this parish on the southern slopes of Bodmin Moor was overwhelmed, and transformed, by a copper-mining boom in the mid-nineteenth century which has been compared, in its intensity and in its social and economic repercussions, to the North American gold rush. Here is A.K. Hamilton Jenkin, for instance: *'On Saturday nights after pay day, the populous villages of Caradon Town, Pensilva, Minions and Crows Nest were crowded with men, and resembled in character the mining camps of Colorado and the Far West.'* There are older historical stories to be told here too; the parish contains the impressive Neolithic chamber tomb of Trethevy Quoit and the decorated and inscribed King Doniert's Stone, which was probably erected by Dumgarth, the last Cornish king to be recorded in what used to

St Cleer Holy Well. MDN.

be called the 'Dark Ages', who drowned in AD875. In the village itself is St Cleer holy well, in a beautiful fifteenth-century building; there used to be a total immersion (or 'bowssening') pool here which was used for the attempted cure of the insane.

St Clement

The peaceful churchtown of St Clement on the Tresillian River (part of the tidal Fal estuary) is still remarkably unspoilt, despite its proximity to Truro. There is a fine walk on an old carriage-drive along the wooded river shore to Tresillian. The churchyard has a slate-faced lych gate (which has, in the past, served as village school, parish vestry room, Sunday school and pigsty) and a rare inscribed stone of the sixth century dedicated to 'Vitalus son of Torricus'.

St Columb Major

This is an attractive town, now that it has been bypassed, with some interesting old buildings, none more so than the largely fourteenth-century parish church. This unusually big, grand building, which includes the tombs of the Arundells of Lanherne in the south chancel aisle, was, Charles Henderson believed, *'among the finest churches in Cornwall'.* Between St Columb and the sea is the beautiful, wooded Vale of Lanherne, where the old Arundell house, in the enchanting village of St Mawgan, is now a Carmelite convent. St Columb is famous for its boisterous Shrove Tuesday celebration of 'hurling' (an ancient game once common in Cornwall), where the teams of Town and Country attempt to hurl a silver-coated applewood ball into each other's goals, which are a mile apart at either end of the town.

St Ewe

The church is mainly fourteenth-century and there is a good little pub in the small churchtown of St Ewe. Nearby at Polmassick there is a successful vineyard; on the other side of the village is the newly-rediscovered garden at Heligan which is thought to be the largest garden restoration project in Europe.

St Germans

The village of St Germans is on the River Tiddy, part of the beautiful estuary of the Lynher which joins the Tamar just downriver from Saltash. The glory of the village is its magnificent Norman church, set in a hollow with two towers and a superb doorway as its west front. This might seem an incongruous setting for such a huge and ancient church, but the parish is still the largest in Cornwall and this church's predecessor was Cornwall's cathedral from AD926, when King Athelstan made Conan the first Cornish bishop, until 1043 when the see was transferred to Crediton, and thence to Exeter in 1050. Down on the river, St Germans Quay was busy in the last century with cargoes of minerals, coal, timber and limestone, and a vigorous trade in roadstone continued until the last war.

St Ives

No wonder people come flocking to St Ives in the summer. It has everything that a seaside resort could wish for: good beaches, views across the bay, a picturesque harbour town huddling in a glorious position, a branch line railway journey from St Erth and still something of a fishing industry (although nothing to what it was – this used to be the principal pilchard fishery in Cornwall) to save it from becoming the victim of its charms. Above all, it has Art. Turner, Whistler and Sickert were amongst the earliest artists to arrive here, then in 1928 the local primitive artist Alfred Wallis was discovered by Ben Nicholson and Christopher Wood. Nicholson, Barbara Hepworth and Naum Gabo settled in St Ives in 1939, and after the war there emerged a younger generation including Peter Lanyon, Roger Hilton and Patrick Heron. This strong and vital artistic tradition, particularly in the field of the abstract avant-garde, led to the siting of the new Tate Gallery here in 1993. The award-winning building is a triumph and the gallery has become one of Cornwall's major attractions, introducing modern art to an entirely new audience. The Barbara Hepworth Museum is fascinating and includes a garden featuring many of her sculptures, whilst the Penwith gallery exhibits the work of many local artists at work today.

St Just in Penwith

This solid, handsome granite town, exposed on the treeless heights just inland from Cape Cornwall, is the most westerly in Cornwall. It has the feel of a place on the edge and of the mining town that it was, with its rows of cottages and surprising number of pubs (one of which, incidentally, is truly the best pub in Cornwall, but it would be foolish of me to say which). The deep mining of tin and copper on the coast here in the nineteenth century was responsible for the growth of St Just from a small churchtown, but tin-streaming in the valleys of Penwith had been going on since the very earliest times. The church has an inscribed stone of the fifth or sixth century, suggesting that this was an early Christian foundation. Across the square is the Plain an Gwarry, a grassy arena where mediaeval Cornish miracle plays were performed, some of them lasting for up to three days.

The Brisons, off St Just. Tim Guthrie

St Just in Roseland

This is a magical place; it has the glory of an old Cornish church by tidal water and in addition what is, as Betjeman wrote, *'to many people the most beautiful churchyard on earth'*. More than that, it has St Just Pool which has somehow resisted all attempts through history to develop it into a dockyard or a commercial port and is still today, as it was when Jack Clemo wrote his haunting poem, a place *'Where boats lounge on mudbanks and wait/For the gurling inwash from Falmouth Bay'*. The name Roseland comes from the Cornish *ros*, meaning 'promontory', and refers to the fertile farming landscape from St Anthony in the south up towards Tregony, and extending to Veryan in the east.

St Ives. Tim Guthrie.

St Just-in-Roseland church. MDN.

Gazetteer

St Keverne

The extensive parish of St Keverne on the eastern plateau of the Lizard lies within the ancient district of Meneage. This name comes from the Cornish for 'monkish land' and is thought to refer to the presence of several Celtic monasteries in the area before the Conquest, although St Keverne is the only place which is known for certain to have had one. The large church has a tower surmounted by a spire which has served as a seamark for centuries. Just offshore, to the east of the churchtown, is the Manacles reef which has a fearsome reputation strengthened by the old belief that the rocks emit a supernatural magnetism which affects ships' compasses, drawing them off course into their deadly clasp. In St Keverne churchyard there is a mass grave which holds most of the 106 people who lost their lives when the *Mohegan* steamed into the Manacles on the evening of October 14 1898, and this is only one of many graves to those who met a similar end.

St Keverne church. MDN.

St Mawes

With its glorious position, curled around a sunny south-facing bay at the mouth of the Percuil, it is hardly surprising that St Mawes was 'discovered' by the leisured classes in Edwardian times. It has a relaxed, holiday atmosphere about it for much of the year, but the bones of the old fishing village that it was, are still there beneath the surface. There is a regular ferry service to Falmouth, and another which crosses the Percuil to St Anthony in Roseland where there is some fine walking country and a lovely little cruciform church hiding behind the big house of Place. St Mawes Castle, built during the reign of Henry VIII like Pendennis across the water, has an unusual cloverleaf design. Although well-placed to deal with a seaborne attack, it was impossible to defend from the landward side and, when besieged by General Fairfax during the Civil War, had no choice but to surrender without a shot being fired.

St Neot

The church of St Neot, standing proud in the small village which nestles below the heights of Bodmin Moor, is famed throughout the country for its stained glass. At least half of the glass in the fifteen windows dates from the fifteenth and sixteenth centuries and depicts saints and angels, the Flood and the story of St Neot (said to have been only four feet tall). Amongst the fine crosses in the churchyard is the shaft of one from the ninth century which is said to be the finest ornamented cross in Cornwall.

St Neot church. MDN.

Rocky Valley near Tintagel. MDN.

Tintagel

No amount of Arthurian frenzy in the village of Tintagel can detract from the simple power of the mediaeval castle on the cliff edge and the earlier, enigmatic ruins on the island beyond; this is a magnificent place, and no wonder it has inspired such enduring traditions. The Victorians popularised the idea of King Arthur's connections with Tintagel, notably Tennyson in his *Morte d'Arthur* and *Idylls of the King;* the opening of the railway to Camelford in 1893 brought the visitors and, soon afterwards, the monumental King Arthur's Castle hotel was built just above Barras Nose. This headland became, in 1897, the first coastal acquisition in England for the infant National Trust. The parish church up on Glebe Cliff is an ancient building on an even older site. Recent excavations suggest that it may have been an important dynastic cemetery of the fifth or sixth centuries and this, together with significant finds on the island, has led the Cornwall Archaeological Unit to conclude that Tintagel is the county's key archaeological site of the early mediaeval period and is now thought to have been a royal stronghold in the early sixth century. The castle itself, owned by the Duchy of Cornwall but managed by English Heritage, was built in the thirteenth century by Earl Richard of Cornwall.

Tregony

This fine looking village, with its broad main street curving down towards the bridge over the Fal, was a busy mediaeval port despite being so far inland. The Fal has suffered particularly badly from silting – it was once navigable even further upstream than Tregony – but the tide began to recede from here in the fifteenth century, taking with it all riverborne trade and Tregony's link to the open sea. During its heyday it is said that there were thirty-six alehouses here, of various descriptions; now there is just one.

Tresillian

The quays at Tresillian have long since lost their busy river traffic and have recently been built over with outsized car showrooms: the final, ironic victory of road transport over water. The bridge at the head of the creek is modern, but there has been a bridge here for centuries and it had its moment of fame on March 10th 1646 when it was chosen for a meeting between the broken Royalist army, under Lord Hopton at Truro, and the victorious Roundheads, under General Fairfax at Tregony. The treaty which was subsequently signed signalled the end of the Civil War in the west.

Truro

It would be hard to imagine a finer capital for Cornwall than this small, beautifully-proportioned city with a long history as a port on the confluence of the rivers Allen and Kenwyn, as a coinage town for the tin industry, as a market town serving a large rural area and as a place of Georgian culture and elegance. Remnants of the old port area where the fresh waters of the Allen and Kenwyn meet the salt of the Fal estuary can still be seen – not all of the quays have been built over with car parks and superstores yet – and there are good warehouses on the river, some of them reused by small businesses. The cathedral, rising magnificently out of the crowded city centre, was built between 1880 and 1910, the first Anglican cathedral to be constructed in England since St Paul's. The new building, designed by J.L. Pearson, incorporated one sixteenth-century aisle from the old parish church of St Mary's which had occupied this spot for six hundred years. Inside, look out for the wonderful painting *Cornubia – Land of the Saints* by the renowned Penwith artist John Miller. The excellent Royal Cornwall Museum in River Street contains extensive collections of Cornish paintings, minerals, mining artefacts and archaeological finds. Lemon Street is, in Pevnser's opinion, *'one of the most completely Georgian streets preserved anywhere'*. At its upper end is the Lander Monument to the Truro brothers who explored Africa; the figure of Richard Lander on top of the column was sculpted by the celebrated Neville Northey Burnard from Altarnun. The granite City Hall on Boscawen Street was built in 1846 in the Italian Renaissance style; following extensive interior remodelling it is set to become a Hall for Cornwall offering unrivalled facilities for theatre, concerts, conferences and markets in the heart of Truro.

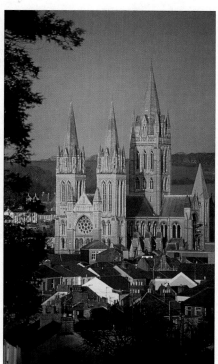

Truro Cathedral. Tim Guthrie.

Veryan

The large church of St Symphorian is set in one of the loveliest of Cornish churchtowns: pub, shop and school amongst the lush trees and gardens. Veryan's famous round houses were commissioned in the early nineteenth century by the Rev. Jeremiah Trist, to a design by the builder Hugh Rowe of Lostwithiel. Tradition has it that they were to protect the village from evil; they have no corners so there is nowhere for the devil to hide, and each has a crucifix on the summit of its thatched roof as an added deterrent. Nare Head to the south is a fine place for walking, with Gull Rock just offshore a notable seabird colony.

Veryan Round House. Cornwall Tourist Board.

Wadebridge

A pleasant shopping-town with a recently pedestrianised main street and a history as a busy river port, the glory of Wadebridge is still, as it has always been, its great bridge across the Camel. There are new bridges on either side of it today, one a footbridge, the other carrying the A39, but this is *the* bridge and it has been described as one of the best mediaeval bridges in England, despite the widening and strengthening works in 1847 and again in 1963 which have changed its character somewhat. It was built in the 1460s on the site of an important but dangerous ford (the town was then simply called Wade, from the English *waed* meaning 'ford') which had a chapel at either end to greet the valiant travellers. The account of the building of the bridge written by John Leland in 1538 still stands as a classic: *'Wher as now Wadebridge is, there was a Fery a 80 Yeres syns, and Menne sumtyme passing over by Horse stoode often in great Jeopardie. Then one Lovebone, Vicar of Wadebridge, movid with pitie began the Bridge, and with great Paine and Studie, good People putting their Help thereto, finished it with xvij fair and great uniforme Arches of Stone. One told me that the Fundation of certein of th'arches was first sette on so quik sandy Ground that Lovebone almost despairid to performe the Bridg ontyl such tyme as he layed Pakkes of Wolle for Fundation.'*

This tradition, of the bridge having been built on wool, is found attached to other bridges and has no evidence to support it. The old railway from Wadebridge to Padstow, and in the other direction to Bodmin, is now the Camel Trail, popular with cyclists and walkers.

Zennor

The village of Zennor is a granite huddle set in the extraordinary landscape of Penwith's north coast, where a narrow coastal shelf between the rugged cliffs and the swelling line of old moorland hills inland (the 'carns') is patterned with a tracery of prehistoric stone-hedged field systems and isolated farmsteads. This feels like a very old place indeed; there has been human settlement in the Zennor area since the early Bronze Age and the echoes of these ancient times are still remarkably strong. As Betjeman put it: *'Nature and prehistory in this treeless parish strewn with granite boulders among the heather make the efforts of modern man, even five hundred years ago, seem small and futile'*. In the church of St Senara is the famous fifteenth-century bench end depicting the Mermaid of Zennor, whose beauty and bewitching singing is said to have lured Matthew Trewhella, a sweet-voiced chorister, to her watery lair in Pendour Cove. Amongst its many literary associations, Zennor is perhaps best known for the year and a half that D.H. Lawrence and his wife Frieda lived here during the Great War – first at the Tinner's Arms in the village and then in a group of cottages at Higher Tregerthen – before being ejected under suspicion of spying for the enemy (Frieda was German-born and they did have an unfortunate penchant for singing German folk songs...). Zennor makes fleeting appearances in some of Lawrence's writing, notably in *Kangaroo*, where he describes *'seeing the light swim above the sea, [Somers] felt he was over the border in another world. Over the border, in that twilight, awesome world of the previous Celts'*.

Zennor. Tim Guthrie.

Newlyn. MDN.

SARDINA PILCHARDUS

by Nick Howell

THE CORNISH PILCHARD (Sardina Pilchardus) is, in reality, a mature Breton sardine and though many people think the Cornish stock has been fished out, in fact it is now in very good shape. The adult 'pilchards' come to breed in Cornish waters between August and December each year and the shoals can sometimes be seen just off the coast. This traditional migration used to bring shoals of fish so vast into Cornwall's many ports and coves that local demand was soon filled. Salting the fish, to preserve it, took advantage of the abundant harvest and exports of salted pilchards are recorded in the mid 15th century. By the mid 17th century exports to France, Spain, Italy and even the Caribbean were being completed and by 1871, Cornwall's biggest export year on record, the annual catch of pilchards reached 16,000 tonnes. (In comparison, the total landings of all vessels in Newlyn, for all species of fish, in 1995 was 11,320 tonnes).

This major and historic industry has left its mark on many coastal areas in Cornwall and it is possible for

The Pilchard Works, Newlyn. MDN.

interested visitors to spot signs of the old industry.

The huers' lookout posts, for instance, remain in a few areas; sometimes a small hut such as can be found on the clifftop at Cadgwith, or a well built granite station as at Newquay or Sennen (the huers were important figures as they acted as guides to the fishing boats, the traditional notice of a pilchard shoal given by the shouting of "hevva, hevva", meaning "found"). Other signs include discarded "pressing stones" which can sometimes be found on beaches. Sea rounded rocks about a foot in diameter, they are

recognisable by a rusty patch the size of a 2p coin, or, rarely, the rusty remains of the old iron hanging hook.

When visiting Cornish coves, if you see a run of six inch square holes in a wall, three feet above the ground, you will be standing in what was once a 'pilchard palace'. The holes used to hold the end of a ten foot beam which had a barrel of salt pilchards underneath it, next to the wall. Used with the beach stones at the other end of the beam, the device formed a lever to press oil out of the fish. Examples can still be seen in St. Ives, Gorran Haven, Cadgwith, Sennen, Mevagissey and Newlyn. Very original palaces remain in Cadgwith and St. Ives and though now lightly converted into tea shops or craft workshops, it is still possible to envisage the vast bulk of pilchards and salt that used to occupy centre stage in the courtyard and the rows of barrels along the walls under the beam presses.

There is only one original Cornish pilchard factory still operating. Situated in Newlyn "The Pilchard Works" is still salting, pressing and packing in traditional wooden barrels and boxes. The product is exported to the same Italian family that started buying from Cornwall in 1905. This "working museum" tells the story of how the vast catches of up to 13m fish were caught and processed and the social, artistic and industrial influences that the pilchard has had on the Cornish economy. Winners of a National award for "outstanding presentation of Britain's heritage" the factory/museum also received a visit from HRH Prince Charles in 1995. The pressing room, built in 1926, is fully operational from June until November, giving a unique insight into how hundreds of Cornwall's fish workers used to be employed.

The press room. Nick Howell.

See details of The Pilchard Works in the Attractions section, Tel. 44 (0) 1736 332 112. Group visits can be arranged for any time during the year from 7.30am until 8pm.
Additional guided tours of Newlyn's Harbour, Fish Market and the cobbled backstreets of the village are offered.
Coaches can be parked by arrangement, in Newlyn Harbour lorry park, 300 yards from the museum.

TATE ST IVES

by Mark Norton

For over 100 years west Cornwall has been a magnet for artists; the area's clear blue light and dramatic coastline an obvious attraction. From the first quarter of the twentieth century, a generation of artists established studios and exhibiting spaces in St. Ives, with Bernard Leach, arguably this country's finest potter, setting up a pottery in the town in 1920. Another resident was Alfred Wallis, a retired mariner, whose untutored painting of ships, lighthouses, harbours and cottages was to have such a profound influence on artists visiting the area.

In 1939, Ben Nicholson, Barbara Hepworth and the Russian sculptor Naum Gabo settled in St. Ives. After the war, a younger generation emerged including Wilhelmina Barns-Graham, Peter Lanyon, John Wells, Terry Frost, Bryan Wynter, Patrick Heron, Roger Hilton and Paul Feiler. Their work was at the forefront of new development in painting and sculpture, and together this group brought international attention to British Art.

Barbara Hepworth sculpture. Tate St Ives.

It is no surprise then, that when an outpost of London's Tate Gallery was first proposed, St. Ives was the obvious choice for its location. Better still, the town's redundant gas works, occupying a spectacular site overlooking Porthmeor Beach, was an ideal location to construct a building that could show works of art in the surroundings and atmosphere in which they were created. The architects for the new building, Eldred Evans and David Shaler, designers of the award-winning Truro Law Courts, were selected in a national architectural competition held in 1990. Their gallery design for a three storey building backing directly into the cliff face, set out to relate the new building to the town itself through the use of compatible local materials, textures and shapes.

Opened in June 1993, over half a million visitors have since visited the gallery, far exceeding initial expectation. Visitors from as far afield as Canada, America and Japan have been drawn to the gallery, its changing programme of displays

Tate St Ives overlooking Porthmeor. Tate St Ives.

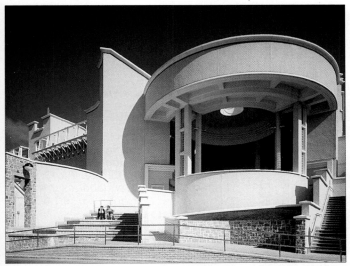

The impressive gallery entrance. Tate St Ives.

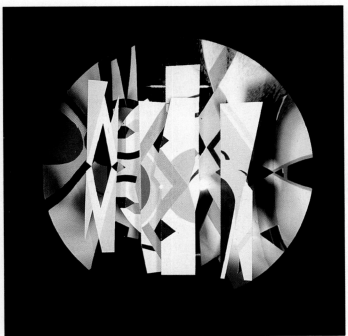

'Imoos VI' Brian Wynter (1965). Tate St Ives.

'St Ives' Alfred Wallis (1928). Tate St Ives.

Patrick Heron window. Tate St Ives.

and exhibitions ensuring a new experience is offered on each visit.

The focus of the building is a glazed rotunda, its form echoing the base of the demolished gas-holder which formerly occupied the site. At the entrance to the gallery is the strikingly impressive coloured glass window, specially designed by Patrick Heron which called for an innovative lamination technique allowing the colours in the stained glass to join, without the need for traditional leading. Manufactured in London, it is the largest unleaded stained glass window in the world.

The building provides five distinct gallery spaces. Two of these are devoted to a chronological overview of the St. Ives School, covering the period from about 1925 to 1975, including archive material, and another two galleries are rather less historical in their approach with a display of ceramics and attempting to communicate the scale and feeling of the St. Ives modernist aesthetic. The fifth gallery space is devoted to small study displays focusing on particular aspects of individual artist's work.

On the roof, as on the deck of a ship about to set sail, is the restaurant. From it the view extends over the rooftops of the town and its harbour, out to sea, along the horizon from Clodgy Point to St. Ives Bay and the Godrevy Lighthouse.

Even with the growth of mass tourism, West Cornwall remains as much a draw for artists as back in the founding days of the St. Ives 'school'. The timeless nature of its maritime landscape is now complemented by the modern and striking form of the Tate which in turn provides inspiration for those wishing to capture on canvas the spirit of St. Ives.

See Attractions section for details of the gallery opening hours.

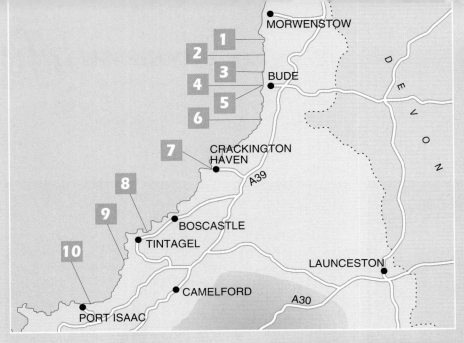

MORWENSTOW
1
2
3
BUDE
4
5
6
7
CRACKINGTON
HAVEN
A39
8
9
BOSCASTLE
TINTAGEL
10
LAUNCESTON
CAMELFORD
A30
PORT ISAAC
D E V O N

5 SUMMERLEAZE

A popular beach with a wide west facing sandy bay as well as a tidal sea water swimming pool for use at low tide. Easy accessibility from adjacent car park.

DIRECTIONS

From A39 Newquay-Bideford road, take A3073 signed Bude and follow signs to Bude Town Centre. Turn right at the mini roundabout signed Car Parks and Beaches. Bear left from main road into car park.

6 WIDEMOUTH SAND

Flat two mile stretch of sand. Though popular with families and surfers, there is usually plenty of room even in high season. West facing. Easily accessible from adjacent car park.

DIRECTIONS

From A39 Newquay-Bude road, turn off for Widemouth Bay. Park overlooking the beach.

(N. only)

7 CRACKINGTON HAVEN

Spectacular scenic area. Beach at high tide is mainly pebbled but a reasonable area of sand is revealed at low tide. West facing. Easily accessible from car park.

DIRECTIONS

From A39 Newquay-Bude road, turn off at Wainhouse Corner, signed Crackington Haven. Once reached, park in small car park adjacent to the river bridge in front of the Coombe Barton Inn.

1 DUCKPOOL

Largely made up of small rocks and pebbles with sand at low tide. West facing. Easy level access from National Trust car park.

DIRECTIONS

From the A39 Bude-Bideford road, turn off half a mile south of the village of Kilkhampton, signed Stibb. Continue through the village and follow the road through a wooded valley. A turn off for the beach is reached just after a narrow bridge across the river. Park adjacent to the beach.

3 NORTHCOTT MOUTH

Attractive west facing beach with mixture of pebbles and sand. Large areas of sand at low tide. Short accessible descent on road from car park to beach.

DIRECTIONS

From the A30 Bude-Bideford road, turn off for village of Poughill. Turn right in the centre of the village signed Northcott Mouth. Follow narrow lanes to the beach, the National Trust car park is on the bend to the left just before the short descent to the beach.

2 SANDY MOUTH

Pebbles in front of cliffs leading to large area of sand, particularly at low tide. Beach is accessible from car park via a slightly inclined path of 200 yards. West facing.

DIRECTIONS

From the A39 Bude-Bideford road, turn off half a mile south of the village of Kilkhampton, signed Stibb. Continue through the village, bearing left after a few hundred yards, signed Sandy Mouth Beach. Continue to the National Trust car park at the bottom of the lane.

4 CROOKLETS

Popular west facing beach with large expanses of golden sand, even at high tide. Very popular with surfers and families alike. Flat easy access from adjacent car park.

DIRECTIONS

From A39 Newquay-Bideford road, take A3073 signed Bude. Follow signs to Bude Town Centre, turning right at the mini roundabout signed Car Parks and Beaches. Continue through town following signs for Poughill, before turning left into car park.

Crackington Haven. MDN

Sandy Mouth. MDN

8 BOSSINEY COVE

Surrounded by high cliffs, this attractive north facing cove is limited as a beach to low tides only. Reached from the parking area via a steep 5-10 minute walk. Unsuitable for pushchairs.

DIRECTIONS

From Tintagel on the B3263, head north to find parking adjacent to a roadside toilet block at Bossiney.

Crooklets. MDN

9 TREBARWITH STRAND

Reasonably large area of sand and rocks at low tide. Easily accessible from parking area via a short walk down the hill. West facing.

DIRECTIONS

From B3314 Delabole Road, turn off signed Trebarwith Strand. Decent sized car park in the hamlet.

Bossiney. MDN

10 PORTGAVERNE

Fairly small stoney beach with sand at low tide. North facing. Accessed via a five minute downhill walk from the parking area on the outskirts of Port Isaac.

DIRECTIONS

From B3314 Delabole road, turn off on to the B3267 for Port Isaac. Park in the car park on the outskirts of the village, jointly used by both Portgaverne and Port Isaac communities and therefore liable to be busy. Follow hill down into Portgaverne.

Trebarwith Strand. MDN

Refreshments.

Toilets may only be open during the summer season.

Lifeguard during summer months.

Dog bans operate between Easter and end of September.

Portgaverne. MDN

31

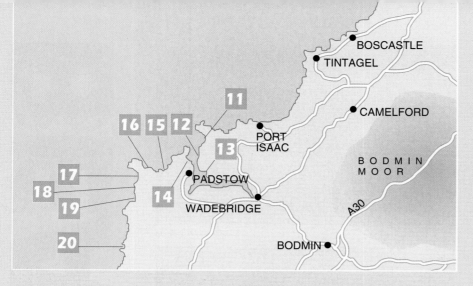

BOSCASTLE
TINTAGEL
CAMELFORD
PORT ISAAC
BODMIN MOOR
PADSTOW
WADEBRIDGE
BODMIN

15 TREVONE BAY

An attractive cove with good areas of golden sand, particularly at low tide. The rocks at adjoining Newtrain Bay offer much in the way of exploring at low tides. Easily accessible from car park. North west facing.

DIRECTIONS

Reached from the B3276 Newquay-Padstow road, turn off to the village of Trevone with parking areas at the bottom of the lane on either side of the cove.

Harlyn Bay. MDN

16 HARLYN BAY

Large crescent of soft golden sand, even at high tide. Surrounded by small dunes. Very sheltered, protected from Atlantic winds by Trevose Head and Cataclews Point. North facing. Level access.

DIRECTIONS

From B3276 Newquay-Padstow road, turn off in the village of St. Merryn, signed Harlyn. Follow road around to the right and park adjacent to the beach just after a small bridge.

11 POLZEATH

Large bay of flat golden sand with plenty of room. Popular with both families and surfers. West facing. Easy access from Polzeath where parking is adjacent to and on the beach.

DIRECTIONS

From A39 Wadebridge-Camelford road, take B3314 signed St. Minver. Follow signs for Polzeath.

Polzeath. MDN

12 DAYMER BAY

Sandy bay of firm sand, surrounded by sand dunes. West facing. Attractive views across Camel Estuary. Car park overlooks the beach.

DIRECTIONS

From A39 Wadebridge-Camelford road, turn off onto the B3314, signed St. Minver. Follow signs for Trebetherick and park adjacent to the beach.

13 ROCK

Continuation of Daymer Bay, situated beside the Camel Estuary and backed by sand dunes. As with most river estuaries, bathers should take great care because of the danger of tidal currents. Straightforward access from car park. West facing.

DIRECTIONS

From the A39 Wadebridge-Camelford road, take the B3314, signed St. Minver. Follow signs to Rock and park adjacent to the beach at the end of the village.

14 ST GEORGES WELL / HARBOUR COVE

Padstow's two closest beaches are St. Georges Well, which has a good area of sand available even at high water, and Harbour Cove, a long stretch of golden sand backed by dunes. Beaches are accessible, but both involve a considerable walk from the parking area. Excellent views across the Camel Estuary. East facing. Facilities in Padstow only.

DIRECTIONS

Park in Padstow's large town car park and take a short walk down into the town. Both beaches can only be reached after a considerable walk from the northern end of the harbour and up through the Memorial Gardens. St. Georges Well is reached after about 10 minutes, Harbour Cove about 20 minutes.

17 CONSTANTINE BAY

Fine crescent of golden sands. Surrounding dunes offer protection when wind blows. West facing. Easily accessible.

DIRECTIONS

From B3276 Padstow-Newquay road, follow signs for Constantine, past Trevose Golf and Country Club, before turning right, signed Constantine Bay. Small car park found at the end of the lane, larger car park available in season.

✕	Refreshments.
♟	Toilets may only be open during the summer season.
◯	Lifeguard during summer months.
🐕	Dog bans operate between Easter and end of September.

Rock. MDN

Trevone Bay. MDN

Constantine Bay. MDN

Daymer Bay. MDN

St Georges Well. MDN

18 TREYARNON BAY

A popular family beach due to the soft, golden sand even at high tide. West facing. Easily accessible from car park.

DIRECTIONS

Follow road for Treyarnon from B3276, Newquay-Padstow road. Follow lane and park in the car park at the bottom of the village.

Treyarnon Bay. MDN

19 PORTHCOTHAN BAY

Large area of flat sand with surrounding dunes. West facing. Car park is across the road from the beach entrance. Beach accessible to pushchairs with a little effort.

DIRECTIONS

On the B3276 Newquay-Padstow road, park in the centre of the hamlet and cross the road to the beach.

Porthcothan Bay. MDN

20 MAWGAN PORTH

Large west facing cove situated between two steep headlands where a river enters the sea. Popular family beach with flat sand at all tides. Accessible for pushchairs with a little effort. Beacon Cove, with no facilities, but much less busy, can be reached by a cliff walk on the southern headland.

DIRECTIONS

On the B3276 Newquay-Padstow road, park behind the shops and cafes with beach access across the road.

Mawgan Porth. MDN

BEACHES

POLZEATH, PADSTOW, CONSTANTINE BAY & MAWGAN PORTH

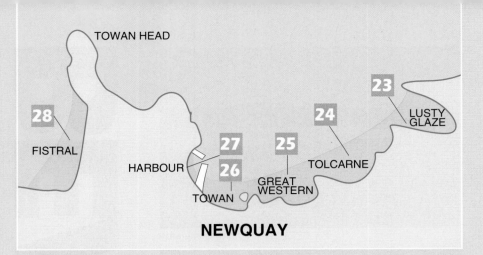

NEWQUAY

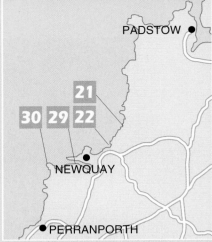

21 WATERGATE BAY

Two mile long west facing stretch of golden sands at the foot of steep cliffs. Though there are several paths down the cliffs, most people choose the easier option of entering in front of the hotels in the valley. Fairly open to direct westerly winds.

DIRECTIONS

On the B3276 Newquay-Padstow road, car parks sited in the valley in front of the hotels.

Porth. MDN

22 PORTH

Large area of flat, golden sands, very popular as a family beach due to safe bathing offered. West facing. Easily accessible from parking area.

DIRECTIONS

On B3276 Newquay-Padstow road, just north of Newquay with parking close to and on the beach.

NEWQUAY

Newquay's excellent beaches have played an important part in establishing the town as Cornwall's largest holiday resort. Consequently, the town can become congested in summer and it is recommended that Newquay's large town car parks are used, all of which provide easy access to the beaches. The 5 beaches of Lusty Glaze, Tolcarne, Great Western, Towan and Harbour form a large crescent below the town. Only Fistral, one of Cornwall's premier surfing beaches and Newquay's largest beach, is west of Towan Head.

23 LUSTY GLAZE

A small cove of sand backed by cliffs. West facing. Popular family beach.

DIRECTIONS

A large parking area overlooking the beach is signed from the Narrowcliff/Henver road (A3058) near the Riviera Hotel.

Tolcarne. MDN

24 TOLCARNE

A large area of sand backed by cliffs. West facing. Popular for surfing.

DIRECTIONS

Park in the main town car parks and proceed to the beach on foot.

25 GREAT WESTERN

West facing surfing beach backed by cliffs.

DIRECTIONS

Park in the main town car parks and proceed to the beach on foot. Access via a path between the Blue Lagoon Leisure Centre and Great Western Hotel.

26 TOWAN

Good sized area of sand and rocks, popular with families and surfers alike. Overlooked by the Newquay Sea Life Centre and Towan Island with its famous suspension bridge. Often busy due to its close proximity to the town centre.

DIRECTIONS

Park in the main town car parks and proceed to the beach on foot. Accessed from the town centre.

Harbour. MDN

27 HARBOUR

Newquay's smallest beach, comprising a small area of sand covered at high tide. Popular with families due to safe, sheltered bathing. North facing.

DIRECTIONS

Park in the main town car parks and proceed to the beach on foot. Accessed from the western end of the town centre.

28 FISTRAL

Located to the west of Towan Head, Newquay's most popular and largest beach is noted for its fine golden sands and excellent surfing conditions. International surfing events are regularly held here. West facing.

Watergate Bay. MDN

DIRECTIONS
As with other Newquay beaches, park in long stay car parks and walk. The small car park adjacent to Fistral is accessed by following signs for Fistral and The Headland, but is often full.

Crantock. MDN

29 CRANTOCK

A popular north west facing beach with a large expanse of golden sand surrounded by large dunes. The River Gannel Estuary, to the north of the beach, should, like most river estuaries, be avoided by swimmers because of river currents. Access through steep dunes is difficult for pushchairs.

DIRECTIONS
From A3075 Perranporth-Newquay road, turn off south of Newquay, signed Crantock. Turn right in village, signed Crantock Beach, and park in either the National Trust or beach shop car parks.

Lusty Glaze. MDN

Great Western. MDN

Porth Joke. MDN

30 PORTH (POLLY) JOKE

An attractive small north west facing cove of good sand, generally less busy than neighbouring beaches due to the short walk from the car park. The path, though unmade, is accessible for pushchairs with effort.

DIRECTIONS
From A3075 Perranporth-Newquay road, turn off for Crantock and follow the road through to the end of the village, signed West Pentire/Porth Joke. Park in the car park at the end of the lane.

Towan. MDN

Fistral. MDN

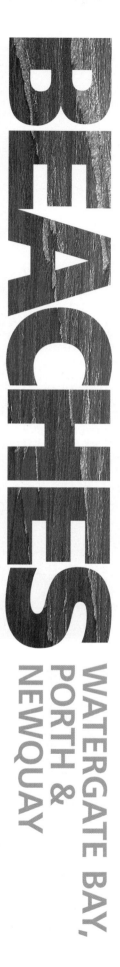

35

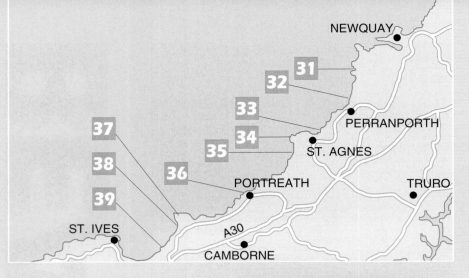

NEWQUAY
31
32
33
37
34
PERRANPORTH
35
ST. AGNES
38
36
PORTREATH
TRURO
39
ST. IVES
A30
CAMBORNE

31 HOLYWELL BAY

Large area of soft golden sands, very popular with visitors and locals alike. The extensive sand dunes surrounding the beach make access for pushchairs difficult. West facing.

DIRECTIONS

From A3075 Perranporth-Newquay road, turn off for Cubert and follow road through village to Holywell. Park in the National Trust car park sited on the left.

Holywell Bay. MDN

32 PERRANPORTH

West facing three mile stretch of fine, golden sands surrounded by high dunes/cliffs. Popular with surfers and families alike. Flat, easy access from Beach Car Park.

DIRECTIONS

From A3075 Redruth-Newquay road, turn off on to the B3284 signed Perranporth. Park in beachside car park or in the overflow car park at the top of Beach Road Hill near Droskyn Point.

Perranporth. MDN

Trevaunance Cove. MDN

33 TREVAUNANCE COVE

Attractive west facing cove of sand and pebbles. Extensive rocks revealed on either side at low tide. Easily accessible down a slight incline from the car park.

DIRECTIONS

From Perranporth take the B3285 to St. Agnes. As you approach St. Agnes, turn off at the sign to Trevaunance Cove. Very small car park situated at the end of the lane.

Chapel Porth. MDN

34 CHAPEL PORTH

Depending on the state of the tides, Chapel Porth possesses a good stretch of flat golden sand. Unfortunately, during near or high tide periods, the beach is reduced to a very small cove. North west facing. Car park overlooks the cove.

DIRECTIONS

Follow B3277 St. Agnes road to the outskirts of the village. Turn left and follow brown National Trust signs for Chapel Porth. Follow signs along narrow road and park at the bottom of the hill adjacent to the beach.

35 PORTHTOWAN

Large north west facing sandy cove flanked by small headlands. Car park adjacent and easily accessible to beach.

DIRECTIONS

From the main Truro-Redruth A30, turn off at Wheal Rose junction signed Scorrier. Follow signs for Porthtowan and turn off for beach after a small bridge. Park at the bottom of lane adjacent to the beach.

36 PORTREATH

Popular north facing family beach of soft fine sand and small shingle backing onto seafront walls. Easily accessible from car park.

DIRECTIONS

From the main A30, take the exit near Redruth, signed Porthtowan and Portreath (B3300). Proceed into Portreath and park adjacent to the beach.

37 GODREVY

North west facing beach with views towards Godrevy Lighthouse. Rocks suitable for exploring revealed at low states of tide.

DIRECTIONS

Godrevy is signed from the B3301 Hayle-Portreath road at a narrow bridge which crosses the Red River adjacent to the Sandsifter Hotel. Proceed up the track to a National Trust car park. An additional car park is located towards the end of the road overlooking the lighthouse. Access to beach via dune paths.

38 GWITHIAN TOWANS

Fine north west facing beach of golden sands, accessible through small sand dunes from the car park.

DIRECTIONS

From the B3301 Hayle-Portreath road, turn left just before the village of Gwithian, signed Gwithian Towans. Car park located at the end of the lane.

Hayle Towans. Tim Guthrie

39 HAYLE TOWANS

Large north west facing area of golden sands adjacent to river estuary making up southern end of sands that stretch up to Gwithian. Straight forward access from parking areas. Avoid swimming in the river estuary due to dangerous currents.

DIRECTIONS

From the A30 Redruth to Penzance roundabout at the northern end of Hayle, enter Hayle by crossing the double mini roundabout. Turn right, signed Phillack, before the Co-op Leo's Superstore. Go through Phillack, past the interestingly named "Bucket of Blood" Public House before reaching The Towans to park in the large car park.

• BEACH SAFETY •

To ensure beach safety, always check tide times, and observe the following flag regulations:

ALL RED FLAG
No bathing permitted.

RED & YELLOW FLAG
Bathe between these flags.

BLACK & WHITE CHECK
Area reserved for malibu and surfcraft only.

Godrevy. Tim Guthrie

Porthtowan. Tim Guthrie

Portreath. MDN

Gwithian Towans. Tim Guthrie

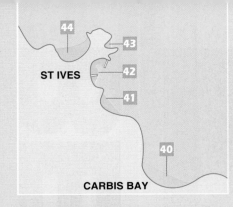

Carbis Bay. MDN

40 CARBIS BAY

Soft, golden sands surrounded by hills affording good protection. Popular north facing family beach due to safe bathing offered. Easy access from parking.

DIRECTIONS
Follow A3074 St. Ives-Hayle road until the turn off signed Carbis Bay Beach and Railway. Proceed to the car park at the bottom of the hill.

ST IVES

One of Cornwall's premier destinations for beachgoers, its popularity leading to severe restrictions on traffic in the town during summer. It is advisable therefore to follow the A3074 into St. Ives and head for the main 1000 space car park from where there is pedestrian access into the town. As a pleasant alternative, park at Lelant and catch the Park and Ride train to St. Ives. This is only a very short rail trip but the scenic view is outstanding. All beaches are accessible from the main part of the town.

41 PORTHMINSTER

A popular beach comprising of a large crescent of soft golden sand with views across St. Ives Bay to Godrevy Lighthouse. Sheltered position and safe bathing available. North east facing.

DIRECTIONS
Park in the town car parks and proceed on foot (adjacent car park only worth trying in low season).

38

42 TOWN (HARBOUR)

A good area of clean sand is revealed at low tide though the beach is completely covered at high tide. South east facing.

DIRECTIONS
Park in the town car parks and proceed on foot.

Harbour. MDN

43 PORTHGWIDDEN

The smallest beach in St. Ives but popular with families due to its sheltered position on the east side of St. Ives Island. Small cove of soft golden sand. East facing.

DIRECTIONS
Park in the town car parks and proceed on foot (adjacent car park only worth trying in low season).

Porthgwidden. Tim Guthrie

44 PORTHMEOR

Wide expanse of soft golden sand on the Atlantic side of St. Ives Island. Popular surfing beach, overlooked by St. Ives Tate Gallery. North facing.

DIRECTIONS
Park in the town car parks and proceed on foot (adjacent car park only worth trying in low season).

Portheras. MDN

45 PORTHERAS

Though a north west facing beach of excellent sand, its inclusion here is something of a warning because of sharp metal fragments embedded in the beach resulting from a dynamited shipwreck. Signs, warning the public of this danger, are clearly visible. A beach therefore not recommended for children.

DIRECTIONS
From B3306 St. Just-St. Ives road, turn off in Pendeen village marked Pendeen Lighthouse. Parking is at the bottom of the lane adjacent to the lighthouse with access to the cove via a fairly rough cliff path eastwards (approx. 10 mins).

46 WHITESAND BAY

An excellent mile long west facing bay of golden sands. Rocks revealed at low tide on either side of the beach. Straight forward access from parking areas. One of only two Blue Flag beaches in Cornwall and highly recommended for surfing.

DIRECTIONS
From the main A30 Penzance-Land's End road, take the turning marked Sennen Cove. There are three car parks; one at either end of Sennen Cove and a large overflow park halfway down the hill.

47 PORTHGWARRA

Picturesque and secluded cove with some sand at low tide. Intriguing arches in the cliffside provide access to tumbled granite boulders, ideal for sunbathing.

DIRECTIONS
From the Newlyn-Land's End road (B3315) near Trethewey, follow signs for Porthgwarra. A narrow road of about 2 miles leads to a parking area near the beach.

48 PORTHCHAPEL

Lovely, sheltered south facing cove of sand surrounded by cliffs. After a 10 minute cliff path walk, access involves a rocky climb down to the beach making it unsuitable for anyone disabled or those encumbered with pushchairs.

DIRECTIONS

From A30 Penzance-Land's End road, turn off on to the B3283 St. Buryan road. Go through the village of St. Buryan, past Treen until you see the signs for Porthcurno. Follow signs for the Minack Theatre and proceed on a narrow road before parking in a car park just before St. Levan Church. Access to the beach is via a 10 minute walk, signed Porthgwarra Cove, opposite the car park entrance.

Porthgwarra. MDN

49 PORTHCURNO

A splendid south east facing cove of fine white sand and turquoise seas. Stunning coastal views. Access is via a five minute walk down an unmade but accessible path from the car park.

DIRECTIONS

From A30 Penzance-Land's End road, turn off on to the B3283 St. Buryan road. Go through the village of St. Buryan, past Treen until you see the signs for Porthcurno. Continue down the hill and park in the car park at the bottom.

50 LAMORNA

Small beach at low tide, adjacent to the harbour and backed by granite boulders. South east facing. Parking adjacent to the harbour.

DIRECTIONS

From the B3315 Newlyn-Land's End road, turn off into the wooded valley. Go past the pub and park overlooking the harbour.

Lamorna. MDN

Porthminster. MDN

Porthmeor. Tim Guthrie

Whitesand Bay. Tim Guthrie

Porthchapel. Tim Guthrie

Porthcurno. Tim Guthrie

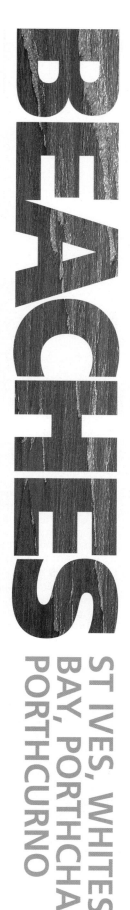

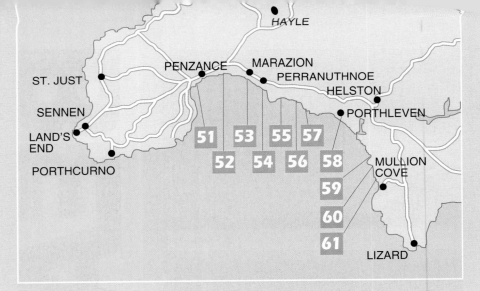

HAYLE

ST. JUST
PENZANCE MARAZION
PERRANUTHNOE
SENNEN HELSTON
LAND'S
END PORTHLEVEN
PORTHCURNO 51 53 55 57
52 54 56 58
MULLION
COVE
59
60
61
LIZARD

55 PRUSSIA COVE

A couple of small coves of grey shingle and rocks. Attractive location, south facing.

DIRECTIONS

From the A394 Penzance-Helston road, turn right at Rosudgeon, signed Prussia Cove. Drive to the bottom of the narrow lane and park in the small car park. From here, proceed on foot down the track, bearing right via an unmade track to Prussia Cove.

56 KENNEGGY SANDS

Secluded bay of sand accessed by a rocky descent with the help of a support rope. Unsuitable for pushchairs. South facing.

DIRECTIONS

Parking as for Prussia Cove. Proceed on foot down the track and follow the coastpath around to the left. Proceed through a gate and take a right fork to the beach. Approx. 10 mins walk.

57 PRAA SANDS

Mile long south west facing stretch of firm golden sands popular for bathing. Easy access from parking area.

DIRECTIONS

From the A394 Penzance-Helston road, turn off for Praa Sands and park at the bottom of the village.

Newlyn/Penzance. MDN

51 NEWLYN/ PENZANCE

Limited, south east facing beaches of pebbles and shingle with some small patches of sand. Largely covered at high tide. The Jubilee Pool, a sea water swimming pool, is available nearby (admission charge). Easy access from parking areas.

DIRECTIONS

From the A30 Hayle-Penzance road, follow the Harbour and Newlyn signs, parking either along the seafront or in one of the small parking areas available.

Long Rock. MDN

52 LONG ROCK

Western edge of sands that stretch around to Marazion, although fairly well covered at high tide. Safe bathing and sheltered position. Easy access from adjacent parking area. South facing.

DIRECTIONS

Follow A30 Hayle-Penzance road, turning off for Long Rock at the Safeway Superstore roundabout. Turn right on the outskirts of the village

signed Long Rock Beach Car Park, over the level crossing and park in the small car park behind the beach.

53 MARAZION

Long crescent of sand overlooking Mounts Bay and sheltered by the National Trust property of St. Michaels Mount. Well liked as a family beach location. Easy access from adjacent parking areas. South west facing.

DIRECTIONS

Follow A30 Hayle-Penzance road, turning off at the Long Rock by-pass roundabout signed Marazion. Park at either the car park adjacent to the railway bridge or in the parking area on the outskirts of Marazion.

54 PERRANUTHNOE

South west facing bay of sand and pebbles, somewhat restricted at high tide. Easy access from parking via steps or slipway.

DIRECTIONS

From A394 Penzance-Helston road, turn off for Perranuthnoe where Bertie Wooster's Restaurant is situated. Proceed to a car park at the bottom of the lane.

Perranuthnoe. MDN

Porthleven. MDN

58 PORTHLEVEN

3 mile south west facing stretch of steeply shelving sand and shingle. Car park 5 mins. walk to the beach. Strong undercurrents make bathing particularly hazardous here.

DIRECTIONS

From Helston take B3304 to Porthleven, turning left after 1.5 miles signed Loe Bar. Follow road into Porthleven outskirts and park in Shrubberies Hill Car Park. 5 minute walk to the beach down a fairly steep incline. Steps down to the beach.

Gunwalloe. MDN

Marazion. MDN

59 GUNWALLOE CHURCH COVE

Attractive west facing cove of sand backed by sand dunes in front of Mullion Golf Course. Small church located to the northern side, much photographed. Easily accessible via a short walk from the National Trust car park.

DIRECTIONS

From A3083 Helston-Lizard road, turn off just after Culdrose Air Base signed Gunwalloe and Church Cove (brown National Trust sign). Follow road for three miles. Large National Trust car park close to the beach.

Prussia Cove. MDN

60 POLDHU COVE

Attractive, sandy west facing cove. Rocks revealed to side of beach at low states of tide. Car park located behind the beach offering easy level access.

DIRECTIONS

From A3083 Helston-Lizard road, turn off signed Cury and Poldhu Cove (3 miles). Parking just behind the beach.

Kenneggy Sands. MDN

61 POLURRIAN COVE

West facing cove of sand flanked by small cliffs on either side. The unmade track and steps leading to the cove make pushchair access very difficult.

DIRECTIONS

From A3083 Helston-Lizard road, turn off on to B3296 to Mullion. Proceed through village, following signs for Mullion Cove before turning right signed Polurrian Cove. As there is no designated parking area, park where able and follow unmade track to cove (5 mins).

Praa Sands. MDN

Polurrian Cove. MDN

Poldhu Cove. Kerrier Tourism Office

BEACHES

MARAZION, PRUSSIA COVE, PRAA SANDS & GUNWALLOE

41

FALMOUTH
A394
HELSTON
HELFORD
MULLION COVE
COVERACK
LIZARD

72 71 70 69 68 67 66 65 64 63 62

turn left onto the B3293 St. Keverne road at the R.N.A.S. Culdrose roundabout. In a few miles, bear right and proceed on the B3294 into the village of Coverack. Parking can be found on the right hand side at the entrance to the village.

Porthoustock. MDN

64 CADGWITH

Two small east facing beaches in front of an attractive fishing village. The main beach is home to the village's fishing boats and consists of grey shingle.

DIRECTIONS

Signed from the A3083 Helston-Lizard road, 8 miles south of Helston. Use the main village car park and follow a signed path (5 mins walk). Accessible by pushchair with a little help.

67 PORTHOUSTOCK

Limited east facing beach of stone and shingle flanked by granite quarry workings. Parking on the beach. Popular with divers departing for the offshore Manacles Rocks.

DIRECTIONS

Take the B3293 to St. Keverne from the R.N.A.S. Culdrose roundabout south of Helston. Follow Porthoustock signs from St. Keverne and park at the bottom of the lane on the beach.

Mullion Cove. MDN

62 MULLION COVE

Very small harbourside beach at low tide only. West facing. The attractive National Trust harbour is the principal reasons to visit the cove. 5 minute inclined walk from the car park.

DIRECTIONS

From the A3083 Helston-Lizard road, turn off on to B3296 signed Mullion. Continue through Mullion village to the Cove. Park on the left with the cove reached after a 5 minute walk.

65 KENNACK SANDS

Large area of sand and rocks, especially at low tide. South east facing. Surrounding grassy areas are a good alternative for sunbathing when the tide is high. Flat and easy access from parking area.

DIRECTIONS

Follow signs for Cadgwith from Helston-Lizard road (A3083). Proceed through village of Kuggar and park at the bottom of a narrow lane overlooking the beach.

68 PORTHALLOW

A limited grey sand beach with stones and shingle. East facing. Attractive, in many ways, more as a fishing village than a bathing area. Cars may be parked alongside the boats on the beach.

DIRECTIONS

From the R.N.A.S. Culdrose roundabout south of Helston, take the B3293 to St. Keverne. Follow Porthallow signs from St. Keverne and park on the foreshore.

Kynance Cove. MDN

63 KYNANCE COVE

A popular, attractive south west facing beach of fine white sand. Though largely covered at high tide, there are many surrounding areas on which to picnic and sit. The beach is reached after a ten minute walk using unmade paths and steps which will prove difficult for those with pushchairs.

DIRECTIONS

Signed (brown National Trust signs) from A3083 Helston-Lizard road, half a mile north of Lizard village.

Kennack Sands. MDN

66 COVERACK

Overlooked by an attractive fishing village, this small east facing beach of sand and rocks is largely covered at high tide. Easily accessible via a short walk from car park.

DIRECTIONS

From A3083 Helston-Lizard road,

69 MAENPORTH

An attractive east facing sandy cove between small headlands. Flat and easy access from adjacent parking.

DIRECTIONS

Follow the main A39 to Falmouth. At the Leo's Superstore roundabout follow signs for beaches. Continue through traffic lights and a further roundabout before turning right into Pennance Road at the Greenlawns Hotel roundabout, signed Cliff Road and All Beaches. At cross roads, follow sign right for Maenporth, shortly passing Swanpool Beach and then turning left at T junction after Falmouth pitch and putt course. Park on the left behind the beach.

Maenporth. MDN

Cadgwith. MDN

70 SWANPOOL

Sheltered east facing sandy cove. Easily accessed from adjacent parking.

DIRECTIONS

Follow Maenporth directions which lead past Swanpool Beach. Park adjacent to beach.

Coverack. MDN

71 GYLLYNGVASE

Falmouth's largest and most popular beach, consisting of a fine crescent of sand backed by well kept gardens. Popular with families for its safe bathing and size. Level access from adjacent parking. South east facing.

DIRECTIONS

Follow directions indicated for Maenporth until the crossroads at Pennance Road is reached. Turn left and follow signs for Gyllyngvase parking.

Porthallow. Kerrier Tourism Office/P Watts

72 CASTLE

A limited area of sand compared with its Gyllyngvase neighbour, but of interest for its extensive rock pools which are worth exploring at low tide. South facing. Adjacent parking allows easy access via short flight of steps.

DIRECTIONS

Follow directions indicated for Maenporth until the crossroads at Pennance Road is reached. Turn left and park on the sea front in Cliff Road.

Swanpool. MDN

Castle. MDN

Gyllyngvase. Tim Guthrie

43

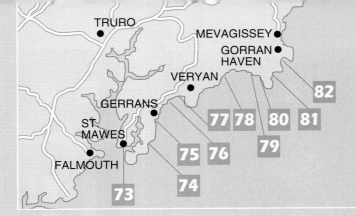

Carne. MDN

St Mawes. MDN

73 ST MAWES

Several small south facing beaches are revealed at lower states of the tide in this small attractive harbourside community. A pleasure trip service (seasonally available) and foot ferry operate between Falmouth and St. Mawes.

DIRECTIONS
1) From A39 Falmouth-Truro road, turn off at Playing Place onto B3289 for King Harry Ferry. After a charged river crossing, continue on B3289 and then join the A3078 at St. Just, signed to St. Mawes.
2) From A39 Truro-St. Austell road, turn off from Probus by-pass on to A3078 signed Tregony/St. Mawes. Follow A3078 for 15 miles to St. Mawes.

74 TOWAN

Rarely crowded south east facing beach comprising of a crescent of sand at the southern end of Gerrans Bay. Accessed via a 250 yard path from parking area.

DIRECTIONS
Follow alternative routes 1 or 2 indicated for St. Mawes. Once on A3078, follow the signs for Portscatho and Gerrans and proceed on the St. Anthony Head road. Park in the National Trust car park at Porth Farm.

75 PORTHCURNICK

South east facing cove of sand just north of Portscatho fishing village. Reached via a five minute walk from the parking area. Other smaller

beaches available in and around Portscatho at low tide. Accessed via coastal path.

DIRECTIONS
Follow alternative routes 1 or 2 indicated for St. Mawes. Once on A3078, follow signs for Portscatho and the Porthcurnick Beach parking area. The beach is at the bottom of a short unmade track leading from the parking area.

Porthcurnick. MDN

76 PENDOWER

Popular south facing family beach of sand. Rocks revealed between Pendower and Carne at lower states of the tide. Access from adjacent parking areas. Excellent views over Gerrans Bay to Nare Head on the one side and Portscatho and beyond on the other.

DIRECTIONS
1) From A39 Truro-St. Austell road, turn off from Probus by-pass onto A3078, signed Tregony/St. Mawes. Pendower is signed left approx. 1 mile after Ruanhighlanes. Park at the bottom of the lane, overlooking the sea.
2) Directions as above following St. Mawes road. Fork left after Esso garage signed Portloe and Veryan. Proceed through Veryan and follow Pendower signs. Narrow lanes lead to a right fork signed to Pendower Beach. Parking next to beach.

Pendower. MDN

77 CARNE

A continuation of Pendower Beach, Carne at low tide offers a good area of sand and shingle with rocks at either end of the beach. However, at periods of high tide the beach is considerably reduced. Good views over Gerrans Bay. South facing.

DIRECTIONS
As Pendower route 2 until right fork signed Pendower Beach. Instead, fork left to Carne Beach. At the bottom of the hill turn left into a sizeable National Trust car park.

78 PORTHOLLAND

Two (East and West) small south facing beaches completely covered at high tide.

DIRECTIONS
Follow Pendower route 2 by forking left at Esso garage. Continue on this road until the Portloe/Portholland and Veryan signs appear before you. Fork left here. Accessed via narrow lanes with West Portholland reached first at the bottom of approach road. East Portholland reached by following road around incline. Parking adjacent to beach.

79 PORTHLUNEY

South facing sandy beach in an attractive cove. Very popular with families throughout the year. Overlooked by Caerhays Castle, a very striking private residence not open to the public. Parking behind the beach allows easy level access.

DIRECTIONS
Follow Pendower route 2 signed Caerhayes. There are narrow lanes to be negotiated with a steep hill leading down to the car park.

44

Porthluney. MDN

Towan. MDN

80 HEMMICK

Fairly isolated small south west facing cove of sand. Limited parking and reached by narrow country lanes.

DIRECTIONS

From A390 Truro-St. Austell road, turn off onto B3287 signed for Tregony. Turn left after about 1.5 miles signed Caerhays and Polmassick. Follow signs for Gorran, from where, take the road signed Boswinger. Turn off to beach where youth hostel indicated, a very narrow road leads down to a small parking area close to the beach. In Summer, a further parking area is situated up the hill on the approach to the beach.

Portholland. MDN

81 VAULT

Secluded and rarely busy, Vault Beach provides a long strip of sand and shingle with rocks at low tide. Access from parking via a 10 minute walk. Though accessible there are probably easier beaches in the area for those with pushchairs. South east facing.

DIRECTIONS

Follow directions to Gorran detailed for Hemmick Beach. Follow signs into Gorran Haven and turn right up Lamledra Hill, a narrow lane just before the main Gorran Haven car park sign. The National Trust car park is on the left at the top of the hill.

Hemmick. MDN

Vault. MDN

82 GORRAN HAVEN

Attractive east facing beach of sand, easily accessed via a slight incline from the car park. Popular with families because of its safe bathing.

DIRECTIONS

From A390 in St. Austell follow signs for Porthpean from between the ASDA Superstore and Mount Charles (signed for Charlestown Shipwreck Centre) roundabouts. Turn left at Lower Porthpean signed Porthpean Beach. Follow the road around and park in the car park on the right just before the Higher Porthpean sign.

Gorran Haven. MDN

BEACHES

ST MAWES, THE ROSELAND PENINSULA & GORRAN HAVEN

45

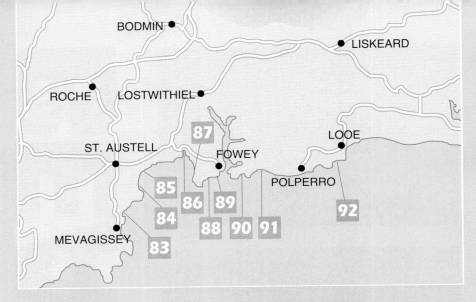

Polridmouth Cove. MDN

88 POLRIDMOUTH COVE

Small sandy south facing cove largely covered at high tide. Reached via a 10 minute walk from the parking area down an unmade track. Accessible by pushchair with some difficulty.

DIRECTIONS

From the A3082 Par-Fowey road, take the turning signed Polkerris and Menabilly. Proceed past Polkerris turning and park at the end of the lane in the National Trust car park. Footpath to Polridmouth.

83 PENTEWAN

Large expanse of sand, over half a mile long. The surrounding area is occupied by the Pentewan Sands Caravan Park which allows visitors to utilise its faciliities upon payment for parking. Flat, easy access to the beach. East facing.

DIRECTIONS

Accessed from the B3273 St. Austell to Mevagissey road, via Pentewan Sands Caravan Park.

84 PORTHPEAN

Attractive east facing beach of sand, easily accessed via a slight incline from the car park. Popular with families because of its safe bathing.

DIRECTIONS

From A390 in St. Austell follow signs for Porthpean from between the ASDA Superstore and Mount Charles (signed for Charlestown Shipwreck Centre) roundabouts. Turn left at Lower Porthpean signed Porthpean Beach. Follow the road around and park in the car park on the right just before the Higher Porthpean sign.

Carlyon Bay. MDN

85 CARLYON BAY

Long south facing bay of soft sand, adjacent at the western end to the amusement/entertainment and leisure complex. Easily accessed from

adjoining parking area. Carlyon Bay is one of only two Blue Flag beaches in Cornwall. Polgaver Bay, at the far eastern end of the bay, was Cornwall's first official naturist beach.

DIRECTIONS

Signed from the A390 in St. Austell (also signed Cornish Leisure World).

Par Sands. MDN

86 PAR SANDS

Large expanse of firm sand and dunes even at high tide. Popular in summer, this south facing beach is easily reached from the adjacent parking area.

DIRECTIONS

From the A3082 Par-Fowey road, turn right in the village of Polmear after passing under a railway bridge. Park in large car park on left in front of the sand dunes.

87 POLKERRIS

Attractive small west facing cove in the shelter of a harbour wall. Popular with families because of its safe bathing. Easily reached from parking area via short, inclined walk.

DIRECTIONS

On the A3082 Par-Fowey road, turn off signed Polkerris and Beach. After 100 yards, turn right to Polkerris and park in a large car park only a short walk away from the beach.

89 READYMONEY COVE

Small sandy south east facing cove overlooking the Fowey Estuary. Limited space at high tide. Accessible by path via a 5 minute walk from parking area.

DIRECTIONS

Follow A3082 to Fowey, turning right where main and beach car and coach parks signed. Continue past main car park to Readymoney Cove Car Park (also signed St. Catherines Castle). Follow lane at the bottom of parking area to the beach. (5 minutes walk).

90 LANTIC BAY

An isolated and attractive cove of sand with some shingle. Views towards Pencarrow Head. Access from car park is not suitable for pushchairs. South facing.

DIRECTIONS

On Polruan to Polperro coast road, locate a small National Trust car park only 50 yards from the path signed for Pencarrow Head (N.T.), one mile east of Polruan. The bay is reached after a 15 minute walk down a steep path. An additional car park, half a mile further on towards Polperro has a toilet block.

✕	Refreshments.
♟	Toilets may only be open during the summer season.
◐	Lifeguard during summer months.
✕	Dog bans operate between Easter and end of September.

91 LANSALLOS

Attractive, rarely busy south facing cove of sand and rocks. Reached by a 20 minute walk down an unmade track, possible, but not easy for pushchairs and involving the crossing of a stile.

DIRECTIONS

From main Polperro roundabout at Crumplehorn, follow signs for Lansallos (2.5 miles). Proceed along narrow lanes and park in the National Trust car park about two hundred yards north of the church. Access to the beach is by way of a path beside the church, although at times this can be muddy.

Lansallos. MDN

92 TALLAND BAY

Limited south facing beach of shingle and rocks with some sand. Easily accessed from parking area.

DIRECTIONS

Follow signs for Talland from main Looe-Polperro road (A387). Proceed on narrow lanes past the church and park in area adjacent to cafe.

Talland Bay. MDN

• BEACH SAFETY •

To ensure beach safety, always check tide times, and observe the following flag regulations:

ALL RED FLAG
No bathing permitted.

RED & YELLOW FLAG
Bathe between these flags.

BLACK & WHITE CHECK
Area reserved for malibu and surfcraft only.

Pentewan. MDN

Porthpean. MDN

Polkerris. MDN

Readymoney Cove. MDN

Lantic Bay. MDN

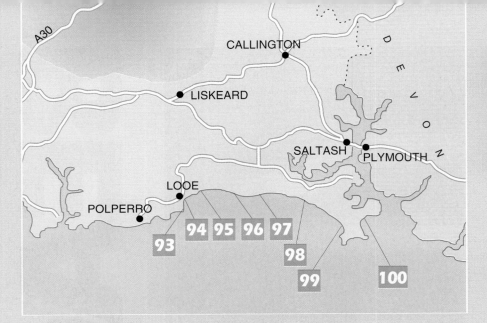

Seaton. MDN

97 DOWNDERRY

South facing beach of sand and pebbles with rocks at low tide. Easy access from parking.

DIRECTIONS

Follow instructions for Seaton and continue on for approx. one mile to the village of Downderry. Park in central part of the village.

Hannafore. MDN

93 HANNAFORE

Strip of shingle and patches of sand with large area of rocks revealed at lower tides. Easily accessible from adjacent parking along the seafront. South east facing.

DIRECTIONS

On arriving in East Looe via the A387, cross the main bridge, turning left immediately into Quay Road. Follow this road around and park beside the main road adjacent to the beach.

94 EAST LOOE

Popular and often crowded, this east facing beach of fine sand is backed by concrete terracing built to counteract particularly high tides. To avoid congestion in the town, parking is a 10 minute flat and accessible walk to the beach through East Looe high street or via the fishing quay.

DIRECTIONS

Follow the A387 into East Looe and cross the main bridge, parking in the signed West Looe Car Park adjacent to the Discovery Centre.

95 MILLENDREATH

Small south facing cove of sand popular with families. The surrounding area is largely occupied by Millendreath Holiday Park which has many facilities open to the visitor. Level, easy access from parking located close to the beach.

DIRECTIONS

From the main Looe-Torpoint road (A387), turn off on to the B3253. Bear left just after Looe Bay Holiday Park and proceed to the car park at the bottom of the lane, adjacent to the beach.

Millendreath. MDN

96 SEATON

Large south facing beach of sand and small pebbles located at the bottom of the River Seaton valley. Level access from parking.

DIRECTIONS

From A387 Looe-Torpoint road, follow B3247 at Hessenford to the bottom of the wooded valley where the beach and parking can be found.

Downderry. MDN

98 PORTWRINKLE

Small south west facing beach of rocks and sand, fairly well covered at high tide. Easy access from parking.

DIRECTIONS

From the Torpoint-Liskeard road (A374), take the B3247 to Crafthole. Follow signs to Portwrinkle and park at the bottom of the hill.

99 WHITSAND BAY

A four mile south west facing stretch of sand and rocks, much of which is covered at high tide. Access from parking areas along the coast road is difficult and involves negotiating fairly uneven paths and flights of steps. Particular care should be taken to prevent being cut off by the incoming tide on this stretch of the coast.

 Refreshments.

 Toilets may only be open during the summer season.

 Lifeguard during summer months.

Dog bans operate between Easter and end of September.

DIRECTIONS

From A374 Torpoint-Looe road, turn off at Antony on to the B3247 signed Millbrook. Proceed onto Whitsand Bay coast road adjacent to Tregantle Fort where there is a large car park with toilets. A further parking area is available a mile east at Sharrow Point where refreshments are available in season. Proceed to beach from cliff paths.

East Looe. MDN

Portwrinkle. MDN

Whitsand Bay. MDN

100 KINGSAND/ CAWSAND

Fairly sheltered small, east facing coves of sand and shingle accessed after a short walk from either the large car park at Cawsand or the parking in Kingsand.

DIRECTIONS

From A374 Torpoint-Looe road, turn off at Antony on to the B3247 signed Millbrook. Follow signs for Cawsand/Kingsand.

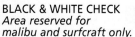

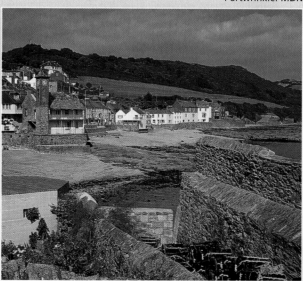

Kingsand. MDN

• BEACH SAFETY •

To ensure beach safety, always check tide times, and observe the following flag regulations:

ALL RED FLAG
No bathing permitted.

RED & YELLOW FLAG
Bathe between these flags.

BLACK & WHITE CHECK
Area reserved for malibu and surfcraft only.

Cawsand. MDN

THE NATIONAL TRUST IN CORNWALL

by Liz Luck

The coastline is the undisputed glory of Cornwall. In its beauty and variety it is incomparable ... and vulnerable: the dramatic rise of tourism in the county in the last hundred years has threatened, at times, to kill the goose that laid the golden egg. It follows that arguably the greatest impact of the National Trust in the South-West has been in the permanent protection from despoliation and development of so many miles of the coast.

The story begins in the very early days. In 1897, just two years after the Trust's foundation, Barras Nose at Tintagel became its first coastal acquisition in England, bought by public subscription as a direct response to the erection nearby of the gigantic King Arthur's Castle Hotel. During the first seventy years, many colossi of the coast came to the Trust through the generosity and far-sightedness of individual donors and groups of local people: the massive, brooding Dodman, for instance, as early as 1919; Pentire Point and The Rumps, saved from bungalows in 1936; the jutting reptilian headland of Cambeak given in 1959.

Despite these early strides, far too much of the coast remained open to attack or had already succumbed to shoddy development. By the time that Enterprise Neptune, the Trust's appeal for the coastline, was

launched in May 1965, it was realised that only vigorous campaigning and fundraising to enable the purchase of land on the open market, where necessary, could begin to save the situation. Neptune began to make a

Volunteers at Nanjulian. Bill Newby/National Trust.

difference immediately - within a year the wild north coast promontory of Park Head had been given as a contribution to the appeal. In the thirty years since then the tempo of acquisition has accelerated steadily, and sometime dramatically. Much of the county's

most spectacular coastal scenery has had its remoteness safeguarded for ever, whilst major landmarks like Cape Cornwall and Lizard Point are shielded from future exploitation. The deep-water estuaries of the south coast are at

particular risk from the pressures of leisure, tourism and housing developments. Since the launch of Enterprise Neptune much progress has also been made in protecting these sensitive areas, although much still remains to be done.

The policy of buying 'one farm

deep' back from the coast originated in Cornwall. Although more expensive, this policy has meant that the entire coastal landscape up to the first skyline is secured, rather than just the narrow cliff stretch. Many of the major areas of Trust ownership on the coast have come about through a slow, delicate process of patient negotiation; piecing together small acquisitions like a jigsaw puzzle, until gradually the whole picture can be seen. That glorious run of unspoilt coast to the east of Polruan on Cornwall's south coast is a notable example; the first piece was in place back in 1936 and the purchase of Townsend Farm in 1991 completed the stretch from Polruan to Lansallos. In recent years the 'jigsaw principle' has been most dramatically successful in the extraordinary prehistoric landscape around Zennor in West Cornwall, now designated as an Environmentally Sensitive Area. The complex and extensive pattern of Trust ownership and covenants in the area began in 1957, but it was in the 1980s that the jigsaw really began to take shape and the national importance of this ancient coastal plateau was recognised.

Management of the coast requires the Trust to take the long view, necessitating hard, sometimes unpopular, decisions to be made: moving a car park or a caravan site,

Towanroath Engine House, Chapel Porth. MDN.

Relaxing at Gillan Creek. D J Flunder/National Trust.

Tintagel Old Post Office. J Hicks/National Trust.

re-routing a path, demolishing an unsightly building. Less publicised are the occasions when the Trust has not shirked the most difficult decision of all - to do nothing but tread softly and leave no trace. In the field of nature conservation, the Trust has led the way in the reintroduction of coastal grazing to encourage the growth of wild flowers; flocks of Manx and Soay sheep, Shetland and Dartmoor ponies cropping near the cliff edge are now a common sight, as are the breathtaking carpets of spring squill, kidney vetch and bird's-foot trefoil which they have allowed to return.

It is no coincidence that it was the people of Tintagel who gave the Trust its first historic house in the county, as well as its first coastal property, for here was a community where the mixed blessings of tourism arrived early, and in spectacular fashion, thanks to Tennyson's popularisation of the Arthurian legend and the opening of the North Cornwall Railway to Camelford. Many of the village's dignified old buildings were sacrificed to the mania for new boarding houses and shops, but the Old Post Office, a rare, small 15th

century manor house, was saved by local people and vested in the Trust in 1903.

Cotehele, owned by the Edgcumbes for nearly 600 years, was, in 1947, the first historic house and estate in the country to be handed over to the Trust in lieu of death duties, through National Land Fund procedures. An invaluable precedent was thus established, largely through the patience and pertinacity of the 6th Earl of Mount Edgcumbe who was determined that the home of his forebears should be preserved.

At Cotehele, where a large and varied estate surrounds one of the least-altered medieval houses in Britain, as well as at Lanhydrock, the Trust in Cornwall pioneered the practice, since widely adopted, of furnishing and exhibiting domestic quarters and workshops as well as the state rooms, revealing to the public every aspect of life on a great estate. The 49 rooms on view at Lanhydrock, which was given in 1953 by the 7th Viscount Clifden, are particularly fine. The fascinating contrast between the richly-furnished Dining Room, Billiard Room and Drawing Room and the 'below stairs' accommodation and

service rooms dramatically evokes a lost world of high Victorian living.

Constraint of space does not allow justice to be done to the amazing variety of great buildings in the county now in the care of the Trust - the sublimely romantic castle on St. Michael's Mount, the classical eighteenth-century beauty of Antony, Elizabethan Trerice with its magnificent Great Hall window - nor to the thousands of humbler dwellings, many of them classics of local vernacular architecture revealing the social history of ordinary people.

The genial climate of Cornwall produces some of the country's finest gardens, many of which - Glendurgan, Trengwainton, Trelissick, Lanhydrock, Cotehele - are now owned and tended by the Trust. Recently, the great storm of January 1990 wreaked terrible damage but much effort and imagination has since gone into repairing and replanting, alongside the constant work needed to keep the gardens alive for future generations.

Some of the great archaeological sites of Cornwall - Iron Age hill forts and cliff castles, burial chambers and settlements from the late Stone Age and Bronze Age - have long been protected by the Trust. They have latterly been joined by impressive remnants of our more recent industrial past, particularly with the active conservation of mine engines and buildings (which would surely have seemed an implausible idea to the Trust's founders back in 1895!). Of particular significance was the gift of Cornish Engines at Pool by the Cornish Engines Preservation Society in 1967.

This catalogue of growth and progress is only possible through the hard work of members, staff and volunteers as well as the all important donations of property and funds. As important, of course, are the properties' visitors, the admission fees ensuring the protection of important and historic buildings and landscapes.

For details of the Trust properties in Cornwall, see the Attractions section.

For membership of the Trust, you can join at almost all properties or shops. Alternatively, telephone the Membership Department on 0181 464 1111, Monday to Friday, 9am - 5.30pm.

Trevean Cliff, Nr Morvah. W Hocking/National Trust.

Treen Castle from Pedn-Vounder. W Hocking/National Trust.

POWERHOUSE HAYLE

by Bret Guthrie

When your long journey through the rich and varied West Country landscape is within a dozen miles or so of Land's End, and you pass through a small town's long street of houses and shops, offering three miles of golden sands, you would hardly believe that you are in a springboard of the Industrial Revolution. But two and a half centuries ago, and up to the late nineteenth century, that is what Hayle was.

It started when the hamlets of Redruth and Camborne became the centre of a mining field producing much of the world's copper, later tin, and a host of other minerals. Mines went ever deeper, and drainage by waterwheel worked pumps, or adits into valleys and the coast became ineffective. Steam engines, first Newcomen's, then Watt's, were introduced which needed coal for fuel.

With a canal in 1769, the port of Hayle could take Welsh sailing coal boats deep into the Angarrack creek where a tide mill was situated and close to where the Co-Op Leo's supermarket is presently sited. Copper ores were smelted nearby from 1755 to 1819, hence Copperhouse, whose cast blocks of black slag were used to build much of the quay walls, hedges and some houses. Later this smelter turned to iron founding, making pumping engines for Cornish and overseas mines, and items such as the chains for the Hungerford and Lambeth suspension bridges in London and Brunel's Albert Bridge in Plymouth.

In 1779 a village blacksmith, John

Hayle Estuary

Harvey, moved to Carnsew at the western end of Hayle to build a foundry that was to make industrial history. There Richard Trevithick, Cornwall's most innovative engineer, made the first steam road carriages in 1801 and 1802; a steam-powered rock drill and a portable engine for farmers. His most important work was the high-pressure boiler, the heart of the true Cornish Engine, which he made for a local mine. The foundry built hundreds of these pumps in the nineteenth century for home and abroad, including those draining the Severn Tunnel and

many for London's waterworks. The greatest was the Cruquius engine, near Heemstede in Holland, with a twelve foot diameter cylinder working eleven beam pumps, operating until 1933. A similar cylinder was cast at Copperhouse and a third at Perran Foundry, to drain the Haarlemmermeer.

In the dunes, gunpowder and dynamite were made for the mines, and cordite for the 1914-1918 war, ending when peace came.

Apart from their major works, what could be made of iron, the foundries would make; everything from nails to cooking ranges and iron steamships. Such industry brought wealth for the Harvey's; three handsome family homes beside the foundry millpond and two more on the hill overlooking the inner estuary; one now the Paradise Park conservation centre. For the craftsmen and middle classes there were terraces of standard Victorian design, overlooking the harbour, and for the rest, terraces of small stone-built two-storeyed homes on the hillsides.

As mining rapidly declined by 1900 so did Hayle's fortunes, forcing it to turn to the "golden sands" to make its living.

The amazing variety of minerals found in the county are well displayed in the Royal Cornwall Museum in Truro, the Camborne School of Mines at Pool, and Cornwall Geological Museum, Penzance. Cornish engines, maintained by the National Trust, are open at Pool and Levant, near Trewellard, while Geevor Mine at Pendeen, one of the last to close, is now a mining museum. The Cruquius engine at Heemstede, Holland, is also preserved for public viewing.

Hayle Viaduct. Tim Guthrie.

Hayle Harbour. Tim Guthrie.

The Copley Arms, Hessenford.

King of Prussia, Fowey.

Cornish Pubs

A LOOK AT SOME OF THE PUBS OF ST AUSTELL BREWERY...

The St. Austell Brewery was founded in 1851 by Walter Hicks, a farmer from Lower Menadue in the Parish of Luxulyan. At the age of 22 Walter mortgaged his farm and set up business as a maltster at Trenance on the north eastern fringes of St. Austell. By 1861 he had moved to Church Street, a few doors down from the White Hart, and was trading as a wine and spirit merchant as well. In 1867 a property known as the 'London Inn' situated at Market Street was offered for sale. Walter Hicks built a 'steam brewery' and dwelling house on the site of the inn, the two of which came to be known in later years as Tregonissey House and still grace the expanse of Market Street, opposite the church, today. At the same time he acquired property running up to No 8 Market Hill for use as offices and a malt house. Because he was the first and the only major brewer to set up in the boom town of St. Austell, Walter Hicks ensured for his company a secure foundation from which the business could only flourish. Such was the brewery's rapid success that it had out-grown these buildings within twenty-five years of their erection. In 1893 the new

brewery was built on a site of two open fields beside Tregonissey Lane on high ground above the town, with spectacular views over the broad sweep of St. Austell Bay. Over the years since then there have been alterations and improvements, but the essential 'brew house' of 1893 is still the working heart of the brewery today.

The business in its early days was carried on under the founder's name, but in 1934 the name of the company was changed to the St. Austell Brewery Co. Ltd. To this day the company remains an independent family firm with nearly all of Walter Hick's numerous descendants involved in the brewery as shareholders and some more actively as directors. Many employees throughout the brewery's history have established impressive family traditions too, having been involved with the company for their entire working lives, thus helping to create the strengths and qualities of a truly independent family firm.

St. Austell Brewery's inns may be found throughout Cornwall, from Penzance to Fowey, Newquay to Looe.

Visitor Centre

Take a guided tour around Cornwall's oldest independent Family Brewery.

Why not spend some time at St Austell Brewery Visitor Centre (see Attractions section, page 122, for details).

The St Austell Brewery has been brewing beer for over 140 years. Many of the original traditions and skills remain at the heart of St Austell beers today. Experience the working brewery, the gleam of old wood, polished brass and copper. Follow the brewing process from raw ingredients to finally, sampling the traditional cask conditioned ales.

Guided tours can be booked on (01726) 66022.

The Old Custom House, Padstow.

The Swan Hotel, Wadebridge.

The Ship Inn, Fowey.

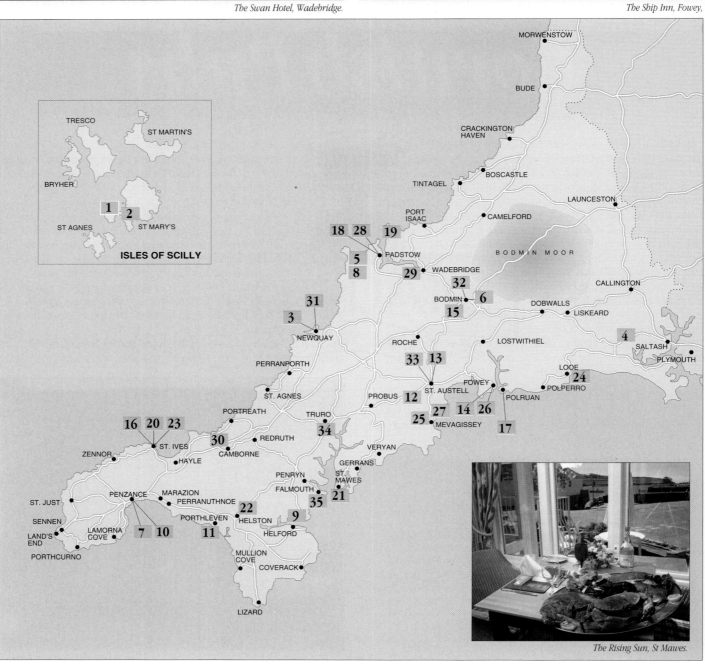

TRESCO

ST MARTIN'S

BRYHER

1   2

ST AGNES   ST MARY'S

ISLES OF SCILLY

MORWENSTOW

BUDE

CRACKINGTON HAVEN

BOSCASTLE

TINTAGEL

LAUNCESTON

CAMELFORD

PORT ISAAC

BODMIN MOOR

CALLINGTON

18 28   19

PADSTOW

5   WADEBRIDGE
8   29

32

DOBWALLS

BODMIN   6

LISKEARD

31   15

3

NEWQUAY

ROCHE   LOSTWITHIEL

4

SALTASH

PLYMOUTH

PERRANPORTH

33 13

LOOE   24

ST. AGNES

PROBUS   12   ST. AUSTELL   FOWEY   POLPERRO

PORTREATH

TRURO   25 27 14 26

PORTREATH   34   MEVAGISSEY 17

16 20 23

ST IVES   VERYAN

ZENNOR   30   REDRUTH

CAMBORNE

HAYLE   GERRANS

ST. MAWES

PENRYN   21

ST. JUST   PENZANCE   MARAZION   FALMOUTH   35

SENNEN   PERRANUTHNOE

LAND'S   LAMORNA   7   10   PORTHLEVEN   22   9

END   COVE   HELSTON

PORTHCURNO   HELFORD

MULLION COVE

COVERACK

LIZARD

The Rising Sun, St Mawes.

56

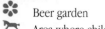 Beer garden

Area where children are welcome

Disabled are advised to phone for details of facilities prior to visit.

The Farmers Arms, St Merryn.

1. **ATLANTIC INN** St. Mary's, Isles of Scilly. (01720) 22323

2. **BISHOP & WOLF INN** St. Mary's, Isles of Scilly. (01720) 22790

3. **CENTRAL INN** Central Square, Newquay. (01637) 873810

4. **COPLEY ARMS** Hessenford, Saltash, PL11 3HJ. (01503) 240209

5. **CORNISH ARMS** Churchtown, St. Merryn, Padstow, PL28 8ND. (01841) 520288

6. **CORNISH ARMS** Crockwell Street, Bodmin. (01208) 75800

7. **DOLPHIN INN** Penzance, TR18 4BD. (01736) 64106

8. **FARMERS ARMS** St. Merryn, Padstow, PL28 8NP. (01841) 520303

9. **FERRYBOAT INN** Helford Passage, TR11 5LB. (01326) 250625

10. **FOUNTAIN TAVERN** St. Clare Street, Penzance, PL28 8NP. (01736) 62673

11. **HARBOUR INN** Commercial Road, Porthleven, TR13 9JB. (01326) 573876

12. **HEWAS INN** Sticker, St. Austell, PL26 7HD. (01726) 73497

13. **HOLMBUSH INN** Holmbush, St. Austell, PL25 3LL. (01726) 68691

14. **KING OF PRUSSIA** Town Quay, Fowey, PL23 1AT. (01726) 832450

15. **LANIVET ARMS** Lanivet, Bodmin. (01208) 831212

16. **LIFEBOAT INN** Wharf Road, St. Ives, TR26 1LF. (01736) 794123

17. **LUGGER INN** Polruan, Nr. Fowey. (01726) 870007

18. **OLD CUSTOM HOUSE INN** South Quay, Padstow, PL28 8BL. (01841) 532359

19. **OYSTER CATCHER** Polzeath Holiday Apartments, Polzeath, Wadebridge, PL27 6TG. (01208) 862371

20. **QUEENS TAVERN** High Street, St. Ives, TR26 1RR. (01736) 796468

21. **RISING SUN** St. Mawes, Truro, TR2 5DJ. (01326) 270233

22. **RODNEY INN** Helston, TR13 8AA. (01326) 572417

23. **SHEAF OF WHEAT** Chapel Street, St. Ives, TR26 2LS. (01736) 797130

24. **SHIP HOTEL** East Looe, PL13 2QR. (01503) 263124

25. **SHIP HOTEL** Mevagissey, St. Austell, PL26 6UQ. (01726) 843324

26. **SHIP INN** Trafalgar Square, Fowey, PL23 1AZ. (01726) 832230

27. **SHIP INN** West End, Pentewan, St. Austell, PL26 6BX. (01726) 842855

28. **SHIPWRIGHTS** North Quay, Padstow, PL26 6UQ. (01841) 532451

29. **SWAN HOTEL** Wadebridge, PL27 7DD. (01208) 812526

30. **TYACKS HOTEL** Camborne, TR14 7DF. (01209) 612424

31. **VICTORIA BARS** King Street, Newquay, TR7 1NB. (01637) 872671

32. **WEAVERS** Honey Street, Bodmin, PL31 2DL. (01208) 74511

33. **WHITE HART HOTEL** Church Street, St. Austell, PL25 4AT. (01726) 72100

34. **WIG AND PEN** Frances Street, Truro, TR1 3DP. (01872) 73028

35. **WODEHOUSE INN** The Moor, Falmouth, TR11 3SA. (01326) 312534

WALKING AREAS & VIEWPOINTS

This section has been designed to take you to the best walking areas and viewpoints in Cornwall. How many times have you heard that a certain place offers lovely views, but have been unable to find out how to get there?

There will be no such problems with these walks as each has been visited by the publishers to ensure accuracy of information to the user. The sketch maps should also be used to help you get your bearings.

For each walking area, an O.S. map reference has been included, referring to the start point car park. This will allow those who like to use O.S. maps the opportunity to familiarise themselves with the walking area before they get there. The new O.S. Explorer series of maps (bright orange cover) are recommended as they cover large areas in great detail. There are currently three, covering parts of Cornwall: 7 Land's End, 8 The Lizard, 9 Bodmin Moor.

As a reminder with map references, remember that the first 3 digits refer to the Easting, that is, the numbers horizontally along the bottom/top of the map, so named because they ADVANCE across the map from left to right or west to east. The last three digits refer to the Northing, that is, the numbers vertically along the side of the map, likewise advancing up the map from south to north.

EXAMPLE

On the Explorer 7 Land's End map, the P marking the parking for Land's End would have a map ref. of 345 251

Easting = 345 Find the number 34 along the bottom (or top) of the map and then count 5/10ths across towards the next number.

Northing = 251 Now find the number 25 on the left (or right) side of the map and count 1/10th towards the next number.

Draw 2 imaginary lines from these points and where they cross, this indicates the exact position referred to by the map reference.

If this section gives you a taste for walking in Cornwall, why not try our other Cornish book, **Classic Walks: Cornwall.** This contains 60 full colour guided walks that allows you to explore on a circular route many of Cornwall's secret places. Distances range from 2 to 6 miles with step by step instructions in addition to nearly 200 colour photographs to whet your appetite. **Classic Walks: Cornwall** is available from just £4.99 *offer limited to U.K. only.* See advert at the back of the book.

WALK TERRAIN GRADE

- ■ **Tough**
- ■ **Moderate**
- □ **Easy**

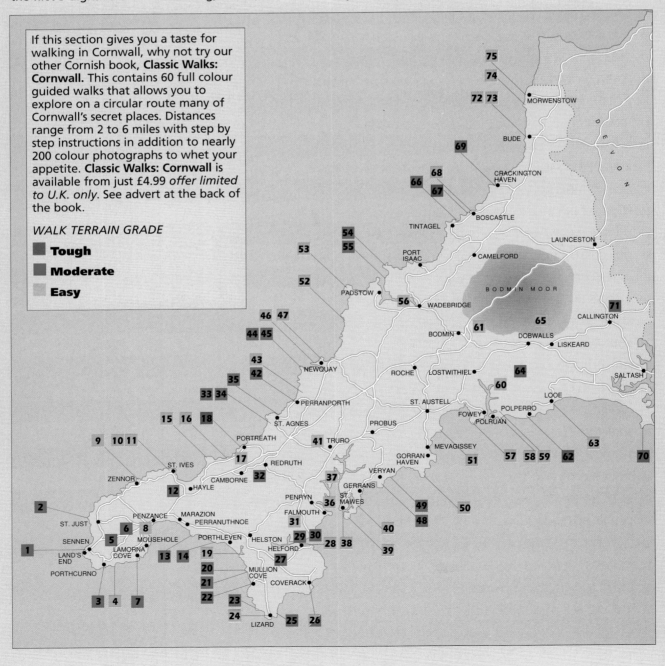

1 SENNEN TO LAND'S END

The climb to Mayon Cliff. MDN

Walk from either one of Sennen Cove's two main beach car parks towards Land's End using the coast path along National Trust owned Mayon Cliff (approx. 1.5 miles). Views across surfing beach of Whitesand Bay, the headland of Cape Cornwall and offshore Brison rocks. Longships Lighthouse can also be seen.

WALK TERRAIN GRADE: MODERATE

MAP REF: EXPLORER 7 Land's End **355 264**

DIRECTIONS: Follow A30 from Penzance towards Land's End. Take Sennen Cove turn off and park in one of the car parks at either end of the village. In high season, an overflow car park is available on the right before the descent to the cove. Refreshments and pub in Sennen. Toilets at both car parks.

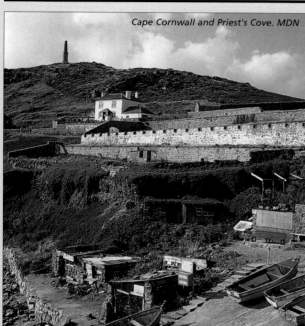
Cape Cornwall and Priest's Cove. MDN

2 CAPE CORNWALL

Bought for the National Trust by H. J. Heinz Ltd. in 1987, England's only cape provides lovely sea views towards Land's End and the offshore rocks of The Brisons. The first mining here, evidence of which can be seen in the tall chimney stack, renovated in 1986, was recorded as far back as 1787 and reached its zenith in the 1850's when underground workings went under the sea as far as The Brisons. The mines were closed in 1889.

WALK TERRAIN GRADE: MODERATE

MAP REF: O.S EXPLORER 7 Land's End **354 318**

DIRECTIONS: Take the A3071 from Penzance to St. Just and follow signs from here to Cape Cornwall. Use a small parking area overlooking the Cape. All facilities in St. Just.

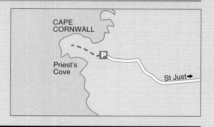

---

3 PEDN-MEN-AN-MERE

Whilst most people parking at Porthcurno will get little farther than its famous beach, just a little more exertion will allow a walk past the open air clifftop Minack Theatre to reach the National Trust headland of Pedn-men-an-mere. This small headland is a wonderful place to admire the striking coastal views of West Penwith.

WALK TERRAIN GRADE: MODERATE

MAP REF: O.S EXPLORER 7 Land's End **355 264**

DIRECTIONS: From the A30 Penzance-Land's End road, follow the B3283 through St. Buryan and past the village of Treen to pick up signs for Porthcurno. Use the car park above the beach. The headland is reached via rocky steps from the beach and by following the coast path past the Minack Theatre.

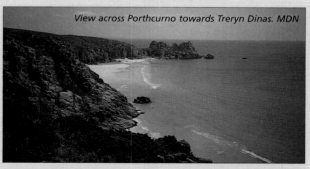
View across Porthcurno towards Treryn Dinas. MDN

The approach to Pedn-men-an-mere from Porth Chapel. MDN

4 TREEN AND LOGAN ROCK

Well used and signed field paths proceed directly from the hamlet to reach the coast path and headland of Treryn Dinas (approx. 0.75 miles). A 60 ton rocking stone on the headland has resulted in its popular name of Logan Rock. Lovely views across turquoise seas towards the white sands of Porthcurno.

WALK TERRAIN GRADE: **EASY**

MAP REF: **O.S EXPLORER 7** Land's End **396 229**

DIRECTIONS: *Take the A30 from Penzance towards Land's End. After passing through the village of Drift, take the B3283 to St. Buryan. Proceed to Treen and drive past the pub to park in a large car park at the end of the hamlet. Toilets, shop and Logan Rock Inn at start point.*

View towards Porthcurno from Logan Rock. MDN

Chapel Carn Brea. MDN

5 CHAPEL CARN BREA

Not to be confused with its namesake near Redruth, Chapel Carn Brea is located in the far west of the county near Land's End and is regarded as England's 'first and last' hill. It rises to a height of 657 ft. and can easily be explored from a small car parking area on its northern side. On clear days, stunning views can be seen of West Penwith and even as far as the Isles of Scilly. The hill, which has been measured as being subject to gales on 97 days of the year, was an important Bronze Age burial site and the summit cairn marks the site of a Medieval chapel dedicated to St. Michael.

WALK TERRAIN GRADE: **MODERATE**

MAP REF: **O.S EXPLORER 7** Land's End **388 284**

DIRECTIONS: *Take A30 from Penzance towards Land's End. Turn off at Crows-an-Wra (signed St. Just) to park on the northern side of the hill and follow the path to the summit.*

6 SANCREED BEACON

A 560 ft. high exposed granite upland covered in gorse and bracken, west of Penzance. As the name suggests, the Beacon was used to light fires during the Napoleonic Wars. Evidence of Bronze Age occupation as well as more recent mining for tin. Extensive views across West Penwith including Mounts Bay and St. Michael's Mount.

WALK TERRAIN GRADE: **MODERATE**

MAP REF **O.S EXPLORER 7** Land's End **414 294**

DIRECTIONS: *From near the village of Newbridge on the A3071 Penzance-St. Just road, follow signs for Sancreed. Sancreed Beacon (signed as an ancient monument) is indicated from the village. Park in a small lay-by and follow the path to the top.*

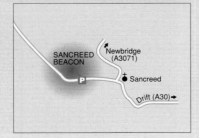

Sancreed Beacon. MDN

7 LAMORNA COVE

Stunning cliff walks both east and west from the cove by way of the coast path. Superb granite landscape and views to Tater-du lighthouse. One of west Cornwall's most beautiful places.

WALK TERRAIN GRADE: MODERATE

MAP REF: O.S EXPLORER 7 Land's End **452 242**

DIRECTIONS:
Take the B3315 from Newlyn to Lamorna. Park overlooking the cove. Refreshments available in season, toilets all year round. Lamorna Wink pub in the valley above the cove.

Lamorna Cove. MDN

St Michael's Mount. Tim Guthrie.

Penzance Promenade. MDN

8 PENZANCE PROMENADE

An unusual walking area in that the walk is essentially urban, albeit with extensive sea views across Mounts Bay towards St. Michaels Mount. Park in the harbour car park at Penzance (near the railway station) and head across the Ross swing-bridge and around the harbour to pass the Jubilee Bathing Pool. From here, enjoy a level walk along Penzance Promenade to Newlyn. Total distance from the car park to Newlyn is approx. 1.5 miles. Suitable for pushchairs and wheelchairs.

WALK TERRAIN GRADE: EASY

MAP REF: O.S EXPLORER 7 Land's End **355 264**

DIRECTIONS:
Take A30 to Penzance and use the Harbour car park near the railway station and Tourist Information Centre. All facilities in Penzance.

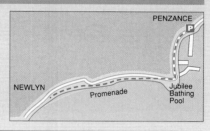

9 ZENNOR HEAD

The ancient settlement of Zennor provides the starting point for an exhilarating and level 1.25 mile return walk to Zennor Head (the coast path on either side of the headland can also be explored though the terrain is much tougher). Views towards Pendeen Watch Lighthouse. Adjacent Pendour Cove is associated with the Zennor mermaid legend.

WALK TERRAIN GRADE: EASY

MAP REF: O.S EXPLORER 7 Land's End **355 264**

DIRECTIONS: The hamlet of Zennor is on the B3306 between St. Ives and St. Just-in-Penwith. A parking area with toilets is provided close to the Wayside Museum. Tinner's Arms pub.

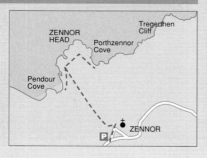

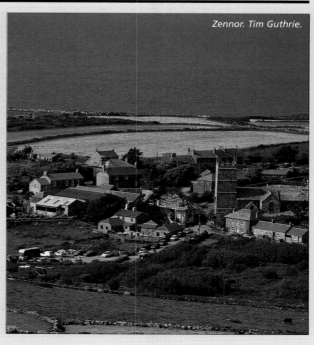
Zennor. Tim Guthrie.

10 WEST FROM ST. IVES

A chance to follow the coast path west from St. Ives for whatever distance required. The rocky headland of Carrick Du is probably the best place to enjoy the view towards the attractive building of the Tate St. Ives. From the car park, walk past the bowling green to find the well marked coast path.

WALK TERRAIN GRADE: **EASY**

MAP REF: **O.S EXPLORER 7** Land's End **515 408**

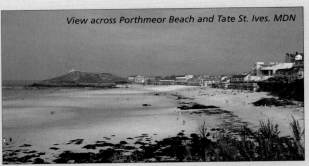
View across Porthmeor Beach and Tate St. Ives. MDN

DIRECTIONS:
Follow signs in St. Ives for the main 1000 space car park. Continue to the double roundabout shortly afterwards and follow signs to Porthmeor Beach (if full, a further car park is passed between the roundabouts and Porthmeor). Toilets and refreshments available at Porthmeor.

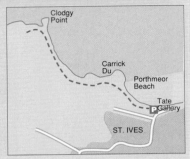

Coast path west of St. Ives. MDN

St. Ives Island and chapel. MDN

11 ST. IVES ISLAND

In fact not an island, but a small headland offering tremendous sea views just a short walk from St. Ives town centre. The Island overlooks the renowned Porthmeor Beach and Tate Gallery St. Ives building, a small chapel on the promontory provides a further point of interest.

WALK TERRAIN GRADE: **EASY**

MAP REF: **O.S EXPLORER 7** Land's End **515 402**

Porthmeor Beach from St. Ives Island. MDN

DIRECTIONS: *In high season, follow signs in St. Ives for the main 1000 space car park and catch one of the frequent minibuses into town. Head down to the harbour and bear left to reach Porthgwidden and The Island. In low season only it may be worth following the one way system around the harbour to reach a small car park at Porthgwidden. Toilets and refreshments throughout St. Ives.*

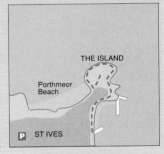

12 TRENCROM HILL

Lying to the south of St. Ives, this 500 ft. high gorse covered summit offers excellent views over St. Ives Bay and the Hayle estuary. It has been in the care of the National Trust since 1946 when it was given as a memorial to the men and women of Cornwall who gave their lives in two World Wars. Trencrom Hill was used in the Iron Age as a hillfort and is reached from a small National Trust car park on its northern side.

WALK TERRAIN GRADE: **MODERATE**

MAP REF: **O.S EXPLORER 7** Land's End **518 360**

Trencrom Hill. MDN

DIRECTIONS:
From the St. Ives end roundabout on the Hayle bypass, turn off for Lelant and bear first left signed Lelant Downs. Parking for Trencrom Hill is signed 1 mile further on.

13 CUDDEN POINT

A glorious section of the coastline on the eastern side of Mount's Bay providing a 1.75 mile coast path walk from above Perran Sands beach to the rocky National Trust headland of Cudden Point. If you want a longer walk, continue on the coast path from Cudden Point to reach the famous Prussia Cove.

WALK TERRAIN GRADE: **MODERATE**

MAP REF: **O.S EXPLORER 7** Land's End **539 295**

DIRECTIONS: From the A394 Penzance-Helston road, turn off for Perranuthnoe (between Marazion and Rosudgeon). Proceed to the car park just above the beach. Toilets in car park and refreshments in season above the beach. Victoria Inn in the village.

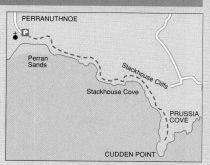

Prussia Cove near Cudden Point. MDN

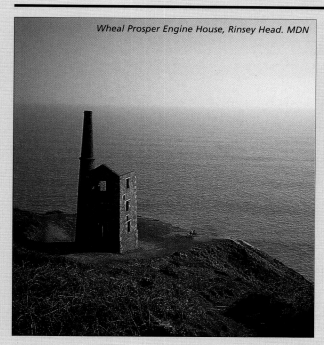

Wheal Prosper Engine House, Rinsey Head. MDN

14 RINSEY HEAD

Small National Trust headland on the eastern edge of Mounts Bay. A mid nineteenth century engine house of the Wheal Prosper tin and copper mine, extensively restored by the National Trust since the property's acquisition in 1969, dominates the cliff. Views towards Mounts Bay.

WALK TERRAIN GRADE: **MODERATE**

MAP REF: **O.S. EXPLORER 7** Land's End **591 271**

DIRECTIONS:
From A394 Penzance-Helston road, turn off in village of Ashton and follow signs for Rinsey. After about 1 mile, an unmade narrow track leads to a small National Trust parking area.

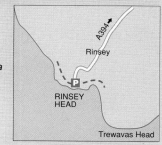

15 GODREVY POINT

Easy coast path walking is available at Godrevy Point, the northern perimeter of St. Ives Bay. A highlight of this walk is the proximity to Godrevy Lighthouse, built in 1859 and inspiration for Virginia Woolf's famous novel 'To the Lighthouse'.

WALK TERRAIN GRADE: **EASY**

MAP REF: **O.S. EXPLORER 7** Land's End **585 423**

DIRECTIONS: From the B3301 Hayle-Portreath road, turn off, signed to Godrevy, adjacent to a narrow bridge close to the Sandsifter Hotel. Park in front of the cafe building. (If full, a N.T. parking area is available further on, nearer the lighthouse). Modern cafe adjacent to car park. Toilets adjacent to the N.T. parking area.

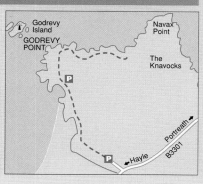

Godrevy. Tim Guthrie.

WALKING AREAS & VIEWPOINTS

16 RESKAJEAGE DOWNS

Known locally as North Cliffs, the gorse covered Reskajeage Downs offer level coast path walking with distant views towards Godrevy Lighthouse. Park overlooking the sea at Basset's Cove and bear left to follow the coastal path for whatever distance required.

WALK TERRAIN GRADE: **EASY**

MAP REF: **O.S. LANDRANGER 203 638 441**

DIRECTIONS: Find the Tehidy Country Park North Cliffs Car Park on the B3301 coastal road between Hayle and Portreath. Head in the Portreath direction for a short distance to find a rough track that leads towards the sea and a National Trust car park at Basset's Cove.

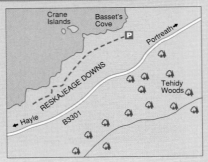

Reskajeage Downs. MDN

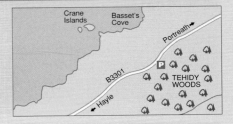

Tehidy Woods. MDN

17 TEHIDY WOODS

Tehidy Country Park is managed by Cornwall County Council who provide free public access to over nine miles of attractive woodland, lake and riverside paths in an area of nearly 250 acres. The woods and much of the surrounding land was originally part of the Bassett family estate whose immense wealth was based on tin and copper mining during the seventeenth and eighteenth centuries. Four walks, varying between 1 and 3 miles, are marked with colour posts.

WALK TERRAIN GRADE: **EASY**

MAP REF: **O.S. LANDRANGER 203 641 438**

DIRECTIONS: On the B3301 coastal road between Hayle and Portreath, use the car park signed Tehidy Country Park North Cliffs car park (1.5 miles from Portreath).

18 RALPH'S CUPBOARD

The popular surfing and family beach at Portreath provides the start point for a two mile return walk to Ralph's Cupboard, a deep chasm caused by a collapsed sea cave that was said to have been occupied by a fearsome sailor eating giant. After an initial climb from the beach to Western Hill, the coast path levels out towards Ralph's Cupboard and provides sea views to the offshore bird colony of Gull Rock.

WALK TERRAIN GRADE: **TOUGH**

MAP REF: **O.S. LANDRANGER 203 655 454**

DIRECTIONS: Portreath is signed from the A30 near Redruth via the B3300. Park in a car park overlooking the beach or beside the wide road approaching the car park. Refreshment facilities and toilets in Portreath.

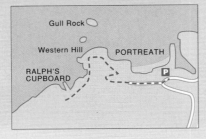

Western Hill, Portreath. MDN

19 LOE POOL

A tranquil and rather special place as well as being Cornwall's largest freshwater lake and a nature reserve for wildfowl. Well used and defined paths allow a 5 mile circular walk around the lake which was formed by the sea creating Loe Bar, a sand and shingle spit that dammed the River Cober.

WALK TERRAIN GRADE: EASY

MAP REF: O.S. EXPLORER 8 The Lizard **654 252**

DIRECTIONS: From the R.N.A.S. Culdrose roundabout on the A3083 south of Helston, take the A394 Penzance road before turning immediately left into Degibna Lane next to the Helston Community Hospital, sited adjacent to the roundabout. A National Trust car park is located at the end of the lane, opposite Degibna Methodist Church.

Loe Pool. MDN

Gunwalloe Church Cove. MDN

20 GUNWALLOE CHURCH COVE

Situated on the western coast of the Lizard Peninsula, Church Cove is a popular bathing beach from where you can use the coast path to explore Halzephron Cliff. 'Halzephron' is Cornish for 'cliffs of hell', a reference to the many shipwrecks in this area which include a Portuguese treasure ship wrecked in the sixteenth century.

WALK TERRAIN GRADE: MODERATE

MAP REF: O.S. EXPLORER 8 The Lizard **659 208**

DIRECTIONS: From the A3083 Helston-Lizard road, turn off 1.5 miles south of Helston and follow signs to Gunwalloe. Parking reached after three miles. Toilets and refreshments (seasonal availability) at Gunwalloe. Halzephron Inn nearby.

Halzephron Inn. MDN

21 MARCONI MONUMENT

A 1.25 mile return walk to the Marconi Monument which marks the spot from where, in December 1901, the first message to cross the Atlantic by wireless was transmitted. Lovely sea views from the coast here, especially in late afternoon when the west facing vantage point benefits from a setting sun.

WALK TERRAIN GRADE: MODERATE

MAP REF: O.S. EXPLORER 8 The Lizard **667 200**

DIRECTIONS: From the A3083 Helston-Lizard road, turn off signed to Cury and Poldhu Cove. Park in car park behind beach. Toilets and refreshments at Poldhu (seasonal availability).

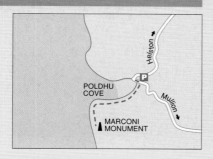

Marconi Monument. MDN

22 MULLION COVE

Mullion Cove is a popular National Trust owned harbour with stout granite walls and enjoyable sea views out towards Mullion Island. Walk around the harbour area or with a little more exertion, Mullion Cliff, reached via the coast path on the southern (left as you look out to sea) side of the cove.

WALK TERRAIN GRADE: **MODERATE**

MAP REF: **O.S. EXPLORER 8** The Lizard **672 182**

Mullion Cove. MDN

DIRECTIONS:
From the A3083 Helston-Lizard road, take the B3296 signed to Mullion. Pass through Mullion village and head for Mullion Cove, parking in a large car park on the left hand side. Refreshments and toilets at Mullion Cove.

Kynance Cove. MDN

23 KYNANCE COVE

Popular Cornish beauty spot on the Lizard Peninsula since Victorian times. Coast path cliff walks available on both sides of the cove, sea views to offshore Asparagus Island. Serpentine rocks found here are some of the oldest on earth; the rock is cut and polished in workshops at nearby Lizard village.

WALK TERRAIN GRADE: **MODERATE**

MAP REF: **O.S. EXPLORER 8** The Lizard **688 133**

DIRECTIONS: From the A3083 Helston-Lizard road, follow brown tourist signs for Kynance Cove (approx. half a mile north of Lizard village). Refreshments and toilets (seasonal availability) at Kynance car park. Cafe (also seasonal opening) at Kynance Cove itself.

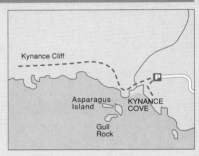

24 LIZARD POINT

If you walk from the centre of the village to the left of the Top House pub (Penmenner Road), you can follow an unmade track to reach the coast path. Turn left and follow the coast path to reach England's most southerly point (Lizard lighthouse nearby). Return via a tarmac road back to the village. Return trip approx. two miles.

WALK TERRAIN GRADE: **EASY**

MAP REF: **O.S. EXPLORER 8** The Lizard **704 126**

DIRECTIONS: Take the A3083 from Helston to Lizard village. A large free car park is available in the centre of the village. Toilets, refreshments and the Top House pub in the Lizard. Refreshments available in season near Lizard Point.

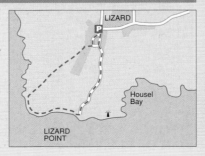

Old lifeboat house, Lizard Point. MDN

25 LANDEWEDNACK

Landewednack Church Cove (not the Church Cove near Mullion) is a simply wonderful little cove from where you can follow the coast path south to Kilcobben cove and its modern lifeboat station. From the car park at the centre of Lizard village, bear left to pass the historic church of St. Wynwallow, England's most southerly place of worship, and descend to reach Church Cove.

WALK TERRAIN GRADE: **MODERATE**

MAP REF: **O.S. EXPLORER 8** The Lizard **704 126**

DIRECTIONS:
Take the A3083 from Helston to the Lizard. A large free car park is available in the centre of the village. All facilities in Lizard village.

Thatched cottage, Landewednack. MDN

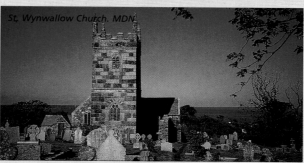
St. Wynwallow Church. MDN

Coverack. MDN

26 COVERACK

Coverack is a quiet, much loved coastal village set around a small harbour on the eastern side of the Lizard Peninsula. The parking area is located at the entrance to the village with a pleasant walk around the bay to the harbour area. For the more adventurous, use the coast path that heads south to reach the headland of Chynhalls Point.

WALK TERRAIN GRADE: **EASY/MODERATE**

MAP REF: **O.S. EXPLORER 8** The Lizard **782 187**

DIRECTIONS: Take the B3293 towards St. Keverne from south of Helston. After a few miles, bear right and proceed on the B3294 into the village of Coverack. Parking can be found on the right hand side at the entrance to the village. All facilities in Coverack.

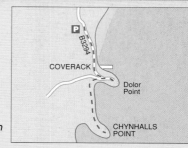

---

27 TRELOWARREN WOOD

Developed with the aid of the Countryside Commission, the Trelowarren Woodland Walk is open, by permission of Sir John Vyvyan, from Easter until the end of September and is detailed in a free leaflet available from the pottery. The walk includes a Victorian Folly, woodlands, gardens and a fogou (an Iron Age underground chamber). Coffee shop and art gallery in Trelowarren House.

WALK TERRAIN GRADE: **MODERATE**

MAP REF: **O.S. LANDRANGER 203 718 238**

DIRECTIONS:
From Helston, take B3293 signed for St. Keverne. Turn off left at village of Garras for Trelowarren.

Primroses. MDN.

Bluebells. MDN.

28 HELFORD RIVER

Located at the northern extreme of the Lizard Peninsula, the Helford River is a lush, largely wooded river estuary famed for its beauty; the tiny hamlet of Helford much photographed and loved by visitors and locals alike. Made famous by Daphne du Maurier's novel of the same name, Frenchman's Creek is owned by the National Trust and is rich in bird life, especially herons. See map for walk directions.

WALK TERRAIN GRADE: **EASY**

MAP REF: **O.S. EXPLORER 8** The Lizard **759 261**

DIRECTIONS: *From the B3293 Helston-St. Keverne road, follow signs for Helford via Newton-in-St. Martin. Park in the car park above Helford village, overlooking the river estuary. Toilets within Helford car park. Cafe, general stores/post office and Shipwright Arms pub in Helford.*

Helford village. MDN

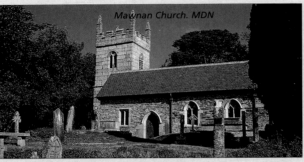

Mawnan Church. MDN

Helford River Estuary. MDN

29 MAWNAN CHURCH

A footpath just to the right of Mawnan Church, leads down to reach the coastal path along the National Trust headland of Mawnan Shear, overlooking the Helford River Estuary. Lovely views can be obtained by either turning left (east) towards Rosemullion Head or right (west) to Durgan.

WALK TERRAIN GRADE: **MODERATE**

MAP REF: **O.S. EXPLORER 8** The Lizard **787 213**

DIRECTIONS: *Follow signs to Mawnan Smith from the A39 Penryn by-pass approach to Falmouth. Bear left at the Red Lion pub in the centre of the village and proceed to a right turn in front of Nansidwell Country House Hotel. Follow the lane to a small parking area in front of Mawnan Church. Red Lion pub in Mawnan Smith.*

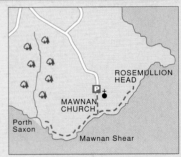

30 ROSEMULLION HEAD

Maenporth Beach is located south of Falmouth and provides the start point for a 3 mile return walk on the coast path to Rosemullion Head. The headland is owned by the National Trust and a believed one time site of an Iron Age cliff castle. Excellent sea views.

WALK TERRAIN GRADE: **MODERATE**

MAP REF: **O.S. EXPLORER 8** The Lizard **790 297**

DIRECTIONS:
From the A39 Penryn by-pass, turn off at the Hillhead roundabout signed to Maenporth. Follow the narrow country lane to park just behind the beach. (If this is full, there is a larger cafe car park on the opposite side of the road).

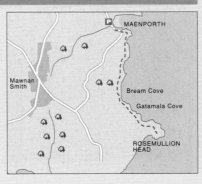

Rosemullion Head. D.J.Flunder/National Trust.

31 ARGAL/COLLEGE RESERVOIRS

The two reservoirs are noted wildlife havens and have enjoyable walks around their shorelines. The Argal walk, overlooked by Mabe Church, is about two miles in length; the 1.75 mile walk around College Water can be reached by a signed half mile walk from the main parking area at Argal.

WALK TERRAIN GRADE: EASY

O.S. MAP REF: LANDRANGER 204 763 328

DIRECTIONS:
Argal and College Waterpark is signed from the A39 Penryn by-pass approach to Falmouth. Picnic area and toilet block at Argal Water parking area.

Argal Reservoir. MDN.

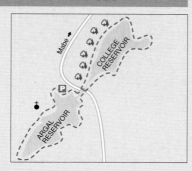
Carn Brea. MDN

Carn Brea Castle. MDN.

32 CARN BREA

Said once to have been home to giants, the 812 ft. summit of Carn Brea (pronounced bray) has an extensive viewpoint with dramatic views towards the north and south coasts as well as across a landscape rich in the remains of disused engine houses, reflecting the area's great industrial heritage. The hill has extensive Neolithic and Iron Age remains as well as a nineteenth century obelisk and a small castle-like Victorian folly that now houses a restaurant.

WALK TERRAIN GRADE: MODERATE

MAP REF: O.S. LANDRANGER 203 684 407

DIRECTIONS: From the A30 Redruth bypass, follow A393 (signed Falmouth) before taking the B3297 (signed Helston). From this road, follow signs for village of Carnkie to find a sign indicating Ancient Monument. A licensed restaurant is to be found at the top of an unmade and rather bumpy track.

33 CHAPEL PORTH

A half mile walk via the coast path from Chapel Porth cove allows close inspection of Towanroath engine house and the disused mine buildings of Wheal Coates Mine, their dramatic cliffside location much loved by photographers and artists.

WALK TERRAIN GRADE: MODERATE

MAP REF: O.S. LANDRANGER 203 698 496

DIRECTIONS: From the A30 near Truro, follow the B3277 to the edge of St. Agnes village. Turn left to follow brown National Trust signs for Chapel Porth. A narrow road leads to a small National Trust car park at Chapel Porth Cove. National Trust toilets and refreshments during the season at the car park.

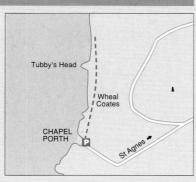

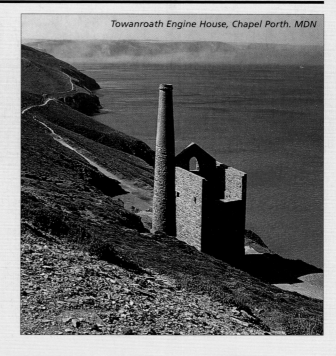
Towanroath Engine House, Chapel Porth. MDN

34 ST. AGNES BEACON

A far reaching viewpoint on the north coast near St. Agnes. 629 ft. heather covered summit soon reached from parking area; views on clear days over 30 miles towards St. Ives and Trevose Head.

WALK TERRAIN GRADE: **MODERATE**

MAP REF: O.S. LANDRANGER 203 **703 502**

DIRECTIONS: From the A30 near Truro, take the B3297 to St Agnes. In St. Agnes village, take the Trevaunance Road turning (just after St. Agnes Hotel, opposite the church). A small parking area is reached on the right after approx. 1 mile. A path is signed from here to the National Trust summit.

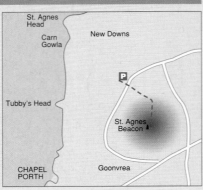

St. Agnes Beacon. MDN

Trevellas Porth. MDN

35 JERICHO VALLEY

The evocatively named Jericho Valley (shown as Trevellas Coombe on O.S. maps) is reached after a short coastpath walk above Trevaunance Cove near St. Agnes. The coastpath is signed on the left next to the Driftwood Spars Hotel; walk to reach Trevellas Porth and then bear right after the road bridge to follow a path up the valley (the stream on your right and the remains of an engine house on your left). Round trip from Trevaunance Cove approx. 2.5 miles.

WALK TERRAIN GRADE: **MODERATE**

MAP REF: O.S. LANDRANGER 204 **721 515**

DIRECTIONS: Take the B3285 from Perranporth to St. Agnes. As you approach St. Agnes, take the turn off signed to Trevaunance Cove. Small car park situated at the end of the lane. Toilets and refreshments in Trevaunance Cove.

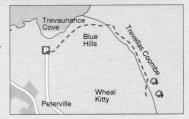

36 TREFUSIS POINT

At the end of the road that leads through Flushing village and away from the quay, find a public footpath that takes you around Trefusis Point to Mylor Churchtown. Tremendous views towards Falmouth and across the Carrick Roads river estuary. The distance to Mylor is approx. 2 miles, the terrain level and easy to walk.

WALK TERRAIN GRADE: **EASY**

MAP REF: O.S. LANDRANGER 204 **799 339**

DIRECTIONS: From the A39 Truro-Falmouth road, turn off at Penryn and follow signs to Flushing. Proceed to find the small quay car park. If full, turn right out of the car park and follow the road as it bears left uphill. Depending on the parking restrictions in operation at the time, park along this road. Toilets and restaurant at Flushing quay, Post Office and two pubs in Flushing. Further refreshments and toilets in Mylor Churchtown.

Flushing. MDN

37 TRELISSICK

This walk is open all the year round and explores woodlands surrounding the National Trust property at Trelissick, one of the Trust's finest gardens and an absolute delight throughout the year. The property borders the River Fal and has a total of 4 miles of woodland paths. The National Trust's informative booklet, 'Coast of Cornwall: Trelissick Woodland Walk', is available from National Trust shops and is an essential guide to the property.

WALK TERRAIN GRADE: **EASY**

MAP REF: **O.S. LANDRANGER 204 836 396**

DIRECTIONS: From Truro follow the A39 towards Falmouth before taking the B3289 at Playing Place (signed King Harry Ferry). Ample parking at Trelissick. Restaurant, shop, exhibition gallery and toilets available when the garden is open (March to Dec.). Admission to garden for non N.T. members.

Trelissick. A. Reekie/National Trust.

St. Mawes. MDN

38 CARRICK ROADS ESTUARY

A delightful section of Roseland Peninsula walking from the boating mecca of St. Mawes. From the car park, head for the castle and follow a waterside path overlooking the Carrick Roads estuary towards Falmouth. Superb views throughout. The path continues for three miles to reach St. Just-in-Roseland church.

WALK TERRAIN GRADE: **EASY**

MAP REF: **O.S. LANDRANGER 204 848 333**

DIRECTIONS: From the A39 Truro-St. Austell road, follow A3078 (signed St. Mawes). Park in the main St. Mawes car park. (Alternatively, use the King Harry Ferry signed from the A39 at Playing Place between Truro and Falmouth. St. Mawes is reached from St. Just-in-Roseland via the A3078). All facilities in St. Mawes.

---

39 ST. ANTHONY HEAD

Coast path walking on either side of the southern extreme of the Roseland Peninsula. St Anthony Head is cared for by the National Trust; a lighthouse and the remains of a coastal artillery battery add interest to the excellent coastal views.

WALK TERRAIN GRADE: **EASY**

MAP REF: **O.S. LANDRANGER 204 847 314**

DIRECTIONS: From the A39 Truro-St. Austell road, take the A3078 (signed St. Mawes). Turn off shortly after the hamlet of Trewithian signed to Gerrans. After Gerrans, follow a narrow lane to St. Anthony Head. (Alternatively, reach Gerrans via the King Harry Ferry signed from the A39 at Playing Place between Truro and Falmouth).

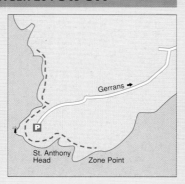

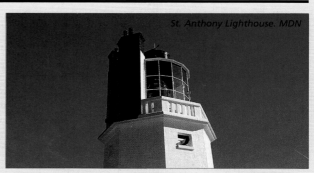
St. Anthony Lighthouse. MDN

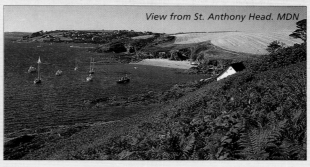
View from St. Anthony Head. MDN

40 KILLIGERRAN HEAD

The National Trust owned Porth Farm can be used as the start point for a 1 mile walk to Killigerran Head in the far south of the Roseland Peninsula. From Porth Farm, head down to Towan Beach and bear right to walk on the coast path.

WALK TERRAIN GRADE: **EASY**

MAP REF: **O.S. LANDRANGER 204 868 328**

DIRECTIONS: *From the A39 Truro-St. Austell road, take the A3078 (signed St. Mawes). Turn off shortly after the hamlet of Trewithian signed to Gerrans. Pass through Gerrans, Porth Farm is reached on the right. (Alternatively, reach Gerrans via the King Harry Ferry signed from the A39 at Playing Place between Truro and Falmouth).*

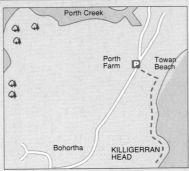

Sheep at Bohortha. MDN

Idless Woods. MDN

41 IDLESS WOODS

Forestry Commission owned woodland, 2 miles north of Truro.

WALK TERRAIN GRADE: **EASY**

MAP REF: **O.S. LANDRANGER 204 822 477**

DIRECTIONS: *Follow signs to Idless from the B3284 Truro-Shortlanesend road, north of Truro.*

42 CLIGGA HEAD

From the car park, head towards the Cellar Cove Hotel and past the Youth Hostel on Droskyn Point to follow the coast path towards Cligga Head. The airfield now used by gliders, just inland from Cligga Head, housed a squadron of spitfires during World War Two.

WALK TERRAIN GRADE: **MODERATE**

MAP REF: **O.S. LANDRANGER 204 756 545**

DIRECTIONS: *Perranporth is situated on the north coast between Newquay and St. Agnes. Use the larger car park up the hill from the car park in front of the beach.*

Perranporth Beach. MDN.

Perranporth Beach. MDN.

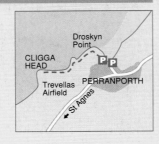

43 ST. PIRAN'S ORATORY

The extensive sand dunes north of Perranporth provide for a 2 mile return trip to the site of St. Piran's Oratory, a sixth century church established by St. Piran, the patron saint of tinners. The church was abandoned in the 11th century and lost below the sand before being 'rediscovered' in 1835. Unfortunately, the elements took their toll on the site and once again the church has been buried beneath the sand. A simple granite stone reached by a few steps is all that can be seen today.

WALK TERRAIN GRADE: **EASY**

MAP REF: **O.S. LANDRANGER 200 774 552**

DIRECTIONS: Take a narrow road adjacent to Toll-gate cottage, found on the B3285 east of Perranporth. Use one of the lay-bys found on this road and walk ahead to find two stone pillars on the left (opposite a road signed to Rose). Follow the white marking stones to the site of the oratory (a large wooden cross is about 100 yds away).

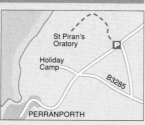

St. Piran's Oratory. MDN

Holywell Bay. MDN

44 KELSEY HEAD

From the car park, head out towards the sea and bear right to find a board walk through the dunes that leads to the coast path and Kelsey Head. Offshore is The Chick where many seabirds nest as well as on the headland. Kelsey Head and much of the surrounding area is cared for by the National Trust.

WALK TERRAIN GRADE: **MODERATE**

MAP REF: **O.S. LANDRANGER 200 767 591**

DIRECTIONS: From the A3075 Perranporth-Newquay road, turn off for Cubert and proceed through village to Holywell. A National Trust car park is situated on the left, near the beach. All facilities at Holywell.

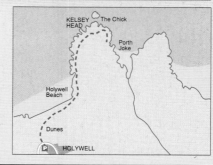

45 PENTIRE POINT WEST

The small National Trust headland of Pentire Point West enjoys marvellous views across Crantock Beach and the River Gannel estuary. It can also be used to provide a 1 mile circular walk around to Porth (or locally Polly) Joke, an attractive and rarely busy bathing cove. A short climb leads back to the car park.

WALK TERRAIN GRADE: **MODERATE**

MAP REF: **O.S. LANDRANGER 200 777 605**

DIRECTIONS: Follow signs to West Pentire via Crantock from the A3075 Redruth-Newquay road, 1 mile south of Newquay.

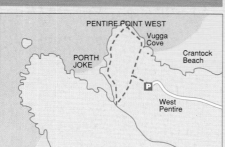

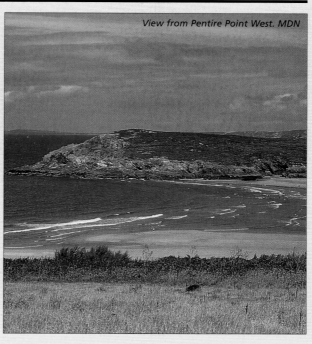

View from Pentire Point West. MDN

46 PENTIRE POINT EAST

An excellent viewpoint close to Newquay, Cornwall's busiest resort. A parking area on the headland allows easy strolling and enjoyable views across the sand dunes of Crantock and the River Gannel river estuary. Level terrain make this headland suitable for all ages.

WALK TERRAIN GRADE: **EASY**

MAP REF: O.S. LANDRANGER 200 **787 615**

DIRECTIONS: Pentire Point East is reached via Pentire Road, through the built up area of East Pentire, south west of the centre of Newquay.

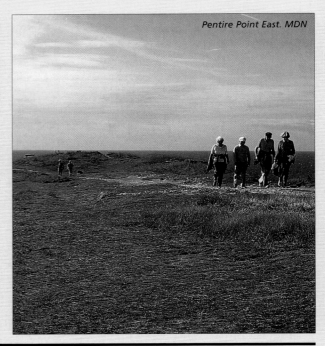
Pentire Point East. MDN

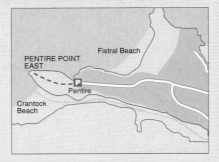
Newquay. MDN

47 TOWAN HEAD

Towan Head is best reached by parking in one of Newquay's main car parks and heading along Fore Street in the direction of the harbour. Take the first right after North Quay Hill (King Edward Crescent) and walk past the Huer's Hut and along the coast to reach Towan Head (approx. 1.5 miles).

WALK TERRAIN GRADE: **EASY**

MAP REF: O.S. LANDRANGER 200 **812 617**

DIRECTIONS: Use one of Newquay's main town car parks. All facilities found close by.

48 NARE HEAD

Nare Head is one of Cornwall's most prominent headlands and a lovely place to marvel at the views across Gerrans Bay. The headland is reached after 1.5 miles by bearing left up the hill from the car park to reach some steps and the coastal path.

WALK TERRAIN GRADE: **MODERATE**

MAP REF: O.S. LANDRANGER 204 **905 383**

DIRECTIONS: From the A39 Truro-St Austell road, take the A3078 (signed St. Mawes). Proceed over Tregony Bridge and stay on the A3078 until a left turn (signed Veryan) immediately after a garage. Leave Veryan village, passing between two of the round houses and follow the narrow lane to Carne Beach. Turn left in front of the beach to park in the National Trust car park. Toilets in the car park.

Carne Beach and Nare Head. MDN

View from Nare Head. MDN

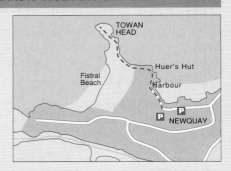

49 PORTLOE AND THE JACKA

Portloe. MDN

A charming village nestling above a small fishing cove with coast path cliff walks on either side. Descend to the cove and bear right away from the Lugger Hotel to follow a path that provides fine sea views (this area is known locally as The Jacka).

WALK TERRAIN GRADE: **MODERATE**

MAP REF: **O.S. LANDRANGER 204 938 398**

Portloe. MDN

DIRECTIONS: From the A39 Truro-St Austell road, take the A3078 (signed St. Mawes). Proceed over Tregony Bridge and stay on the A3078 until a left turn (signed Veryan and Portloe) immediately after a garage. Follow signs to Portloe and descend to find a small car park on the right hand side. Lugger Hotel, Ship Inn, tea rooms and toilets in Portloe.

Cross on Dodman Point. MDN

50 DODMAN POINT

This imposing Cornish headland has a mystery and magic all of its own, the large granite cross at its tip erected by a local rector in 1896 to aid seafarers. The Dodman is also site of the 'Bulwark', a bank and ditch some 2,000 feet long and Cornwall's largest earthwork. The work of the National Trust allows visitors easy access to the headland and a 1.7 mile return walk from the car park at Penare.

WALK TERRAIN GRADE: **EASY**

MAP REF: **O.S. LANDRANGER 204 999 404**

DIRECTIONS: Follow signs for Gorran from the B3273 just north of Mevagissey. Shortly after Gorran High Lanes follow signs for Boswinger. Very narrow lanes lead past Hemmick Beach to reach a National Trust car park at Penare.

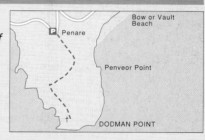

51 BLACK HEAD

Acquired by the National Trust in 1986, the 12 acre promontory of Black Head, like most Cornish headlands, was fortified with earthworks by Iron Age settlers. The headland cannot be accessed on certain weekends (usually Sundays) between Sept. and April due to its use as a firing range. Advance notice and red flags warn of such an occurrence. Extensive coastal views.

WALK TERRAIN GRADE: **EASY**

MAP REF: **O.S. LANDRANGER 204 034 487**

DIRECTIONS: Take the Porthpean turning from the A390 in St. Austell between the ASDA Superstore and Mount Charles roundabouts. Continue straight ahead before bearing left to follow signs for Trenarren where there is a small parking area. Walk ahead (signed Public Bridleway) on a well defined path. Black Head is reached after approx. 20 mins.

View from Black Head. MDN

52 PARK HEAD

An interesting coastal headland, not far up the coast from Newquay and overlooking the famous rock stacks of Bedruthan Steps. Two banks and a ditch across the neck of the headland show the site was defended by Iron Age settlers over 2,000 years ago. From the parking area, follow the footpath signs out to Pentire Steps and Park Head (a little short of 2 miles return trip).

WALK TERRAIN GRADE: **EASY**

MAP REF: **O.S. LANDRANGER 200 854 707**

DIRECTIONS: Take the B3276 north coast road from Newquay, passing through Mawgan Porth. 1 mile after the National Trust viewpoint across Bedruthan Steps at Carnewas, turn left at a small white sign indicating Pentire Farm and Park Head. Park up the lane on the right hand side.

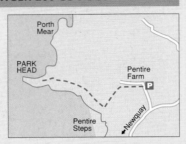

View to Park Head across Bedruthan Steps. MDN

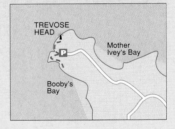
Trevose Head. MDN

53 TREVOSE HEAD

Dramatic cliff views and excellent coastal path walking on a headland midway between Newquay and Padstow. The automated lighthouse is testament to the treacherous nature of the coastline here.

WALK TERRAIN GRADE: **EASY**

MAP REF: **O.S. LANDRANGER 200 851 764**

DIRECTIONS: Trevose Head is signed from St. Merryn on the B3276 between Newquay and Padstow. Pass Mother Ivey's Bay Caravan Park and use a toll road to reach a parking area on the headland.

54 PENTIRE POINT/THE RUMPS

The Rumps is one of Cornwall's most magnificent headlands, its distinctive outline reached via a narrow isthmus with ditches and ramparts that were built in the Iron Age to enhance its natural defensive capabilities. Pass around Pentireglaze Haven and follow the coast path to Pentire Point and The Rumps. Return by farmland paths and a right turn opposite Pentire Farm to complete a 3.5 mile circular walk.

WALK TERRAIN GRADE: **MODERATE**

MAP REF: **O.S. LANDRANGER 200 937 797**

DIRECTIONS: Take the B3314 from Wadebridge signed to Polzeath. Shortly after the Porteath Bee Centre, turn right for New Polzeath and park in the main car park (there are also a number of spaces overlooking the bay).

The Rumps. MDN

55 DAYMER BAY

From Daymer Bay beach car park, bear left to explore the dome shaped Brea Hill and adjacent sand dunes. The hill provides lovely views across the glorious Camel estuary and towards Padstow and Stepper Point.

WALK TERRAIN GRADE: MODERATE

MAP REF: O.S. LANDRANGER 200 929 777

DIRECTIONS: *From the roundabout on the A39 at the northern end of Wadebridge, take the B3314 (signed Polzeath and Rock). After approx. 3.5 miles, turn left signed to Pityme and Rock. After reaching the Pityme Freehouse at St. Minver Lowlands, turn right into Trewiston Lane and follow signs for Trebetherick. From here, turn left to follow a narrow lane signed to Daymer Bay. Park overlooking the beach. Seasonal refreshments and toilets at car park.*

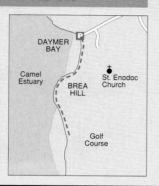

Brea Hill, Daymer Bay. MDN

Cyclists on the Camel Trail. MDN

56 THE CAMEL TRAIL

One of Cornwall's best recreation routes, and something of a rarity as it is ideal for cyclists. The Camel Trail is based on the old Padstow to Bodmin railway line, its conversion from track bed to recreational route undertaken by Cornwall County Council in 1980. The total length of the trail is 17 miles with perhaps the most popular section being the 5 miles between Padstow and Wadebridge, principally because of its superb views across the River Camel estuary.

WALK TERRAIN GRADE: EASY

DIRECTIONS: *Brown tourist signs indicate the Camel Trail in Padstow, Wadebridge & Bodmin. Cycle hire available at Padstow and Wadebridge.*

57 GRIBBIN HEAD

Gribbin Head forms the eastern end of St. Austell Bay and the western approach to the important port of Fowey. The Gribbin is immediately recognisable by its red and white striped daymark tower, built in 1832 by Trinity House to help mariners. From Menabilly car park, head down the farm track to Polridmouth Cove before turning right to explore the headland.

WALK TERRAIN GRADE: EASY

MAP REF: O.S. LANDRANGER 204 095 511

DIRECTIONS: *From the A3082 Par-Fowey road, turn right shortly after Polmear (signed Polkerris). Continue straight ahead and park at Menabilly Barton car park.*

Gribben Head Daymark. MDN

58 PENCARROW HEAD

A National Trust headland offering excellent walking and coastal views, just to the west of Polperro. The headland divides Lantic and Lantivet Bays and is easily reached from a nearby National Trust parking area.

WALK TERRAIN GRADE: **EASY**

MAP REF: O.S. LANDRANGER 201 **149 514**

DIRECTIONS: On the Polruan to Polperro coast road, about 1 mile east of Polruan is a small National Trust parking area. The path to Pencarrow Head is a short distance away.

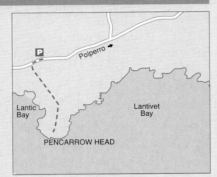

Pencarrow Head. MDN

'Hall Walk' view of Fowey estuary. MDN

59 THE 'HALL WALK'

The 'Hall Walk', which runs from Bodinnick to Penleath Point, was created by the Mohun family of Hall and dates from at least the sixteenth century. It provides stunning views across Fowey and its estuary and the narrow wooded creek of Pont Pill.
Cross the River Fowey via the Bodinnick Ferry and walk uphill past the Old Ferry Inn. Approx. 100 yards past a tiny church on the right, turn right and follow the path to the Q memorial.

WALK TERRAIN GRADE: **EASY**

MAP REF: O.S. LANDRANGER 200 **126 522**

DIRECTIONS: Head for Fowey on the A3082 from Par, near St. Austell. At a cross-roads, take the B3269 signed for Bodinnick Ferry. Park in a car park adjacent to the ferry. Toilets and refreshments nearby. Old Ferry Inn at Bodinnick.

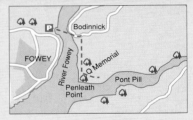

'Hall Walk' view of Fowey. MDN

60 LERRYN CREEK

If you enjoy creekside walking through lush woodlands, Lerryn Creek is unlikely to disappoint. The woods on the northern side of the creek are owned by the National Trust and can easily be accessed for level and firm underfoot walking. At low tide use the stepping stones across the river, but at high tide, it will be necessary to cross the sixteenth century road bridge.

WALK TERRAIN GRADE: **EASY**

MAP REF: O.S. LANDRANGER 200 **140 571**

DIRECTIONS: From the A390 St. Austell-Liskeard road, on the eastern edge of Lostwithiel, follow signs to Lerryn. Cross the narrow road bridge at the entrance to the village and follow the road right to the main car park. Refreshments and toilets nearby.

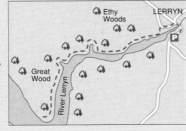

Lerryn Creek. MDN

61 CARDINHAM WOODS

Managed since 1922 by the Forestry Commission, Cardinham Woods offers extensive public access to both walkers and cyclists. Four walks can be traced, ranging from between 2 and 3 miles with such names as the 'Bluebell Walk' and 'Silvermine Trail'.

WALK TERRAIN GRADE: **EASY**

MAP REF: **O.S. LANDRANGER 200 098 636**

DIRECTIONS: From Bodmin take the A38 for 2 miles to reach the A30/A38 roundabout. 400 yards beyond the roundabout, turn left and follow signs to Cardinham. Refreshments during the summer at Callywith Cottage, adjacent to the car park. Cycle hire also available.

Cardinham Woods. MDN

Polperro. MDN

62 POLPERRO

Polperro's delightful harbour area is a great attraction to the many visitors. A good way to admire the view is to take steps to the rear of the nearby Blue Peter Inn, waymarked "To the cliff". Use the coast path for whatever distance you require.

WALK TERRAIN GRADE: **TOUGH**

MAP REF: **O.S. LANDRANGER 201 205 515**

DIRECTIONS: The A387 into Polperro ends at the main village car park (Crumplehorn). From here, walk down into the village and stay on the right hand side of the harbour. Toilets and refreshments at car park. All facilities in Polperro.

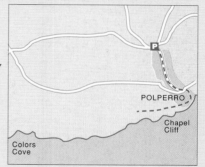

63 KILMINORTH WOODS

The heavily wooded slopes of the West Looe River have a well marked riverside path (signed to Watergate) that is easily found from the far western end of Looe's main car park.

WALK TERRAIN GRADE: **EASY**

MAP REF: **O.S. LANDRANGER 201 252 538**

DIRECTIONS: Take the A387 to Looe and park in the main town car park at West Looe (also signed Discovery Centre). Toilets and refreshments adjacent to the Discovery Centre.

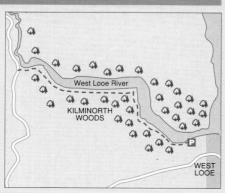

West Looe River. MDN

64 DEERPARK WOOD

Forestry Commission owned woodland with forest trails and picnic areas. Approx. 6 miles north of Looe and Polperro.

WALK TERRAIN GRADE: **MODERATE**

MAP REF: O.S. LANDRANGER **198 604**

DIRECTIONS: Head south from the A390 Lostwithiel-Liskeard road on the B3359 at Middle Taphouse. After approx. 2 miles, turn left signed to Deerpark Forest.

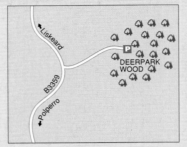

Golitha Falls. Tim Guthrie.

65 GOLITHA FALLS

Ancient woodlands sitting astride one of Cornwall's most important rivers, the Fowey, first mentioned in the Domesday Book. Now managed by English Nature, there are a series of waymarked tracks with the small falls reached after a 10 minute walk. Particularly impressive after periods of heavy rainfall.

WALK TERRAIN GRADE: **EASY**

MAP REF: O.S. LANDRANGER 201 **227 690**

DIRECTIONS: From the A38 at Dobwalls, head north following signs for Dobwalls Adventure Park. Proceed past the park and follow signs for Golitha Falls. After a short distance, turn left across a small bridge and park on the right hand side. Toilet block in car park.

66 ROCKY VALLEY

A dramatic, steep sided valley of great beauty. The river has cut its way through an abrupt slate landscape, forded in several places by small wooden footbridges that allow you to follow the river to the sea. As you descend through the valley, look out for labyrinth like rock carvings (near ruined buildings) that are believed to date from the Bronze Age, some 4,000 years ago.

WALK TERRAIN GRADE: **MODERATE**

MAP REF: O.S. EXPLORER 9 Bodmin Moor **074 891**

DIRECTIONS: Use a small parking area for about 15 cars located on the B3263 Tintagel-Boscastle road between the settlements of Bossiney and Trethevy. A path is signed from the parking area past the trout farm and Trevillet Mill coffee shop (seasonal opening) to the valley.

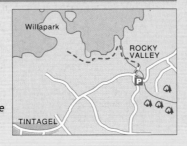

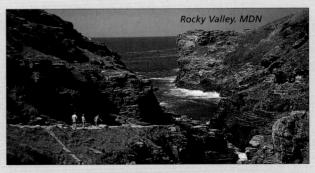

Rocky Valley. MDN

Rocky Valley. MDN

67 BOSCASTLE CLIFF WALKS

The tortuous inlet of Boscastle Harbour provides the starting point for splendid cliff walks both north and south. If heading north, keep the river to your left and climb gradually to reach Penally Hill with its distinctive fish shaped weathervane. An arguably better view of the inlet can be gained by crossing the river left to reach the boat moorings at the bottom of the harbour. Climb to reach the distinctive white coastguard building on the Willapark headland. Before your walk, visit the excellent visitor centre in the car park (free admission) that details the natural history of this area.

WALK TERRAIN GRADE: **TOUGH**

MAP REF: **O.S. EXPLORER 9** Bodmin Moor **101 914**

DIRECTIONS: Follow signs to Boscastle from the A39 Bude-Camelford road. Park in the large car park in the centre of the village next to the North Cornwall Visitor Centre (toilets). Refreshments in the village.

Boscastle. MDN

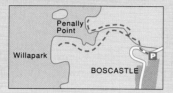

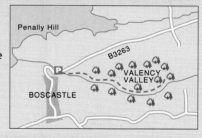
Valency Valley. MDN

68 THE VALENCY VALLEY

The National Trust safeguards 100 acres of the wooded Valency Valley, a tranquil and lovely place in which you can walk upstream for about a mile by the side of the Valency River. Well signed public rights of way continue to St. Juliot's Church, the location where the then architect, Thomas Hardy, met his first wife Emma Gifford whilst overseeing the church's restoration.

WALK TERRAIN GRADE: **EASY**

MAP REF: **O.S. EXPLORER 9** Bodmin Moor **101 914**

DIRECTIONS: Follow signs to Boscastle from the A39 Bude-Camelford road. Park in the large car park in the centre of the village next to the North Cornwall Visitor Centre. Toilets in the car park. Refreshments throughout the village.

69 CRACKINGTON HAVEN

Crackington Haven is the start point for towering cliff walks on National Trust land both north and south from the cove. To the south is the promontory of Cambeak and Strangles Beach, the latter overlooked by High Cliff, at 731 feet, Cornwall's highest cliff. To the north, Pencannow Point provides classic coastal views.

WALK TERRAIN GRADE: **MODERATE**

MAP REF: **O.S. LANDRANGER 190 143 968**

DIRECTIONS: Follow signs to Crackington Haven from Wainhouse Corner on the A39 between Bude and Camelford. Use a small car park adjacent to the river bridge in front of the Coombe Barton Inn. Toilet block, cafes and beach shop also.

Crackington Haven. MDN

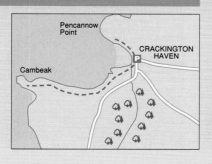

70 RAME HEAD

One of Cornwall's grandest headlands with far reaching views across the adjacent Whitsand Bay and towards the entrance to Plymouth Sound. A small stone chapel dedicated to St. Michael, dating from the twelfth century, is situated at the top of the headland on the believed site of a Celtic hermitage.

WALK TERRAIN GRADE: **MODERATE**

MAP REF: **O.S. LANDRANGER 201 421 488**

DIRECTIONS: *Take the B3247 to Millbrook and follow signs for Kingsand/Cawsand. Head for the hamlet of Rame and use a small car park close to Rame Head. All facilities in Kingsand/Cawsand.*

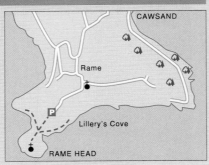

View from Rame Head. MDN

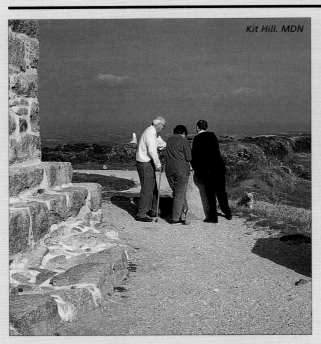

Kit Hill. MDN

71 KIT HILL

A 1000 ft. summit offering extensive views towards Dartmoor, Bodmin Moor and across the Tamar Valley towards Plymouth Sound. Three directional viewfinders are sited beside the summit's tower. The hill was extensively mined for tin, copper and arsenic before being donated to the people of Cornwall as a country park by HRH Prince Charles in 1985.

WALK TERRAIN GRADE: **MODERATE**

MAP REF: **O.S. LANDRANGER 201 384 714**

DIRECTIONS: *From the A390 1 mile east of Callington, turn left signed to Kit Hill. After less than half a mile, turn left and follow a track to the parking area.*

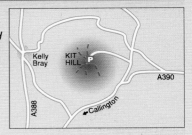

72 BUDE CANAL

A level waterside walk suitable for families, pushchairs and wheelchairs. A tarmac towpath follows the course of the canal for about two miles to Helebridge, crossing from the right hand side at Rodd's Bridge. The canal was originally used to transport fertilisers inland, although was largely abandoned from the 1880's.

WALK TERRAIN GRADE: **EASY**

MAP REF: **O.S. LANDRANGER 190 210 059**

DIRECTIONS: *Head into Bude from the A39 south of Stratton. Take the first exit on the first mini roundabout you come to and park in the Crescent car park where there is a large and interesting visitors' centre. Toilets in car park, ample refreshment facilities in Bude.*

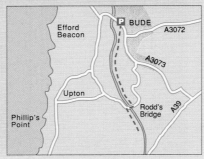

Bude Canal. MDN

73 COMPASS POINT

An enjoyable walk can be had on the coast path at Compass Point immediately south of Bude. Built here is an unusual eight sided storm tower after which the point derives its name. An information board details the tower's history. From the car park, cross the bridge in front of the Falcon Hotel and turn right alongside the canal. A wooden kissing gate at the end of the cul-de-sac leads to a right turn allowing exploration of the coast path overlooking Bude's breakwater.

WALK TERRAIN GRADE: **EASY**

MAP REF: O.S. LANDRANGER 190 **210 059**

DIRECTIONS: Head into Bude from the A39 south of Stratton. Take the first exit on the first mini roundabout you come to and park in the Crescent car park where there is a large and interesting visitors' centre. Toilets in car park, refreshment facilities readily available in Bude.

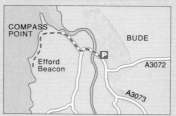

Compass Point, Bude.

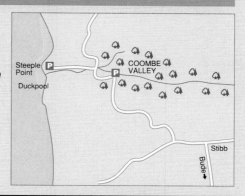

74 COOMBE VALLEY

Forestry Commission owned wood with woodland walk about 4 miles north of Bude. Can be combined with a visit to the National Trust owned Steeple Point at nearby Duckpool.

WALK TERRAIN GRADE: **EASY**

MAP REF: O.S. LANDRANGER 190 **213 116**

DIRECTIONS: Follow signs for Coombe from the A39 Bude-Bideford road half a mile south of Kilkhampton. Pass through village of Stibb and follow Forestry Commission signs.

---

75 MORWENSTOW

This is a truly interesting area to walk with much to see. Situated in the far north of Cornwall, Morwenstow has a lovely old church, where its former vicar, the Rev. Hawker, a famous Victorian eccentric, is credited with making popular the Harvest Festival. The graveyard contains the figurehead of the Caledonia, wrecked in 1843, just one of many shipwrecks for whose crews Hawker tried to ensure a Christian burial. By walking along the 450 foot high Vicarage Cliff, you can find Hawker's Hut, built of driftwood and used by him to watch for shipwrecks. Return back along the cliff or descend to the Tidna valley and turn left to complete a 1.5 mile circular walk.

WALK TERRAIN GRADE: **EASY**

MAP REF: O.S. LANDRANGER 190 **207 154**

DIRECTIONS: From the A39, just over 2 miles north of Kilkhampton (north of Bude), follow signs to Morwenstow and use a parking area between Rectory Farm and the church. Refreshments at Rectory Farm available during the season. The Bush Inn pub is nearby.

Caledonia figurehead, Morwenstow graveyard. MDN

Carn Galver. Clive Vincent.

Lamorna. Clive Vincent

CORNISH LIFEBOAT STATIONS

by Sue Denny

The Royal National Lifeboat Institution operates 14 lifeboat stations in Cornwall, all of which have a long and distinguished history. Whenever lifeboats are mentioned, Cornwall is the county which immediately springs to mind, with its picturesque fishing villages and the lifeboat stations at their heart. Whilst the technology has certainly changed, as have those picturesque villages, the volunteer spirit of the lifeboat service has not. A tour of the lifeboat stations would take in some of the prettiest, roughest and most dangerous coastline in the country.

LOOE is the second newest lifeboat station in Cornwall, having been re-established in 1992. The D class inflatable inshore lifeboat is capable of 29 knots, has a crew of two or three, can be quickly launched and is capable of working close inshore amongst rocks and surf. Since the lifeboat station was re-established the lifeboat has launched, on average, once a month.

FOWEY has the first 25 knot 14.26m (46ft 9in) Trent class all-weather lifeboat to go on station in Cornwall. This new class of lifeboat, together with the larger 17m Severn class lifeboat, will eventually replace all the lifeboats which lie afloat.

FALMOUTH, established in 1867, has two lifeboats. The all-weather lifeboat is an Arun class *Elizabeth Ann*. The Atlantic 21 rigid inflatable *Falmouth Round Table* was provided as a result of local fundraising within the organisation.

THE LIZARD lifeboat station is situated on a tongue of rock at the foot of a 140 feet high cliff. There are over two hundred steps between the car park and the boathouse floor! The Lizard currently operates a Tyne class lifeboat *David Robinson* capable of 18 knots.

St Ives Lifeboat station. Picture courtesy of Xpelair/RNLI.

MARAZION lifeboat station was established in 1990 in order to provide cover during the busy summer months. It operates a D class inflatable inshore lifeboat, provided from an appeal by the South West Federation of Sea Anglers.

PENLEE lifeboat station has a heroic and tragic history, for it was here in 1981 that all eight crew of the lifeboat *Solomon Browne* lost their lives when she was wrecked while assisting the coaster *Union Star*.

SENNEN COVE lifeboat station currently operates a Mersey class lifeboat *The Four Boys*, which was partly funded by an appeal launched by the families of four boys who were swept out to sea off Land's End. A D class inflatable lifeboat also operates from the station.

ST IVES lifeboat station also has a distinguished and tragic history. In January 1939 the lifeboat launched to the aid of an unknown vessel. The lifeboat capsized near Clodgy Point and when she righted four men were missing. In 1993/94 a new boathouse and slipway were constructed, in order to accommodate the Mersey class lifeboat *The Princess Royal (Civil Service No 41)* which is launched from a carriage. The boathouse has won a number of architectural awards and is built of traditional Cornish materials.

ST AGNES is one of seven lifeboat stations in the UK and Republic of Ireland to have a lifeboat provided by the viewers of BBC television's children's programme 'Blue Peter'. The first appeal for lifeboats was made in 1964 and there have been four since.

NEWQUAY lifeboat station was established in 1860 and operates two inshore lifeboats. In 1994 the old Seaman's Mission was demolished and a joint RNLI boathouse/Seaman's Mission was constructed. The new boathouse provides housing for both the 'D' and Atlantic 21 class lifeboats, as well as crew facilities and souvenir sales outlet.

PADSTOW lifeboat station is another old station with a distinguished history. The Tyne class lifeboat launches down a slipway in Mother Ivey's Bay, Trevose Head, some 2 miles from Padstow, so the volunteer crew, when summoned by their pagers, meet in the centre of the village and are ferried to the lifeboat station in a unique RNLI mini-bus, complete with blue flashing light. The lifeboat station is spectacularly situated and can be reached by stairs or an 'outside' lift, which is not an experience for the faint hearted!

ROCK is the newest lifeboat station in Cornwall, having been established in 1994 in order to deal with the increasing numbers of people using the estuary for water activities, who required a fast response. The D class inflatable lifeboat has certainly proved vital during the hot summers of the past few years.

PORT ISAAC lifeboat station was first established in 1869 but closed in 1933 and re-opened in 1967 as an inshore (D class) lifeboat station.

BUDE lifeboat station was established in 1837 and closed in 1923. The RNLI re-opened the station in 1966 as an inshore lifeboat station and a D class inflatable, which can deal with the surf and work close inshore to the beaches and the cliffs, is on station.

During 1995 Cornish lifeboats launched 376 times and saved the lives of 102 people.

14m Trent class lifeboat. Picture courtesy of Rick Tomlinson/RNLI.

CORNWALL AIR AMBULANCE

by Richard Taylor

Cornwall's Air Ambulance, the first dedicated helicopter emergency medical service to operate in the UK, was brought into service in 1st April 1987.

The county lends itself ideally to an operation of this kind, having a widely scattered population, many living in remote and isolated rural communities, far from the nearest accident and emergency facilities at either Plymouth or Truro. During the summer months Cornwall's narrow, winding roads often become clogged with holiday traffic, making access for a road ambulance very difficult and turning any subsequent trip to hospital with a patient into a very daunting and drawn out process. The beaches, clifftops and moorland areas where many accidents occur, are also frequently inaccessible by road.

The Cornwall Air Ambulance makes short work of such difficulties. From its base at RAF St. Mawgan, near Newquay, it can reach any part of the county within 20 minutes, regardless of traffic conditions. Its skid landing gear enables it to cope with any type of terrain which is likely to be encountered and the compact dimensions of the aircraft, coupled with a high degree of manoeuvrability, allows it to land safely in even the most confined areas.

Despite its relatively small size, the Air Ambulance carries all the immediate care, monitoring and resuscitation equipment found on a

Picture courtesy of Tim Guthrie.

normal front-line ambulance. There is also sufficient room on board for two stretcher patients and to provide them with treatment whilst airborne. As well as the pilot, the helicopter is crewed by two paramedics whose services are provided by the Westcountry Ambulance Service. There is currently a pool of twenty paramedics who work on the Air Ambulance on a rota basis, the remainder of their time being spent on the road ambulances around the county.

The Cornwall Air Ambulance is not reserved for use in specially selected types of incident. It is operated by the Ambulance service as an integral part of its resources. Both road and air crews work closely together to provide the public with the best possible response in the event of an emergency.

In the nine years since its launch the Air Ambulance has flown over 7000 missions, transporting victims of sudden serious illness or traumatic injuries to hospital from all parts of Cornwall and, on occasions when the need has arisen, The Isles of Scilly. The speed of the helicopter has provided an extra dimension to the Ambulance Service's resources in the county. Had it not been available when needed, it is certain that a number of the patients it has carried would not have survived. It has also made an appreciable difference to the long-term recovery prospects of a great many others.

Picture courtesy of David Brenchley/Bernard White.

ANCIENT CORNWALL

by Mark Norton

Cornwall has some of the finest prehistoric remains in Britain. As on Dartmoor in neighbouring Devon, these are largely, though not exclusively, concentrated on upland moors; Bodmin and West Penwith are the principal location of Cornwall's antiquities, their lack of use for agriculture or development ensuring their preservation for posterity.

Many of the sites listed below are at the heart of the magic and mystery that is Cornwall. Isolated standing stones, intriguing stone circles and quoits stand patiently in the Cornish mist, their exact reason for construction lost over time and now the subject of intense academic speculation.

A number of these sites are freely accessible to the visitor. For full directions on how to get to them, refer to the relevant section containing that antiquity.

CHAMBER TOMBS Also known as quoits or barrows and largely dating from around 4,000 years ago. Most consist of a large capstone resting on smaller upright stones and are believed to have contained more than one occupant. It has always been believed that they were covered with a mound of earth though this has been questioned more recently. Good examples include **Lanyon Quoit** near Penzance, **Chun Quoit** near Morvah and **Trethevy Quoit** near St. Cleer on Bodmin Moor.

STONE CIRCLES Perhaps the most widely discussed with regard to precise purpose, the Cornish stone circles are of course smaller in scale than their more famous counterparts at Stonehenge and

Duloe stone circle. MDN.

Avebury, but similarly thought to have been constructed for some form of ceremonial purpose. The best examples are the **Merry Maidens** near Lamorna and **The Hurlers**, an intriguing line of three stone circles on Bodmin Moor. A further circle worth a visit is at **Duloe**, near Looe, unusual in that the erected stones are of quartz.

STANDING STONES These often accompany stone circles though they can be found individually throughout Cornwall. Generally placed in position at least a thousand years before the birth of Christ: a good example are **The Pipers**, located in a field on the opposite side of the road to the Merry Maidens. More intriguing is

Men-an-Tol, a circular stone with a round hole regarded in the past for its healing properties.

INSCRIBED STONES Dating from much later than the standing stones, inscribed stones are generally associated with commemorating or recording the burial sites of Cornish chieftains

and leaders. The best two examples are **Men Scryfa** near Penzance and **King Doniert's Stones** near Dobwalls.

IRON AGE HILLFORTS AND CLIFF CASTLES It is generally thought that the Iron Age (circa 1000 BC onwards) was a particularly turbulent period because of the emphasis given to the construction of settlements with defensive positions, many of which can clearly be traced today. Classic hillfort sites include Castle-an-Dinas near St. Columb and Trencrom Hill near St. Ives. Cliff castles were built wherever headlands or promontories could be protected through the building of ditches and embankments. Best examples include Dodman Point, Park Head, Logan Rock, Black Head and The Rumps.

IRON AGE VILLAGES Occupied until around the time of the Roman invasion in the first century AD, these settlements often have fougous (pronounced foogoo), an underground passage variously regarded as hiding holes, tombs or storage chambers. Chysauster Settlement is Cornwall's most famous example, although Carn Euny near Sancreed, cared for by English Heritage is also well worth a visit. Situated on the Trelowarren Estate near Helston is Halliggye Fougou.

For further details, see the following sections:
IT'S FREE! - Lanyon Quoit, Trethevy Quoit, Merry Maidens, The Hurlers, Duloe Stone Circle, Men-an-Tol, Men Scryfa, King Doniert's Stones, Castle-an-Dinas, Carn Euny & Halliggye Fougou.
WALKING AREA AND VIEWPOINTS - Trencrom Hill, Dodman Point, Park Head, Logan Rock, Black Head & The Rumps.
ATTRACTIONS - Chysauster

Lanyon Quoit. MDN

Carn Euny. MDN.

CLASSIC CORNISH FISHING VILLAGES

by Mark Norton

Two industries, mining and fishing, lie at the heart of understanding how Cornwall has developed over the last couple of hundred years. Though both industries have largely declined compared to their peaks in the nineteenth century, and with only one tin mine remaining compared to over 300 in 1850, fishing remains an important, if low scale, activity in the county. Just as mining resulted in the development of towns such as Redruth and Camborne, fishing ensured that small communities would develop around coves where harbour walls could be constructed, boats landed and a living made.

Nowadays, however, most fishing in Cornwall consists of local boats, working relatively close inshore with an emphasis on crab, lobster and seasonal fishing for species such as mackerel.

The modern fishing industry in Cornwall is centred on Newlyn, England's most important port for landing fish, and to a far lesser extent at Looe and Padstow. Each of these places is well worth a visit in its own right and with this in mind the following fishing villages have been chosen to illustrate 'typical' Cornish fishing communities:

BOSCASTLE Treacherous inlet below towering cliffs on the north coast near Tintagel. One of relatively few fishing communities in this part of Cornwall as the coastline has few inlets capable of supporting a harbour. The attractive National

Cadgwith. MDN.

Trust harbour area is freely accessible to visitors.

CADGWITH Photogenic fishing village on the southern end of the Lizard Peninsula. Important pilchard fishery in the nineteenth century.

COVERACK Popular village on the eastern side of the Lizard Peninsula. Small harbour area with stout granite walls from which there are fine views across the bay.

MEVAGISSEY Retains an active fishing industry with an extensive complex of harbour walls ideal for exploration by visitors. In the nineteenth century, Mevagissey had a reputation for excellence in boat building; smuggling was an important supplement for fishermen.

MOUSEHOLE An archetypal Cornish fishing village centring on a small harbour with views across Mounts Bay to St Michael's Mount. Visitors are attracted here throughout the year, the harbour extensively decorated with lights at Christmas.

MULLION COVE A one time flourishing pilchard fishery with impressive granite harbour walls built in the 1890's. Now largely owned by the National Trust.

POLPERRO A much loved and picturesque harbourside community with an established fishing industry since the thirteenth century. Narrow streets of whitewashed cottages add to the visual attraction.

PORTHLEVEN A fishing village since medieval times. The extensive harbour area that can be seen today results from a plan in the nineteenth century to develop it into a major port.

PORT ISAAC North coast fishing village with narrow streets crowding around a small cove. Park in the car park on the Portgaverne side of the village and follow a marked path to the harbour.

PORTLOE A narrow rocky inlet on the Roseland Peninsula famed for its attractiveness and lack of commercialism. Small scale fishing activity remains, watched over by narrow whitewashed cottages and the Lugger Hotel.

Mousehole. MDN.

Newlyn. MDN.

IT'S FREE!

A selection of things to see and do in Cornwall that won't break the bank!

The ideas contained in the **IT'S FREE** section are based around activities that are essentially free to do with no admission charge or payment required for the core activity. (All costs involving retail purchases, travel, parking and refreshments are excluded).

For ease of reference, the **IT'S FREE** ideas have been organised broadly west to east. Use the map below to identify the location of each suggestion.

A SHORT NOTE ON THE ENTRY DETAILS:

OPENING HOURS   Though all opening hours have been verified, in the low season (September to May) it would often be worthwhile to ring before making a long journey.

DISABLED ACCESS   If in doubt, ring prior.

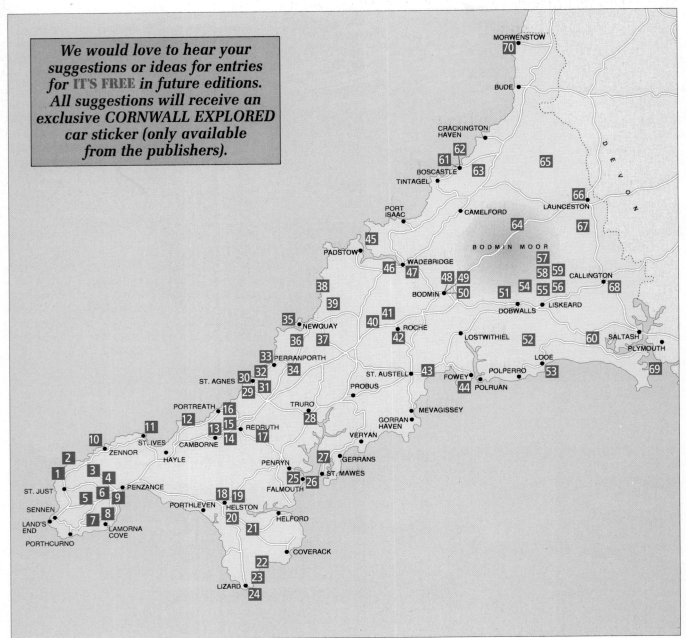

We would love to hear your suggestions or ideas for entries for IT'S FREE in future editions. All suggestions will receive an exclusive CORNWALL EXPLORED car sticker (only available from the publishers).

1 CROWNS ENGINE HOUSES

ADDRESS/LOCATION
Botallack, near St. Just-in-Penwith.

DIRECTIONS
Botallack is on the B3306 north of St. Just. A lane leading north west from the village will lead to a path to the engine houses.

OPENING HOURS
Any reasonable time.

DISABLED ACCESS
No

Crowns, Botallack. Tim Guthrie.

DETAILS
A testament to the bravery and daring of the Cornish mining industry, these two engine houses are dramatically located above the sea on a cliffside ledge. The mine workings stretched for over half a mile out to sea; it was here that the miners could famously hear the sound of boulders shifting on the sea bed above them.

2 PENDEEN GEM & JEWELLERY WORKSHOP

ADDRESS/LOCATION
Pendeen. TR19 7DP. (01736) 788217

DIRECTIONS
Located on the B3306 coast road between St. Ives and Lands End.

OPENING HOURS
Daily, 10am-6pm, later in Summer.

DISABLED ACCESS
Yes.

DETAILS
Jewellery workshop with handmade jewellery using local gem stones where possible. Adjacent crafts and mining exhibition as well as "The Pound and Ounces" Cornish fudge shop.

3 MEN-AN-TOL/ MEN SCRYFA

ADDRESS/LOCATION
Near Madron.

DIRECTIONS
From the B3306 St. Just-St. Ives road, turn south, just east of Morvah signed towards Penzance and Madron. A small roadside parking area is reached after approx. 1 mile. 10 min signed walk to Men-an-tol, Men Scryfa further 5 mins.

OPENING HOURS
Any reasonable time.

DISABLED ACCESS
No.

DETAILS
Men Scryfa is a standing stone with a Latin inscription commemorating "Rialobran, the son of Cunoval", believed to have been a 6th century chieftain. **Men-an-Tol** is a stone noted for its round hole, said to cure children of rickets and other ailments which involved the passing of the naked child through the hole three times. Also known as the Devil's Eye.

Men-an-Tol. MDN.

4 LANYON QUOIT

ADDRESS/LOCATION
Near Madron.

DIRECTIONS
From B3306 St. Just-St. Ives road, turn south, just east of Morvah, towards Penzance and Madron. A couple of roadside parking areas are reached after approx. 2 miles, the quoit being 50 yards from the road.

OPENING HOURS
Any reasonable time.

Marcus Way/National Trust

DISABLED ACCESS
No.

DETAILS
Famous chamber tomb with the top slab measuring over 15' by 10'.

5 CARN EUNY

ADDRESS/LOCATION
Near Sancreed, west of Penzance.

DIRECTIONS
Follow brown tourist signs from Drift on the A30 west of Penzance. Narrow country lanes with passing places bring you to a small parking area from where it is a 5 min walk.

OPENING HOURS
Daylight hours.

DISABLED ACCESS
No.

DETAILS
Well preserved Iron Age courtyard village, maintained by English Heritage. The farming hamlet was occupied from 500BC until 300AD; there is also an excellent example of a fougou, an underground chamber, the exact purpose of which is unknown.

6 DRIFT RESERVOIR

ADDRESS/LOCATION
Near Penzance.

DIRECTIONS
From A30 Penzance-Land's End road, turn off in small village of Drift signed towards Sancreed. A small parking area overlooking the reservoir is found after a short distance on the right hand side.

OPENING HOURS
Daylight hours.

DISABLED ACCESS
Yes.

DETAILS
For a relaxing picnic, why not head for Drift Reservoir where a parking and picnic area has been created overlooking the dam.

7 MERRY MAIDENS

ADDRESS/LOCATION Near Lamorna.

DIRECTIONS From Newlyn, follow the B3315 towards Lamorna. Continue past the turn off for Lamorna valley and park in one of the small lay-bys. The circle is in a roadside field, accessed by a stile.

OPENING HOURS Any reasonable time.

DISABLED ACCESS No.

DETAILS 19 stones, in a circle of over 70 feet in diameter, they are said to be maidens turned to stone as a punishment for dancing on a Sunday.

8 LAMORNA POTTERY

ADDRESS/LOCATION Lamorna, Nr. Penzance. TR19 6NY. (01736) 810330

DIRECTIONS On the B3315 Newlyn to Lands End road.

OPENING HOURS 7 days a week, mid Feb to Oct 31st, 10am-5.30pm.

DISABLED ACCESS Yes.

DETAILS Working pottery since 1947 with gift shop, boutique and restaurant. Visitors able to have a go at throwing a pot on the wheel in school holidays (charged for).

9 NEWLYN ART GALLERY

ADDRESS/LOCATION New Rd, Newlyn, Nr. Penzance. TR18 5PZ. (01736) 363715

DIRECTIONS Newlyn Art Gallery is the first building on the left at the Penzance entrance to Newlyn.

OPENING HOURS Mon to Sat, 10am-5pm, including Bank Holidays.

DISABLED ACCESS Full disabled access including ramp access and lift.

DETAILS Overlooking Mount's Bay, the Gallery presents nine major exhibitions a year of contemporary work featuring artists of regional, national and international importance. Lecture series and related educational events for each exhibition. Gallery shop and coffee point.

10 ST SENARA CHURCH

ADDRESS/LOCATION Zennor village.

DIRECTIONS Zennor is on the B3306 west of St. Ives.

OPENING HOURS Daylight hours.

DISABLED ACCESS With a little help.

DETAILS The small 12th century church is famous for its carved bench end of a mermaid. Legend has it that Matthew Trewhella, a local squire's son and chorister, was lured to his doom in nearby Pendour Cove by the mermaid after she heard him sing. A male voice is still said to be heard at the cove

11 LEACH STUDIO POTTERY

ADDRESS/LOCATION Upper Stennack, St. Ives. (01736) 796398

DIRECTIONS On St. Just to St. Ives road. (B3306) above St. Ives town.

OPENING HOURS All year, Mon to Fri, 10am-5pm. Easter through summer, Sats, 10am-5pm also.

DISABLED ACCESS One step to be negotiated then studio accessible.

DETAILS Exhibition of Bernard Leach Pottery as well as Janet Leach and Trevor Corser Pottery. Showroom and retail area.

12 HELL'S MOUTH

ADDRESS/LOCATION Near Hayle.

DIRECTIONS Between Hayle and Portreath on the B3306 (detached roadside cafe near parking lay-by).

OPENING HOURS Any reasonable time.

DISABLED ACCESS No

DETAILS Sheer drop in the National Trust owned cliffs near Godrevy. Adjacent parking allows a chance to view the spectacle, take care as the cliffs are treacherous. Seabird colonies also.

13 MINERAL TRAMWAYS DISCOVERY CENTRE

ADDRESS/LOCATION Old Cowlin's Mill, Penhallick, Carn Brea, Redruth. (01209) 612917

DIRECTIONS Nr Carn Brea Leisure Centre in Redruth.

OPENING HOURS 10am-4pm (Sat. 1pm-4pm, closed Mons)

DISABLED ACCESS Yes.

DETAILS Discover Cornwall's fascinating industrial past; the old mineral tramways, the mines and ports they served and the people and places at the one time centre of one of the world's biggest tin and copper mining areas. Waymarked trails and leaflets help explore this landscape.

14 C.S.M. GEOLOGICAL MUSEUM

ADDRESS/LOCATION
Camborne School of Mines, Pool, Redruth. TR15 3SE. (01209) 714866

DIRECTIONS
A3047 at Pool, turn into Cornwall College campus and right again to C.S.M. car park.

OPENING HOURS
All year, Mon to Fri, 9am-5pm except Bank Holidays and Christmas/New Year season.

DISABLED ACCESS
To ground floor displays only.

DETAILS
Displays of rocks and minerals from around the world. Art gallery showing mainly local artists both well known and newcomers. Shop. Coffee available.

15 TESCAN SHEEPSKIN

ADDRESS/LOCATION
Carn Tannery, Wilson Way, Redruth. TR15 3RX (01209) 214101

DIRECTIONS
A30 to Redruth or Camborne, then the A3047 to Pool Industrial Estate and Wilson Way.

OPENING HOURS
Mon to Fri, 9am-5pm, Sat 10am-5pm. Sunday 10am-5pm. Open all year (except Christmas and Good Friday). Pottery viewing Mon to Fri only, 10am-4pm.

DISABLED ACCESS
Yes.

DETAILS
Sheepskin and pottery shops. 300 seater coffee shop. Small charge for use of potters wheel.

16 CORNISH GOLD CENTRE

ADDRESS/LOCATION
Tolgus Mill, Nr. Portreath. TR6 4HN. (01209) 218198

DIRECTIONS
Turn off the A30 at Redruth exit and head towards Portreath on the B3300. Gold centre is 1 mile on left.

OPENING HOURS
June to Aug, weekdays, 9.30am-10pm. Weekends, 9.30am 5.30pm. Rest of the year, daily, 9.30am-5.30pm.

DISABLED ACCESS
Yes.

DETAILS
Gold retail showrooms holding the largest collection of gold jewellery in the West Country. Goldsmiths can be seen at work, there is also a coffee shop with both indoor and outdoor facilities.

17 GWENNAP PIT

ADDRESS/LOCATION
Near St. Day, Redruth.

DIRECTIONS
Follow brown tourist signs from A30 near Scorrier.

OPENING HOURS
Pit: daylight hours. **Visitor centre:** Spring bank holiday to end of Sept., Mon-Fri 10am-12.30pm and 2pm-4.30pm. Sat 10am-12.30pm. Sunday services between July and August at 2.30pm.

DISABLED ACCESS
No.

DETAILS
One of John Wesley's favourite places for preaching in Cornwall, receiving 18 visits between 1762 and 1789. The natural amphitheatre was created by underground mine workings and was capable of holding a congregation of many thousands. There is also a small visitor centre.

18 CORONATION BOATING LAKE

ADDRESS/LOCATION
Helston.

DIRECTIONS
The boating lake (adjacent parking) can be found immediately after turning onto the Porthleven road (A394) from Helston.

OPENING HOURS
Daylight hours.

DISABLED ACCESS
Yes.

DETAILS
Well kept gardens and boating lake with lots of ducks to feed. Tennis, putting and lakeside cafe (seasonal opening). Lakeside walk (the level path is suitable for pushchairs and wheelchairs) as well as free childrens activity area.

19 HELSTON FOLK MUSEUM

ADDRESS/LOCATION
Market Place, Helston. TR13 8TH. (01326) 564027

DIRECTIONS
Directly behind the Guildhall which is in the centre of Helston.

OPENING HOURS
All year, Mon-Sat, 10.30am-1pm, 2pm-4.30pm except Wed when 10.30am-12 noon only.

DISABLED ACCESS
Steps to front door, but side access available. Disabled very welcome.

DETAILS
The museum's emphasis is on the former trades and industries which flourished in and around Helston during the 19th and early 20th centuries. Exhibitions throughout the year, mainly art. Museum shop selling minerals, jewellery and local books.

20 R.N.A.S. CULDROSE VIEWING AREA

ADDRESS/LOCATION Culdrose, Helston.

DIRECTIONS Signed from the B3293/A3083 roundabout south of Helston.

OPENING HOURS Any reasonable time.

DISABLED ACCESS Yes.

DETAILS Small viewing enclosure overlooking Europe's largest military helicopter base. Adjacent toilets, cafe and shop.

21 HALLIGGYE FOUGOU

ADDRESS/LOCATION Near Garras, south east of Helston.

DIRECTIONS The Trelowarren Estate is indicated by a large sign in the village of Garras on the B3293 Helston-St. Keverne road. The fougou is signed on the road to Trelowarren and has no designated parking area.

OPENING HOURS Any reasonable time.

DISABLED ACCESS No.

DETAILS Halliggye fougou is an English Heritage maintained site on the Trelowarren Estate on the Lizard Peninsula. It lies within an earthwork enclosing a settlement that was occupied in the late Iron Age and early Roman periods circa 200B.C.-400A.D.

22 KENNACK POTTERY

ADDRESS/LOCATION Kennack Sands, Ruan Minor, Near Helston. TR12 7LX. (01326) 290592

DIRECTIONS From Helston, take the A3083 Lizard road turning left onto B3293. After Goonhilly Satellite Station, turn right for Kennack Sands. In Kuggar, turn left, Pottery beside Treasure Island gifts and beach shop.

OPENING HOURS
Peak season: Mon-Sat, 9am-7pm, Sun, 9am-7pm. Rest of season: Mon- Sat, 9am-7pm, Sun, 10am-5.30pm. Winter: Daily, 9am-5pm but advisable to phone first.

DISABLED ACCESS Yes.

DETAILS Pottery with opportunity for D.I.Y. modelling as well as sales area of Michael Hatfield ceramic models and locally made crafts. Tea room available. Try your hand at throwing a pot (small charge).

23 DEVIL'S FRYING PAN

ADDRESS/LOCATION Near Cadgwith, Lizard Peninsula.

DIRECTIONS Use Cadgwith's main car park and follow signed path to village. Turn right and follow the coast path sign that leads through the gardens of 'hillside' (permitted path). Walk up the lane and turn left to follow signs for Devil's Frying Pan (roughly 10-15 mins walk from car park).

OPENING HOURS Any reasonable time.

DISABLED ACCESS No.

DETAILS The Devil's Frying Pan is a 200 foot hole in the cliffside caused by the collapse of a sea cave. At high tide the sea bursts through under the arch that forms the outer perimeter.

24 LIZARD LIGHTHOUSE

ADDRESS/LOCATION (01326) 290431

DIRECTIONS Take the A3083 from Helston into Lizard village. Follow the lighthouse signs down a narrow lane to the National Trust owned car park adjacent to the lighthouse.

OPENING HOURS From Easter, 2pm til 1 hour before sunset.

DISABLED ACCESS No.

DETAILS Access can sometimes be made to the light but is strictly at the keepers discretion and it is advisable to telephone first (e.g. the lighthouse is closed to the public when the foghorn is operational). No admission charge is made but most visitors donate to lighthouse funds.

TO CONFIRM THE LOCATION OF INDIVIDUAL ATTRACTIONS, USE THE MAP ON PAGE 90

MATCH THE ATTRACTION NUMBER AGAINST THE RELEVANT COLOURED SQUARE.

25 FALMOUTH ART GALLERY

ADDRESS/LOCATION
Municipal Buildings, The Moor, Falmouth. TR11 2RT. (01326) 313863

DIRECTIONS
Take A38 to Falmouth centre. Follow signs to car parks, gallery situated above public library in Municipal Buildings.

OPENING HOURS
Mon-Fri, 10am-4.30pm, Sat, 10am-1pm.

DISABLED ACCESS
Not at present.

DETAILS
Changing programme of exhibitions during the year, together with a selection on display from the Town's permanent collection.

26 CASTLE DRIVE & PENDENNIS HEAD

ADDRESS/LOCATION
Falmouth.

DIRECTIONS
Signed from central Falmouth.

OPENING HOURS
Daylight hours.

DISABLED ACCESS
Yes.

DETAILS
Castle Drive provides a short one way drive around Pendennis Point, one of Cornwall's most interesting viewpoints. A small parking area near the beginning allows views across Falmouth docks where giant tankers can often be seen under repair. By

Tim Guthrie.

continuing to the car park at the end of Pendennis Head, views can be enjoyed across the Carrick Roads Estuary towards St. Anthony Lighthouse as well as across Falmouth Bay towards Rosemullion Head. The Little Dennis Blockhouse can also be explored from the car park.

27 ST JUST-IN-ROSELAND CHURCH

ADDRESS/LOCATION
Roseland Peninsula, north of St. Mawes.

DIRECTIONS
Signed from the A3078 St. Mawes road. Alternatively, use King Harry Ferry (signed between Truro and Falmouth in the A39) to reach the Roseland and follow B3289.

OPENING HOURS
Daylight hours.

DISABLED ACCESS
Possible although help will be needed due to steep inclines.

DETAILS
Cornwall's most photographed church, situated creekside amidst lush, palm fringed gardens. Parking area (with toilets) provides easy access to this tranquil setting.

28 TRURO CATHEDRAL

ADDRESS/LOCATION
21 Old Bridge Street (Cathedral Office), Truro. TR1 2AH. (01872) 76782

DIRECTIONS
Central Truro.

OPENING HOURS
Daily, 7.30am-6pm.

DISABLED ACCESS
Via Cathedral shop (ramp) though no disabled toilets.

DETAILS
Cornwall's only cathedral and the first Anglican cathedral to have been built in England since St. Paul's, the site having been a place of worship for many centuries, albeit in four different buildings. Completed in 1910, it has a shop, toilets, refectory and guide tape for the blind.

29 PRESINGOLL BARNS

ADDRESS/LOCATION
Penwinnick Road, St. Agnes. TR5 0PB. (01872) 553007. (01872) 553170 for pottery only

DIRECTIONS
From Chiverton Cross Roundabout on the A30, take the B3277 to St. Agnes. Presingoll Barns is situated a further 2 miles on the right.

OPENING HOURS
End May to end Oct, 9.30am-6pm. Nov to May, 10am-5pm.

DISABLED ACCESS
Yes except the pottery showroom which is upstairs.

DETAILS
Candle making, carving and dipping plus shop; working pottery and shop; fudge making; farmyard gift shop; D.I.Y. pot making and plate decorating and cafe. Childrens play area.

30 ST AGNES MUSEUM

ADDRESS/LOCATION
Penwinnick Road, St. Agnes. TR5 0PA.

DIRECTIONS
From the A30, take the B3277 to St. Agnes, free parking in the village.

OPENING HOURS
April to September, daily, 10.30am-5pm.

DISABLED ACCESS
After initial entry steps (2), the ground floor of the museum is accessible to wheelchairs.

DETAILS
Local history of the Parish of St. Agnes from fishing to folklore, tin mining to turtles. Exhibitions and displays include a video display showing films about St. Agnes, including a journey on the old branch line.

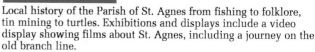

IT IS ADVISABLE, ESPECIALLY IN THE SEPTEMBER TO MAY LOW SEASON, TO CONFIRM OPENING ARRANGEMENTS BEFORE MAKING A LONG JOURNEY.

31 IMAGES OF CORNWALL

ADDRESS/LOCATION
Peterville, St. Agnes.
(01872) 553674

DIRECTIONS
Adjacent to road signed
for beach (Trevaunance
Cove) in St. Agnes.

OPENING HOURS
All year, Mon-Sat,
9.30am-5.30pm (closed
Weds between Christmas
& Easter).

DISABLED ACCESS
Gallery: Yes, once initial 6 steps negotiated. **Images of Cornwall:** Yes.

DETAILS
Images of Cornwall: Cornish tin and Celtic pewter jewellery and gifts including Cornish framed prints, Cornish textiles, pottery, candles, biscuits and fudge. **Saffron Gallery:** Exhibition of traditional Cornish paintings by local artists including Nancy Bailey and Monica Childs. Galley coffee shop for Cornish cream teas and refreshments.

32 TREVAUNANCE COVE CRAFT WORKSHOPS

ADDRESS/LOCATION
Trevaunance Cove, St. Agnes. Enquiries (01872) 552428

DIRECTIONS
Proceed to St. Agnes and follow signs for the beach. The workshops are on the right, 200 yards from the cove with a large free car park opposite.

OPENING HOURS
Summer 10am-5pm. Best to ring in Winter to determine opening arrangements.

DISABLED ACCESS
Yes.

DETAILS
Craft workshops in purpose built building with wide range of gifts and locally made items for sale. Includes two art galleries, a pottery, jewellery and tarot card reading and associated art.

33 PERRANZABULOE FOLK MUSEUM

ADDRESS/LOCATION
Oddfellows Hall, Ponsmere Rd, Perranporth.

DIRECTIONS
Signed from central Perranporth.

OPENING HOURS
Every day except Saturday during Summer season and Easter Holidays, 11am-1pm and 2pm-5pm.

DISABLED ACCESS
At present approached by staircase.

DETAILS
Exhibition of local history including agriculture, mining etc. as well as St. Pirans Oratory and the natural history of the area.

34 KERNEWEK POTTERY FACTORY SHOP

ADDRESS/LOCATION
Goonhavern, nr.
Perranporth. TR4 9QQ.
(01872) 573505

DIRECTIONS
On A3075, in centre of
Goonhavern.

OPENING HOURS
June to Sep, weekdays,
from 9am.

DISABLED ACCESS
Yes.

DETAILS
Large factory pottery shop. Toilets.

35 HUER'S HUT

ADDRESS/LOCATION
Near Towan Head, Newquay.

DIRECTIONS
Western end of Newquay bay near the Atlantic Hotel.

OPENING HOURS
Any reasonable time.

DISABLED ACCESS
Yes.

DETAILS
A small whitewashed building that was at the heart of an industry now declined. The Huer kept watch for shoals of pilchards and would direct fishermen through the cry of "hevva, hevva" meaning "found".

36 TRENANCE BOATING LAKE

ADDRESS/LOCATION
Boating lake & gardens.

DIRECTIONS
From the Goonhavern-
Newquay road (A3075),
proceed across
roundabout towards
Newquay on Trevemper
Road. The boating lake
is accessed from the
next roundabout.

OPENING HOURS
Daylight hours.

DISABLED ACCESS
Yes.

DETAILS
Large, attractive boating lake (boating charged for) and well kept gardens overlooked by a cafe. The lakeside path is level and suitable for pushchairs and wheelchairs.

IT IS ADVISABLE, ESPECIALLY IN THE SEPTEMBER TO MAY LOW SEASON, TO CONFIRM OPENING ARRANGEMENTS BEFORE MAKING A LONG JOURNEY.

37 NEWQUAY PEARL

ADDRESS/LOCATION
Quintrell Downs, Nr. Newquay. TR8 4LE. (01637) 872991

DIRECTIONS
Situated at the crossroads where the A392 from Newquay meets the A3058 at Quintrell Downs.

OPENING HOURS
March to Jan 3rd, Mon to Sun, 9.30am-5.30pm. Sun, 10.30am-4.30pm

DISABLED ACCESS
All on ground level with toilet facilities.

DETAILS
Thousands of square feet devoted to pearls and pearl jewellery where workshop staff are at hand for designing jewellery to specification. Coffee shop.

38 BEDRUTHAN STEPS

ADDRESS/LOCATION
The Count House, St. Eval, Nr. Newquay. PL27 7UP. (01637) 860563

DIRECTIONS
On the Newquay-Padstow coast road (B3276).

OPENING HOURS
30th March to 31st Oct, daily, 10.30am-6pm.

DISABLED ACCESS
Yes, with help usually on hand.

DETAILS
The newly restored staircase gives access to the justly famous beauty spot of Bedruthan Steps (not N.T.). Views from the Trust's clifftop also available from adjacent to an information centre and shop/tea room housed in the count house of the former Carnewas Iron Mine. Although access to the viewpoint and information centre is free, there is a parking charge for non National Trust members.

39 THE BONSAI NURSERY

ADDRESS/LOCATION
St. Mawgan Village, Nr. Newquay. TR8 4ET. (01637) 860116

DIRECTIONS
A3059 (from St. Columb Major roundabout to Newquay) turn right at signs "Newquay Airport" and "St. Mawgan". Turn right at "St. Mawgan" signpost.

OPENING HOURS
Every day, 10am-6pm.

DISABLED ACCESS
Yes.

DETAILS
Bonsai nursery display and retail area, gardens. Adjacent tea rooms and gift shop.

40 SCREECH OWL SANCTUARY

ADDRESS/LOCATION
Trewin Farm, Indian Queens, TR9 6HP. (01726) 860182

DIRECTIONS
Signed from the A30 nr Indian Queens.

OPENING HOURS
Daily, 10am-5pm.

DISABLED ACCESS
Yes.

DETAILS
Rescue and rehabilitation centre for sick and injured owls. Guided tours by sanctuary staff as well as a gift shop and refreshments. The sanctuary is funded solely by donations from the public and proceeds from the gift shop.

41 CASTLE-AN-DINAS

ADDRESS/LOCATION
Near St. Columb.

DIRECTIONS
From the A39/A3059 roundabout south of St. Columb, follow signs for Castle-an-Dinas. After 2.25 miles, turn left at sign and park at the top of the track.

OPENING HOURS
Any reasonable time.

DISABLED ACCESS
No.

DETAILS
Iron Age fort location comprising three concentric rings, hedges and ditches atop a 700 foot hill. The fort occupied a strategic position overlooking key trade routes; its defensive capability was enhanced by just one entrance into the site. Occupied around 2,000 years ago.

42 ROCHE ROCK

ADDRESS/LOCATION
Near Roche.

DIRECTIONS
Turn off A30 at Victoria for Roche (B3274 for St. Austell). Use a small car park next to the Rock Inn pub. Walk down the lane towards the rock, access the site via a small gate.

OPENING HOURS
Any reasonable time.

DISABLED ACCESS
No.

DETAILS
The granite outcrop is only a short walk from the main road and rises to a height of approx. 60'. Built into the rock, and seeming to 'grow' from it, are the remains of a 14th century chapel.

43 MID CORNWALL GALLERIES

ADDRESS/LOCATION
St Blazey Gate, Par. PL24 2EG. (01726) 812131

DIRECTIONS
On the A390, 3 miles east of St. Austell.

OPENING HOURS
Mon to Sat throughout the year, 10am-5pm.

DISABLED ACCESS
Yes

DETAILS
Crafts council selected art gallery with exhibitions of contemporary fine art and craftwork including paintings, ceramics, jewellery, sculpture, woodwork and leather. 8 or 9 exhibitions are held per year with work from national and South West artists and craftworkers. Small coffee shop.

44 ST CATHERINES CASTLE

ADDRESS/LOCATION

Nr Readymoney Cove, Fowey.

DIRECTIONS

Take the A3082 to Fowey and follow signs to the car park for Readymoney Cove. Proceed down track from the bottom of the car park to the cove. The castle remains overlook the estuary and can be accessed by a short path from the beach.

OPENING HOURS

Any reasonable time.

DISABLED ACCESS

No.

DETAILS

English Heritage remains of one of a series of castles built by Henry VIII to protect the south coast from French invasion.

45 ST ENODOC CHURCH

ADDRESS/LOCATION

Between Trebetherick and Rock on the north coast near Padstow.

DIRECTIONS

From A39 Wadebridge-Camelford road, take B3314 (signed St. Minver). Follow signs for Trebetherick and park overlooking Daymer Bay beach. It is only a short walk to the church, signed from the approach lane to the car park.

John Betjeman's grave. Cornwall Tourist Board.

OPENING HOURS

Daylight hours.

DISABLED ACCESS

Access involves using an unmade lane and a slight incline across a golf course (permitted path).

DETAILS

The tiny thirteenth century church of St. Enodoc occupies a picturesque location overlooking the Camel Estuary and is now famed as the final resting place of the former poet laureate, Sir John Betjeman, who lived for a time in nearby Trebetherick. His grave is on the right hand side as you enter the graveyard.

46 ST BREOCK GALLERY

ADDRESS/LOCATION

St. Breock, Nr. Wadebridge. PL27 7JS. (01208) 812543

DIRECTIONS

Take turning off A39 (Wadebridge bypass) to St. Breock, 1/2 mile south of Royal Cornwall showground.

OPENING HOURS

Mon to Sat, 10am-5pm.

DISABLED ACCESS

No.

DETAILS

Art and craft centre with 19th and 20th century watercolours, antique and reproduction furniture as well as local crafts and objets d'art.

47 JOHN BETJEMAN CENTRE

ADDRESS/LOCATION

Southern Way, Wadebridge. PL27 6AF. (01208) 812392

DIRECTIONS

Central Wadebridge.

OPENING HOURS

Mon to Fri, 10am-5pm, Sat, 10am-12 noon. Closed bank holidays.

DISABLED ACCESS

Yes.

DETAILS

Memorabilia room to the poet laureate, John Betjeman.

48 BODMIN MUSEUM

ADDRESS/LOCATION

Mount Folly, Bodmin. PL31 2DQ.

DIRECTIONS

Tourist signs, parking in town centre.

OPENING HOURS

April to Sept, Mon to Sat, 10am-4pm. October, Mon to Sat, 11am-3pm. Closed Bank Holiday Mondays.

DISABLED ACCESS

No.

DETAILS

History of Bodmin up until the end of Second World War. Cornish kitchen.

49 THE CANDLE SHOP

ADDRESS/LOCATION

Art Candles, Dunmere Road, Bodmin. PL31 2QN. (01208) 73258

DIRECTIONS

Situated on the A389 Bodmin to Wadebridge road about 800 yards from the three mini roundabouts.

OPENING HOURS

Open all year. Weekdays, 10am-6pm. Easter to September, Sat, 10am-5pm, Sun, 11am-6pm.

DISABLED ACCESS

Yes.

DETAILS

Cornwall's largest selections of candles and holders made on the premises. Some pottery also made on site.

50 ST PETROC'S CHURCH

ADDRESS/LOCATION

Priory Road, Bodmin. (01208) 73867

DIRECTIONS

Located adjacent to the main road on the eastern side of Bodmin.

OPENING HOURS

2-3 days per week in summer. Usually Mondays, Wednesdays and Fridays.

DISABLED ACCESS

Via side access, ramps required - ring prior to arrange.

DETAILS

Cornwall's largest parish church dating from 1470 and located on the site of previous Celtic and Norman places of worship. Contains the impressive casket, placed here in 1956, that once contained the bones of Saint Petroc.

51 ST NEOT POTTERY

ADDRESS/LOCATION
The Old Chapel, St. Neot, Nr. Liskeard. PL14 6NL. (01579) 320216

DIRECTIONS
From A30 at Jamaica Inn to St. Neot. From A38 at Halfway House or at Twowatersfoot signed to St. Neot.

OPENING HOURS
Mon to Sat, 10am-5pm (sometimes later in summer). Restricted opening in winter.

DISABLED ACCESS
Some steps but wheelchair access possible.

DETAILS
Studio pottery and sales showroom of pottery made on the premises in converted chapel in the heart of St. Neot Village. French spoken.

52 DULOE STONE CIRCLE

ADDRESS/LOCATION
Duloe village, north of Looe.

DIRECTIONS
On the B3254, north of Looe, in the village of Duloe just north of the church. As there is no designated parking area, park where possible and follow the signed track to the circle.

OPENING HOURS
Any reasonable time.

DISABLED ACCESS
No.

DETAILS
8 stones constructed, unusually, from quartz.

53 SOUTH EAST CORNWALL DISCOVERY CENTRE

ADDRESS/LOCATION
Millpool, Looe. PL13 2AF. (01503) 262777

DIRECTIONS
In Looe's main car park.

OPENING HOURS
Closed Jan/Feb. Mar to May and Oct to Dec, Mon to Fri, 10am-4pm. Closed Sat, Sun 11am-3pm. June to Sept, Mon to Fri, 10am-6pm. Sat, 1pm-5pm, Sun 10am-5pm.

DISABLED ACCESS
Full access with lift and toilets.

DETAILS
Visitor centre promoting green tourism in South East Cornwall. Photographic exhibition, video presentation as well as modern information centre. Well stocked shop and year round mail order service. Bookings and information for Project Explore events. Centre staffed by volunteers.

54 KING DONIERT'S STONES

ADDRESS/LOCATION
Near Dobwalls.

DIRECTIONS
From the A38 in the centre of Dobwalls, turn north signed Siblyback Water and Dobwalls Adventure Park. Proceed past the latter and follow signs towards St. Cleer from where a small parking area on the right hand side will be found adjacent to the stones.

OPENING HOURS
Any reasonable time.

DISABLED ACCESS
No.

DETAILS
Inscribed with words that translate into 'Doniert ordered this cross for the good of his soul', these stones commerate a ninth century king believed to have drowned in the River Fowey.

55 ST CLEER WELL

ADDRESS/LOCATION
St Cleer, north of Liskeard.

DIRECTIONS
Signed within St Cleer on the southern edge of Bodmin Moor.

OPENING HOURS
Any reasonable time.

DISABLED ACCESS
Yes.

DETAILS
Beautiful fifteenth century building, the waters contained within were used to help cure insanity.

56 TRETHEVY QUOIT

ADDRESS/LOCATION
Near St. Cleer

DIRECTIONS
Signed from the village of Tremar adjacent to St. Cleer, south of Bodmin Moor.

OPENING HOURS
Any reasonable time.

DISABLED ACCESS
No.

DETAILS
Largely dating from the Bronze Age, the exact reason for these circles is very much disputed, though most theories involve at least some belief in them being used as a place of worship. Probably built before 2000 B.C., Trethevy Quoit is a well preserved example, a feature unusual in east Cornwall.

57 THE CHEESEWRING

ADDRESS/LOCATION

Bodmin Moor.

DIRECTIONS

From a small parking area on the east side of the village of Minions, follow a track through the Hurlers stone circles. The Cheesewring is situated on the edge of the granite quarry, reached after a 20 minute walk.

OPENING HOURS

Any reasonable time.

DISABLED ACCESS

No.

DETAILS

Situated on a moorland rich in prehistoric settlement, the quarry produced a fine silver grey granite utilised extensively for buildings in London. The Cheesewring rock formation, found on the quarry edge, has been formed as a result of natural erosion; the larger flattish rocks balancing precariously on top of smaller ones.

58 THE HURLERS

ADDRESS/LOCATION

Bodmin Moor.

DIRECTIONS

Reached after a short walk up an unmade track from the parking area on the outskirts of Minions on Bodmin Moor.

OPENING HOURS

DISABLED ACCESS

DETAILS

Line of 3 stone circles with diameters between 108' to 140' and dating from about 1500 B.C. The associated legend is somewhat similar to that of the Merry Maidens but in this instance, men were turned to stone, for playing the game of Hurling on a Sunday.

Hurlers. Cornwall Tourist Board.

59 MINIONS HERITAGE CENTRE

ADDRESS/LOCATION

Minions.

DIRECTIONS

Near village of Minions on Bodmin Moor.

OPENING HOURS

Daily, 10am-dusk.

DISABLED ACCESS

No.

DETAILS

Excellent and well researched exhibition detailing the mining industry and local history of Bodmin Moor and the area around Minions. Uniquely located in a restored engine house.

60 KERNOW MILL

ADDRESS/LOCATION

Trerulefoot, Saltash. PL12 5BL. (01752) 851898

DIRECTIONS

From Plymouth over Tamar Bridge on the A38 to Trerulefoot roundabout. From Torpoint, take A387. From Liskeard, A38.

OPENING HOURS

Retail: Mon-Sat, 10am-6pm, Sundays 11am-5pm. **Coffee Shop:** Mon to Sat, 9.30am-5.30am, Sundays 11am-4.30pm.

DISABLED ACCESS

3 access doors. Wheelchair on site.

DETAILS

Cornish craft workshops and quality woollen knitwear and country/outdoor clothing. Cornish gifts and food section, working waterwheel and coffee shop.

61 BOSCASTLE VISITORS CENTRE

ADDRESS/LOCATION

Cobweb car park, Boscastle, PL35 0HE. (01840) 250010

DIRECTIONS

In the centre of Boscastle.

OPENING HOURS

Daily. Summer 10am-5pm, Winter 11am-3pm.

DISABLED ACCESS

Yes.

DETAILS

Informative visitors centre detailing the geography, history and geology of the north Cornwall coast. Audio visual display, children's activity area, aerial views of the coast and retail area. Information on walking and weather also.

62 THE OLD FORGE

ADDRESS/LOCATION

Boscastle Harbour, Boscastle. PL35 0HD. (01840) 250353

DIRECTIONS

Situated in harbour area of Boscastle.

OPENING HOURS

30th March to 31st October, 10.30am-6pm.

J Hicks/National Trust.

DISABLED ACCESS

Limited access due to small size of shop and two steps.

DETAILS

Information centre and shop housed in National Trust owned blacksmith's forge. Fine walks on nearby National Trust owned cliffs surrounding Boscastle Harbour.

63 ST JULIOT'S CHURCH

ADDRESS/LOCATION Near Boscastle, north Cornwall.

DIRECTIONS Signed from the B3263 east of Boscastle (leave A39 near Wainhouse Corner).

OPENING HOURS Daylight hours.

DISABLED ACCESS With help.

DETAILS Medieval church famed for its connection with the writer Thomas Hardy. Originally trained as an architect, Hardy arrived in 1870 to supervise the restoration of the building. Staying at the local rectory, Hardy met and began courting Emma Gifford, the rector's sister-in-law. Their marriage saw him concentrate on his writing; the novel 'A Pair of Blue Eyes' is clearly influenced by the landscape and people of nearby Boscastle.

64 CHURCH OF ST. NONNA

ADDRESS/LOCATION Altarnun, Bodmin Moor.

DIRECTIONS Signed from the A30 at Trewint.

OPENING HOURS Daylight hours.

DISABLED ACCESS Some steps.

DETAILS Cornwall's 'Cathedral of the Moor', a fifteenth century building dedicated to St. Nonna, the mother of St. David, patron saint of Wales. Impressive barrel-roof, carved rood screen and bench ends. Beautiful setting adjacent to a 500 year old granite packhorse bridge.

65 TAMAR GLASS

ADDRESS/LOCATION Unit 2c, North Petherwin Workshops, North Petherwin, Nr. Launceston. PL15 8TE. (01566) 785527

DIRECTIONS 2 miles from Egloskerry off A395, 6 miles north of Launceston off B3254.

OPENING HOURS Easter to end Sept, Mon to Fri, 10am-5pm, (closed 1-2pm). Ring for appointment during winter.

DISABLED ACCESS Yes.

DETAILS Watch glass blowers at work, showroom and gift shop with quality seconds for sale.

66 LAWRENCE HOUSE MUSEUM

ADDRESS/LOCATION 9 Castle St., Launceston. (01566) 773277

DIRECTIONS From A30, approach town centre. Turn right oppposite castle to multi storey car park. Walk through castle grounds, museum is in Castle St.

OPENING HOURS April to Sept, weekdays, 10.30am-4.30pm. Oct 1st to mid Oct, 11am-2pm.

DISABLED ACCESS No.

DETAILS Museum of local history in 10 rooms of a Georgian Town House built in 1753 and now leased from the National Trust. Winner of Gulbenkian National Award 1993. Sales area.

67 LAKESIDE GALLERY

ADDRESS/LOCATION Lezant, Launceston. (01579) 370760

DIRECTIONS South of Launceston off A388.

OPENING HOURS Daily, 10am-5pm.

DISABLED ACCESS Yes.

DETAILS Specialist gallery dealing in fantasy and symbolist painting. Permanent exhibition of Tolkien illustrations from The Lord of The Rings and The Hobbit. Sales of prints, etchings and paintings.

68 DUPATH HOLY WELL

ADDRESS/LOCATION Near Callington.

DIRECTIONS Follow signs from the A388 near Callington. Park at a farm entrance, taking care to avoid obstructing farm vehicles. 75 yard signed walk.

OPENING HOURS Mid Mar to mid Oct., weekdays 9.30am-1pm, 2pm-6.30pm. Suns 2pm-6.30pm. Mid Oct. to mid Mar, weekdays 9.30am-1pm, 2pm-4pm. Suns 2pm-4pm.

DISABLED ACCESS No.

DETAILS Largest and best preserved building of its kind in Cornwall. Maintained by English Heritage, the early 16th century well's waters were said to cure whooping cough.

69 MOUNT EDGCUMBE COUNTRY PARK

ADDRESS/LOCATION Cremyll, Torpoint. PL10 1DT. (01752) 822236

DIRECTIONS From A374 to B3247 via Millbrook.

OPENING HOURS All year, dawn to dusk.

DISABLED ACCESS Toilets and wheelchairs at Cremyll shop and house. Limited access to some areas.

DETAILS 800 acre landscaped country park, jointly managed by Cornwall County Council and Plymouth City Council. Wild deer herd and five historic and formal gardens. Orangery Restaurant, shop and toilets.

70 HAWKER'S HUT

ADDRESS/LOCATION Vicarage Cliff, near Morwenstow.

DIRECTIONS Morwenstow is signed from the A39 Bude-Bideford road north of Kilkhampton. Park near the church and walk towards the sea before following the coast path left. Hawker's Hut is found on the cliffside after about 5 mins walk.

OPENING HOURS Any reasonable time.

DISABLED ACCESS No.

DETAILS The National Trust's smallest property, Hawker's Hut is nothing more than a small shelter built of driftwood. The reason for its interest is that it was built by Rev. Hawker, a famous Victorian eccentric and previous incumbent of the church. Hawker spent much of his time at the hut smoking opium and composing poems as well as watching for shipwrecks, the victims of which he was keen to provide a Christian burial for.

LITERARY CORNWALL

by Liz Luck

The litany of famous writers who have lived and worked in Cornwall, or whose work has been influenced by the time they spent here, is an extraordinary testimony to the inspirational power of place, and of *this* place in particular, which has long been recognized as being somehow different, a land apart.

The Victorians began the trend, with Alfred Lord Tennyson's *Morte d'Arthur* and later *Idylls of the King* being largely responsible for the transformation of the hamlet of Trevena into the bustling Arthurian mecca of Tintagel that we know today. Thomas Hardy met his first wife, Emma, whilst restoring the church of St Juliot near Boscastle and this part of North Cornwall influenced much of his poetry as well as providing the setting for his novel *A Pair of Blue Eyes*. He wrote of Cornwall that 'the place is pre-eminently ..... the region of dream and mystery'. Further up the coast, at wild Morwenstow near the Devon border, lived the idiosyncratic Parson Hawker. In his driftwood hut on Vicarage Cliff he wrote poetry and smoked pipes of opium; he is best known today for penning what has become Cornwall's anthem, *The Song of the Western Men* ('And shall Trelawny live, or shall Trelawny die?').

In this century it has been Daphne du Maurier, above all others, who has brought a vivid sense of Cornwall to a worldwide audience. Novels such as *Rebecca*, *My Cousin Rachel*, *Jamaica Inn* and *Frenchman's Creek* are strongly influenced by Cornish landscape and history and it is not hard for lovers of her work to seek out the places that inspired her. She lived for most of her adult life at Menabilly, near Fowey, and was

Jamaica Inn. MDN.

fortunate enough in her youth to meet and be helped in her writing by Sir Arthur Quiller-Couch, a towering figure in Cornish life and literature who wrote novels, short stories and poetry and was the first Professor of English Literature at Cambridge. His friend Kenneth Grahame was a frequent visitor to Fowey and the harbour makes an unmistakable appearance in *The Wind in the Willows* as 'the little grey sea town I know so well'.

Another writer who has made Cornwall a familiar place to countless people is Sir John Betjeman, the late Poet Laureate who was a regular visitor to Trebetherick on the Camel estuary throughout his life and whose love for North Cornwall sings out in his poems for all to hear. Look out too for his *Cornwall - A Shell Guide*, published in 1964, which is a pure delight. The intense poetry of Jack Clemo, for much of his life both blind and deaf, was profoundly influenced by the 'scarred and erie landscape' of Clay Country, north of St Austell; Charles Causley still lives and works in Launceston, his birthplace and the inspiration for many of his poems, ballads and children's stories; whilst the wonderful poems and short stories

View from Q's memorial across Fowey estuary. MDN.

of A.L. Rowse, often overlooked in favour of his more celebrated volumes of history, autobiography and literary criticism, are full of the landscape of his childhood near St Austell and his later home on the coast at Trenarren.

Television adaptations of the Poldark novels of Winston Graham and the Wycliffe detective stories of W.J. Burley, both deeply rooted in place, have given Cornwall's coastal and rural landscape a new and more immediate popularity; meanwhile the hugely successful Cornish historical sagas of E.V. Thompson have yet to be screened, but it can only be a matter of time.

PLACES TO VISIT

Those places with an asterisk are covered within the Walking Areas and Viewpoints section.

*MOREWENSTOW: The National Trust preserves Hawker's Hut on the cliffs; his church of St. Morwenna & St. John is just inland; alongside is the vicarage he built

St Juliot's church, Boscastle. MDN.

with its chimneys modelled on his favourite church towers.

*BOSCASTLE: The Valency Valley, the church of St. Juliot and the coastline (Beeny Cliff) all have

strong Hardy connections.

*FOWEY: Ferryside at Bodinnick (can be viewed across the river from Fowey) was Daphne du Maurier's first home in Cornwall; Menabilly can be glimpsed from the coast path as it climbs up to Gribbin Head; Fowey T.I.C. is particularly informative on the du Maurier connections; Quiller-Couch lived at the Haven on the Esplanade and his memorial overlooks the harbour at Penleath Point; Kenneth Grahame was married in the church of St. Fimbarrus.

*FRENCHMAN'S CREEK: On the Helford River, part-owned by National Trust, footpaths from Helford Village.

JAMAICA INN: Old coaching inn at Bolventor on Bodmin Moor. *(See Attractions section).*

TREBETHERICK: Betjeman's grave is in the churchyard of St. Enodoc; he lived at Undertown and, later, Treen in the village; the beach and cliff names nearby will be familiar from his poems. (*A visit to St. Enodoc Church is covered in the It's Free! section).*

SUGGESTED FURTHER READING
Cornwall's Literary Heritage Peter Stanier, Twelveheads Press 1992
Cornwall Literary Trails Cornish Tourist Board 1992
Visitors to Cornwall Ida Procter, Dyllansow Truran 1982

Hawker's Hut, Morwenstow. MDN.

St Enodoc church, final resting place of Sir John Betjeman. MDN.

CORNISH ENGINE HOUSES

by Mark Norton

For the majority of first time visitors to Cornwall, particularly if heading west from Truro, one of the most intriguing and impressive sights in the landscape are the Cornish engine houses. Standing on the horizon like miniature castles, engine houses have become as synonymous with Cornwall as clotted cream and pasties. Their construction dates back to a time when Cornwall was at the heart of the world's tin and copper supplies (some two thirds of total world output was being mined here during the 1850's) and led the world in its mining expertise and technical innovation.

Underground mines had been developed from around the fifteenth century although these were not deep and were often achieved by digging tunnels into exposed cliff faces in order to find the tin or copper bearing lodes. In order to exploit the ore deposits buried deep inland, a way would have to be found to prevent the continuous flooding of the shafts which became a major problem in the county.

Ding Dong Mine, near Madron. MDN.

The answer was steam power. Thomas Newcomen had built the world's first commercial steam engine in 1712, a design made more efficient by the work of James Watt fifty years later. Although these engines were further developed from 1800 onwards, it would take the son of a Cornish miner to make the breakthrough that would allow the Cornish mines to go deeper. The patenting of a high pressure engine by Richard Trevithick (now regarded as a hero in Cornwall - Trevithick Day is celebrated in Camborne each April), ensured that much greater quantities of water could be pumped from the mines and enabled more lodes of ore to be exploited. At its peak in the 1850's, the Cornish mining industry was utilising some 650 Cornish engines to pump water, crush the ore and to lift the ore and miners to the surface. The expertise that developed in Cornwall was exported around the world; the great Cornish foundries such as the Williams' Perran Foundry at Perranarworthal and Harvey's of Hayle were building engines for work in Europe, America and Australia.

However, discovery of massive tin and copper deposits in South America and Asia in the 1870's led to a collapse in the Cornish mining industry. Massive emigration followed and mines closed in large numbers. At the end of their working lives, most engines were dismantled for scrap and the engine houses that protected them left to the elements or dismantled for building material. Fortunately, some enlightened individuals saw that an important part of Cornwall's, indeed Britain's heritage was gradually being lost. As a result, the Cornish Engines Preservation Society was set up in 1935 to try and protect those structures remaining. The society, renamed the Trevithick Society after the great man himself, was for example, instrumental with the National Trust in the preservation of the engine at the world famous Levant Mine near St. Just-in-Penwith.

Wheal Coates, near Chapel Porth. MDN.

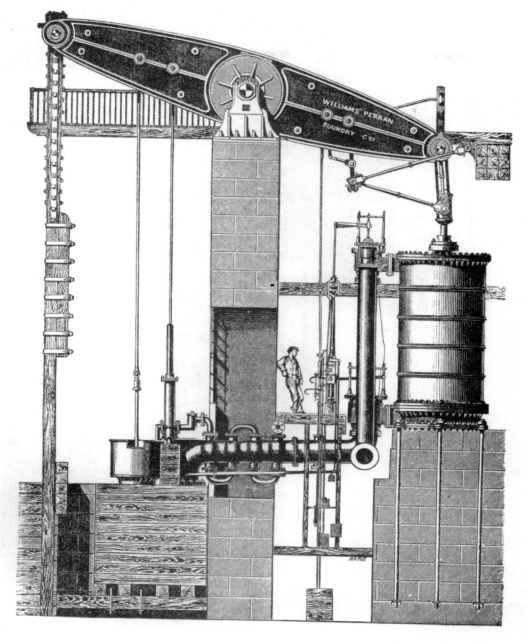

Elevation of Taylor's Pumping Engine. Reproduced from the Williams' Perran Foundry Co. Illustrated Catalogue 1870 courtesy of the Trevithick Society.

The famous Taylor's Engine was manufactured in 1840 and was able to raise 95,750,000 lbs of water 1 foot high by the combustion of one bushel of coal.

Details of how to get to the following engine houses are detailed below.

WHEAL PROSPER, Rinsey
(Walking Areas & Viewpoints)

LEVANT, St. Just-in-Penwith
(Attractions)

WHEAL COATES, St. Agnes
(Walking Areas & Viewpoints)

EAST POOL WHIM, Redruth
(Attractions)

CROWNS, Botallack
(It's free!)

Today, as a result of the Trevithick Society and National Trust's efforts, nearly 200 engine houses survive in Cornwall in some recognisable form (though only one mine, South Crofty at Camborne - the last working tin mine in Europe, continues the proud tradition of Cornish mining).

The following engine houses are good examples and available for close inspection.

WHEAL PROSPER, Rinsey. Copper mine engine house, closed in 1865. Restored by the National Trust in 1971 who were so concerned to ensure it was retained in its original form that an old local quarry was reopened to provide the correct stonework.

LEVANT, St. Just-in-Penwith. One of the great names of Cornish mining and a working mine for over a century before its closure in 1930. The building was restored by the National Trust; a team of volunteers from the Trevithick Society - 'the Greasy Gang' - responsible for bringing the engine back to working order.

Richard Trevithick
(b.1771 - d.1833)

WHEAL COATES, St. Agnes. The Towanroath Engine House of the Wheal Coates Mine dates from the early 1870's. Sited on a 200 foot cliff (the shaft in front of the engine house is over 600 feet deep!), the tin mine was not particularly successful in Cornish terms and closed only 20 years after opening.

EAST POOL WHIM, Redruth. The restored whim (winding) engine was set in motion again by the National Trust in 1975, having been idle for over 50 years. It was designed for lifting men and ore from a depth of 1,500 feet and was originally built in 1887 at the nearby Camborne foundry.

CROWNS, Botallack. Two engine houses, dramatically situated on a rocky ledge above the sea, bear testament to the daring bravery of generations of Cornishmen who were involved in the battle for tin.

A DIRECTOR'S PARADISE

by Sue Craig

Cornwall, with its stunning and diverse landscape, has provided a wealth of film locations for over 50 years. The spectacular coastline, picturesque fishing villages, bleak moorland and mining heritage offer a natural beauty which cannot be recreated in the studio. With a total of 29 episodes, the acclaimed BBC drama series 'Poldark' used this scenery to dramatic effect. In 1996, HTV brought the Poldark dynasty to life once more with 'Poldark - Stranger From the Sea'; again location filming took place throughout Cornwall. Foreign producers also find the area irresistible. The German company, Frankfurter Filmproduktion, for example, shot four Rosamund Pilcher stories entirely in Cornwall, including locations in St Ives, Mousehole and Penzance.

Stately homes, many belonging to the National Trust, are frequently used by film makers looking for an

Wycliffe. Courtesy of Mike Alsford/HTV/SWFC.

authentic period set and Cornwall with its historic houses has played host to several major productions in the 1990s. Locations for 'The Three Musketeers', Walt Disney's £13m feature starring Charlie Sheen and Keifer Sutherland, included the Boconnoc Estate and Lanhydrock both near Bodmin. Trevor Nunn's sumptuous version of 'Twelfth Night', with Helena Bonham-Carter, Ben Kingsley, Mel Smith and Nigel Hawthorne also filmed at Lanhydrock, plus Cotehele and the Elizabethan mansion Prideaux Place.

North Cornwall hosted two major feature films in 1996. 'Oscar and Lucinda', an Australian production starring Ralph Fiennes which filmed at Boscastle, Prideaux Place, Trebarwith, Morwenstow and Crackington Haven. And, Phoenix Pictures $15m 'Amy Foster', based on a story by James Conrad, starring Sir Ian McKellen, Kathy Bates, Vincent Perez and Rachel

Blue Juice. Courtesy of Liam Longman/Skreba-Creon Films/SWFC.

Three Musketeers. Courtesy of Walt Disney/SWFC.

version of 'Moll Flanders' shot at Turnaware Bar on the River Fal and the BBC's 'The Lord of Misrule' used Fowey as a principle location. Visitors to the historic Georgian harbour at Charlestown may also have seen the quayside 'dressed' by the Moll Flanders crew to become a bustling period set enhanced by the magnificent tall ships moored alongside. Charlestown is a particularly versatile location - in the 1976 blockbuster 'The Eagle Has Landed' it was successfully transformed to represent German-occupied Alderney.

Cornwall's unique castles have added intrigue to many dramas. The Gothic elegance of the 19th Century Caerhayes, nestling amongst the woodland on the coast near Veryan, represented Manderley in the BBC 1970's version of Daphne du Maurier's Rebecca and can be seen once more in the new Poldark. St Michael's Mount added spine-tingling authenticity to Dracula, and Tintagel, with its mythical grandeur, provided a realistic backdrop for MGM when they filmed 'Knights of the Round Table' nearly 50 years ago. More recently this location, spiced with mystery and legend, was woven into the script of an American film, 'Guinevere's Gift', shot in 1997.

Twelfth Night courtesy of Alex Bailey/Fine Line Pictures/SWFC.

Weisz. The Amy Foster crew transformed Portquin, a tiny harbour near Port Isaac, into a small hamlet by constructing a church and additional cottages. During the summer months, walkers on nearby Pentire Point, owned by the National Trust, may have been surprised to find an isolated cottage perched on the cliffs - another set built for Amy Foster. It is not marked on any maps and has now, of course, been removed.

Surfers have been challenging the waves on Cornwall's north coast for many years. In 1994, the young surfing community which had evolved around St Ives inspired film-makers Carl Prechezer and Peter Salmi to produce the feature film 'Blue Juice'. Surfing scenes in this movie were supplemented by a one-week shoot in Lanzarote and the entire cast, including stars Sean Pertwee, Catherine Zeta Jones and Ewan McGregor spent a week taking surfing lessons prior to filming!

The gentle sloping, wooded estuaries along the south coast have welcomed several film production units. The popular HTV drama series 'Wycliffe' filmed in and around Truro, the Granada TV

Lanyon Quoit. W Hocking/National Trust.

Porthcurno. Tim Guthrie.

CYCLING

CAMEL TRAIL

Location Between Padstow and Bodmin via Wadebridge. Bridge Bike Hire at Wadebridge (01208) 813050

Directions Signed in Padstow, Wadebridge and Bodmin.

Opening Hours Trail any reasonable time. Bridge Bike Hire 363 days a year, 9am-5pm in the season (please phone for Winter hours).

Details Cornwall's premier cycling route, based on the old Padstow to Bodmin railway line, its conversion from track bed to recreational route undertaken by Cornwall County Council in 1980. The total length of the trail is 17 miles with perhaps the most popular section being the five miles between Padstow and Wadebridge (lovely views over Camel Estuary). Bridge Bike Hire at Wadebridge is the trail's biggest bike depot with over 250 bikes including mountain bikes, tourers, tandems, trikes and child trailers (it is often advisable to book in advance to ensure availability).

CARDINHAM WOODS

Location Near Bodmin. Glynn Valley Cycle Hire (01208) 74244

Directions Take A38 (signed Liskeard) from A30 at Bodmin. 400 yards beyond roundabout, turn left and follow signs to Cardinham.

Opening Hours Cycle hire is open Easter, Bank Holidays, Cornish school holidays and all Sundays. June to September, every day. 10am to 5pm.

Details Set in the Forestry Commission owned Cardinham Woods, the 4.5 mile cycle trail is designed for family groups and is on mostly gentle gradients. The trail winds its way along a valley bottom through scenic woodland with picnic tables available along the waymarked route. Refreshment facilities June to September.

HALLAGENNA FARM CYCLE HIRE

Location St Breward on Bodmin Moor (01208) 850439

Directions St Breward is signed from the A30 near Bodmin.

Opening Hours Throughout the year. In season 8am-8pm. In Winter best to phone and confirm opening arrangements.

Details Located at historic Hallagenna Farm on Bodmin Moor with choice of individual cycle hire and devise your own route, or, as part of a four hour cycle ride with a guide to show you the historical sights of the moor as well as sites of special scientific interest and picturesque views. These guided tours need to be booked in advance. Foreign visitors and all ages catered for.

KILMINORTH WOODS

Location West Looe.

Directions Proceed to West Looe main car park. Trail starts at far western end of car park.

Opening hours Any reasonable time.

Details Bridlepath through Kilminorth Woods at West Looe. Signed to Watergate (1.3 miles). Further information from the South East Cornwall Discovery Centre overlooking the car park (01503) 262777 - see Attractions section for details of opening hours.

PENTEWAN VALLEY TRAIL

Location The Pentewan Valley Trail is situated just to the north of Mevagissey, starting at the village of Pentewan. Cycle hire (01726) 844242.

Directions From the B3273 St Austell-Mevagissey road, turn off for Pentewan. The start of the trail is on the left hand side immediately after a narrow bridge. There is a car park in Pentewan village, in Summer use a larger car park opposite the entrance to Pentewan Sands Caravan Park.

Opening Hours Trail open any reasonable time. Cycle hire April to Sept, 9.30am-dusk.

Details One of Cornwall's newest cycle trails, offering a 2.3 mile course through wetland and woodland alongside the White River. Traffic free cycling, ideal for the whole family. A leaflet from the cycle hire depot at the start of the trail, details a quiet country lane extension of about a mile to reach the Polgooth Inn.

Pentewan Valley Trail.

Camel Trail.

Attractions

Cornwall has a wide variety of quality attractions, from historic houses to wildlife parks, steam railways to flying lessons. These are of a very high standard and offer an exciting day out for all the family.

For ease of reference, each attraction has been put into one of four colour coded groups.

The attractions are organised broadly west to east from Land's End to the Tamar River. This allows you to locate attractions concentrated together in particular parts of the county. Alternatively, the attraction numbers can be found on the map below, allowing a straight forward indication of its location. If one particular attraction is required, use the index.
Golf courses, horse riding, cinemas, leisure centres and fishing are detailed seperately.

A SHORT NOTE ON THE ENTRY DETAILS:

DIRECTIONS In most cases, the directions are detailed from the nearest 'A' class road.

OPENING HOURS Though all opening hours have been verified with the attractions concerned, in the low season (Sept-May) it will often be worthwhile to ring before making a long journey.

DISABLED ACCESS If in doubt, ring prior.

ACTIVITIES/FACILITIES As well as the primary activities at the attraction, the details include ancillary facilities such as coffee shops etc.

🐕 Dog access OK   🐕 Dog access prohibited

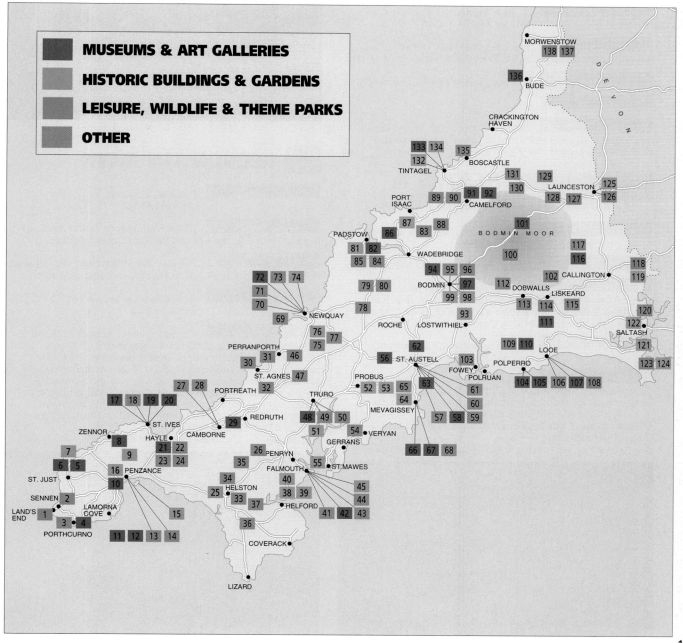

MUSEUMS & ART GALLERIES

HISTORIC BUILDINGS & GARDENS

LEISURE, WILDLIFE & THEME PARKS

OTHER

1 LAND'S END

ADDRESS & TELEPHONE
Sennen. TR19 7AA.
(01736) 871501

DIRECTIONS
End of A30, 11 miles
from Penzance.

OPENING HOURS
Daily except Christmas,
10am-dusk.

DISABLED ACCESS Yes

ACTIVITIES/FACILITIES One of Cornwall's most famous landmarks set in an unrivalled position on the far West clifftops. Last Labyrinth multi sensory theatre, clifftop walks, R.S.P.B. bird watching facilities, animal farm, working craftsmen, art gallery, indoor and outdoor entertainment, childrens adventure play area, miniature village, bees observation hive, restaurant and cafeteria, horse drawn transport and souvenir shops. Man against the Sea exhibition, smellorium and lifeboat experience. Visitors can stay at the Land's End Hotel (England's First and Last).

2 LAND'S END AERODROME

ADDRESS & TELEPHONE St. Just, Penzance. TR19 7RL.
(01736) 788771

DIRECTIONS From the A30 Penzance-Land's End road, turn right at Crows-an-Wra. The airfield lies one mile beyond.

OPENING HOURS It is advisable to ring for availability.

DISABLED ACCESS Yes.

ACTIVITIES/FACILITIES Scenic pleasure flights around Land's End and other sights of West Penwith. Trial flying lessons also available. Cafe, bar and viewing terrace.

3 MINACK THEATRE & EXHIBITION CENTRE

ADDRESS & TELEPHONE Porthcurno, Nr. Penzance. TR19 6JU.
(01736) 810694

DIRECTIONS A30 to Penzance, B3283 to Porthcurno.

OPENING HOURS **Theatre:** Performances Mon to Fri at 8pm, matinees Wed, Fri at 2pm (01736) 810181 for info. line. **Exhibition:** Easter to Sept, 9.30am-5.30pm. Oct, 10am-4.30pm. On matinee days the exhibition may close from noon-2.15pm.

DISABLED ACCESS Access to exhibition and viewing balcony for performances.

ACTIVITIES/FACILITIES Cliff top open air theatre overlooking the sea with 17 week season of plays and musicals by top British amateur companies. Exhibition centre containing photographs, models and audio visual displays telling the history of the Minack's founder, Rowena Cade, and the theatre she built. Gift shop and refreshments.
Dog Access: On leads during the day but not at performances.

Murray King/Minack Theatre.

4 PORTHCURNO MUSEUM

ADDRESS & TELEPHONE Porthcurno. (01209) 612142

DIRECTIONS Take A30 from Penzance towards Land's End. Turn off for St. Buryan and follow signs to Porthcurno. Park at Cove.

OPENING HOURS Fridays April to October, Wednesdays and Fridays July to Sept. Tours begin every hour, on the hour from Cable Hut at the top of Porthcurno beach, or entrance to public car park if raining. First tour at 11am, last tour 3pm.

DISABLED ACCESS Complete access apart from the toilet.

ACTIVITIES/FACILITIES The submarine cable that landed on Porthcurno beach in 1870 was the start of a world spanning telegraph system that led to Porthcurno becoming the largest cable station in the world. In World War II, tunnels were blasted out of the granite hillside and the station moved underground before its eventual closure in 1970. Guided tours (see opening hours) last 75 minutes. Guided tours at other times by appointment only (ring for details). **Dogs:** Guide dogs only please.

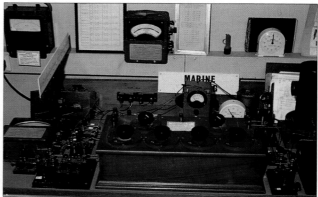

5 GEEVOR TIN MINE

ADDRESS & TELEPHONE Pendeen, Penzance. TR19 7EW.
(01736) 788662

DIRECTIONS B3306 road from St. Just to Zennor, at Pendeen, or follow the signs on the A3071 from Penzance.

OPENING HOURS Full site, Mar to Oct, Sun to Fri, 10.30am to 5pm (last tour at 4pm). Nov to Feb., museum and shop only.

DISABLED ACCESS Access to museum, please ring for further details.

ACTIVITIES/FACILITIES The last tin mine to work in Penwith, bringing to an end a tradition in the area of over 2000 years. Now administered by the Trevithick Trust, Geevor has an excellent museum with a 3 dimensional model of the underground workings. Regular tours by expert guides are given around the surface plant as well as an underground exploration of an adit mine. Craft and book shop as well as the 'Count House Cafe'. Please ring for further information, booked parties, educational visits and out of season tours.
Dog Access: Yes if on a lead except for the cafe.

6 LEVANT BEAM ENGINE

ADDRESS & TELEPHONE
Trewellard, Pendeen, Nr. St. Just. (01736) 786156

DIRECTIONS
1 mile west of Pendeen, on B3306 St. Just-Zennor road.

OPENING HOURS
Easter, May and Spring Bank Hols, Sun and Mon; June, Wed, Thurs, Fri and Sun; July to end of Sept, Sun to Fri, 11am-5pm.

DISABLED ACCESS
No.

ACTIVITIES/FACILITIES
Situated on a cliff edge, 5 miles from Lands End, the oldest beam engine in Cornwall is being driven once more by steam, thanks to an extensive programme of restoration and rebuilding by the National Trust and members of the Trevithick Society. Built in 1840, the 27" whim engine hoisted ore from the famous Levant Mine, one of the great names in Cornish history.
Dog Access: Guide dogs only.

Andrew Besley/National Trust

7 PENDEEN LIGHTHOUSE

ADDRESS & TELEPHONE
Pendeen. Telephone enquiries to Geevor Tin Mine (01736) 788662

DIRECTIONS
Signed from the B3306 St. Just-St. Ives road in the village of Pendeen.

OPENING HOURS
Opening Hours: April to October, Mon-Sat, 11am-5pm.

DISABLED ACCESS
To the engine room only.

ACTIVITIES/FACILITIES
Now administered by the Trevithick Trust, Pendeen Watch Lighthouse is open to the public for tours of the light as well as the engine room that provides power for the largest surviving fog signal in Britain.

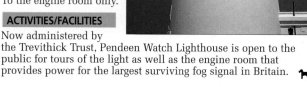

- **MUSEUMS & ART GALLERIES**
- **HISTORIC BUILDINGS & GARDENS**
- **LEISURE, WILDLIFE & THEME PARKS**
- **OTHER**

8 WAYSIDE FOLK MUSEUM

ADDRESS & TELEPHONE
Zennor, Near St. Ives. TR26 3DA. (01736) 796945

DIRECTIONS
West of St. Ives on the B3306 coastal road to St. Just and Lands End.

OPENING HOURS
April to Sept, daily, 10am-6pm plus evenings in high season. October, Sun to Fri, 11am-5pm.

DISABLED ACCESS
Limited access for disabled.

ACTIVITIES/FACILITIES
The oldest private museum in Cornwall covering every aspect of life in Zennor and district from 3000B.C. through to the 1930's. Miller's Cottage (kitchen and parlour), Mill house, Wheelwrights and Blacksmiths plus exhibits on farming, fishing, mining, and domestic life. 3 working waterwheels. Cornish crafts and bookshop with riverside tea garden and children's museum quiz trail.

9 CHYSAUSTER ANCIENT VILLAGE

ADDRESS & TELEPHONE
Nr. Gulval, Penzance. (0831) 757934 - (Summer only).

DIRECTIONS
From Penzance, 2.5 miles north west of Gulval off B3311.

OPENING HOURS
April to Sept, 10.00am-6.00pm. Oct, 10am-4pm.

DISABLED ACCESS
No.

Cornwall Tourist Board

ACTIVITIES/FACILITIES
Iron Age village of 8 oval 'houses' grouped around a central courtyard. Fougou (underground passage) also. Shop, picnic area and toilets. (Shop open Summer only). Steep approach track with high steps. English Heritage maintained.
Dog Access: On leads.

10 THE PILCHARD WORKS

ADDRESS & TELEPHONE
Newlyn, Penzance. (01736) 332112

DIRECTIONS
2 miles west of Penzance on the A30, turn left to Newlyn.

OPENING HOURS
Easter to November, Mon. to Sat., from 10am

DISABLED ACCESS
No due to flights of steps within the museum.

ACTIVITIES/FACILITIES
The last working salt pilchard factory in the country, combining the fascinating social, industrial and artistic heritage of the fishing industry within a working factory that appeals to all age groups. National award for 'outstanding presentation of Britain's heritage'.
Dogs: No but dogs can be secured at the front of the museum.

11 TRINITY HOUSE NATIONAL LIGHTHOUSE CENTRE

ADDRESS & TELEPHONE
The Old Buoy Store, Wharf Road, Penzance. TR18 4BN. (01736) 360077

DIRECTIONS
Into Penzance on A30, take seafront road in town with museum situated on right, opposite docks.

OPENING HOURS
Opening Hours: Every day from April to Oct, 11am-5.00pm (last tour 4.30pm).

DISABLED ACCESS 75% of exhibits (including video room and lighthouse quarters) accessible by wheelchair.

ACTIVITIES/FACILITIES Museum detailing the story of the men and equipment dedicated to maritime safety. Includes reconstructed lighthouse room as well as audio visual history of Eddystone Rock Tower. Souvenir shop.
Dog Access: Yes if well behaved and on a lead.

12 PENLEE HOUSE ART GALLERY AND MUSEUM

ADDRESS & TELEPHONE Morrab Road, Penzance. TR18 4HE. (01736) 363625

DIRECTIONS Park in one of the central car parks and proceed on foot, the museum is set back in a park in Morrab Road.

OPENING HOURS Mon to Fri, 10.30am - 4.30pm. Sat, 10.30am-12.30pm.

DISABLED ACCESS Full disabled access from July 1997.

ACTIVITIES/FACILITIES The museum has been established in its present location since 1949, having originally been established in the town since 1839. Following a major restoration programme which saw the gallery reopen in July 1997, displays detail the area's nature, archaeology and history and include a number of refurbished galleries using the latest computer technology. The Art Gallery houses the largest collection in west Cornwall including work by the famous Newlyn School of Artists. Gift/book shop and coffee shop. **Dog Access:** Guide dogs only.

13 BRITISH INTERNATIONAL

ADDRESS & TELEPHONE Penzance. TR18 3AP. (01736) 363871

DIRECTIONS The heliport is situated 1 mile east of Penzance, alongside the main A30.

OPENING HOURS Flights are operated daily, except Sunday, throughout the year.

DISABLED ACCESS Contact heliport for details.

ACTIVITIES/FACILITIES Scheduled helicopter operator with flights from Penzance heliport to St. Marys and Tresco on the Isles of Scilly. Local pleasure flights operated during the summer.
Dog Access: Contact heliport for details.

Tim Guthrie

14 ISLES OF SCILLY STEAMSHIP CO. LTD.

ADDRESS & TELEPHONE Quay St., Penzance. TR18 4BD. (01736) 362009

DIRECTIONS A30 to Penzance, then to Lighthouse Pier.

OPENING HOURS **High season:** 8am-9pm, **Low season:** 8am-5pm.

DISABLED ACCESS Best to prebook in high season to ensure.

ACTIVITIES/FACILITIES Day trips to Isles of Scilly aboard Scillonian III. Bar, buffet shop and exhibition on Island life. **Dog Access:** Yes on a lead.

Mike Newman/Isles of Scilly Steamship Co

15 ST. MICHAEL'S MOUNT

ADDRESS & TELEPHONE Marazion, Penzance. TR17 0EF. (01736) 710507. (01736) 710265 (tide/ferry info.).

DIRECTIONS Half a mile south of A394 at Marazion with access on foot over causeway at low tide. During summer months by ferry at high tide (return tickets should not be taken).

OPENING HOURS April-October, Mon-Fri, (shop and restaurant open daily), 10.30am-5.30pm. Last admission 4.45pm. November-end March: during the winter it is essential to telephone one or other of the numbers given above before setting out, in order to ascertain the opening arrangements for that day.

DISABLED ACCESS No.

ACTIVITIES/FACILITIES Granite island topped by embattled 14th century castle, home of the St. Aubyn family for over 300 years. Sub tropical vegetation on Mount's slopes. Harbourside community was originally an ancient trading place for tin and other Cornish goods but features today as shops and restaurants.

Andrew Besley/National Trust

16 TRENGWAINTON

ADDRESS & TELEPHONE

Penzance. TR20 8RZ. (01736) 363021

DIRECTIONS

2 miles north west of Penzance, half a mile west of Heamoor on the Penzance-Morvah road (B3312). Half a mile off St. Just road (A3071).

OPENING HOURS

March to October Wed, Thurs, Fri, Sat and Bank Holiday Mons, 10.30am-5.30pm. Closes at 5pm in March and October.

Andrew Besley/National Trust

DISABLED ACCESS

Wheelchair access and availability.

ACTIVITIES/FACILITIES

The garden of mainland Britain perhaps most favoured for the cultivation of exotic shrubs and trees. The most tender flourish in the mild maritime climate and are further protected by a unique complex of five walled gardens. A most beautiful place throughout the year, and a plantsman's delight. The house is not open. **Dog Access:** Guide dogs only.

17 ST. IVES MUSEUM

ADDRESS & TELEPHONE

Wheal Dream, St. Ives. (01736) 796005

DIRECTIONS

Museum is adjacent to harbour.

OPENING HOURS

Mid May-Oct, Mon. to Fri, 10am-5pm, Sat., 10am-4.30pm, Sun,2pm-4.30pm.

DISABLED ACCESS

First floor access via back door allows 75% of museum to be seen.

ACTIVITIES/FACILITIES

St. Ives Museum exhibits include art, militaria, Victorian dress, mining, fishing, mercantile marine and Hain Steamship Co. with models. Large selection of early photography as well as exhibits on G.W.R. Railway, R.N.L.I., geology and the police/fire brigades. Use St. Ives main car parks.

18 ST IVES AQUASPORTS

ADDRESS & TELEPHONE

The New Lifeboat Slip, The Wharf, St. Ives. (01736) 793001/798934. Mobile (0836) 765090

DIRECTIONS

Take A30 to St. Ives.

OPENING HOURS

9am till dusk, daily

DISABLED ACCESS

No.

ACTIVITIES/FACILITIES

Self drive motor boats (half hourly and hourly-carry up to 5 persons), jet ski hire (including wetsuit and lifejacket), parascending, powerboat trips and banana boat rides.

19 TATE GALLERY

ADDRESS & TELEPHONE

Porthmeor Beach, St. Ives. TR26 1TG. (01736) 796226

DIRECTIONS

From A30, signed to St. Ives.

OPENING HOURS

April 1st to Sept. 30th, Mon to Sat, 11am-7pm, Sun & Bank hols, 11am-5pm. Oct. 1st to Mar. 31st, Tue to Sun, 11.00am-5pm. Closed Mons & Christmas.

DISABLED ACCESS

Yes.

ACTIVITIES/FACILITIES

Owned by Cornwall County Council, Tate Gallery St. Ives occupies a spectacular site overlooking Porthmeor Beach. A four storey building, the Tate provides 5 gallery spaces in which to display distinct groups of work. There is also an education room, parent and baby room, bookshop and restaurant/cafe.

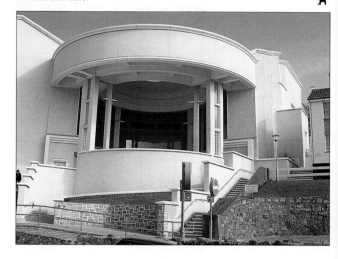

20 BARBARA HEPWORTH MUSEUM

ADDRESS & TELEPHONE

Barnoon Hill, St. Ives. TR26 1TG. (01736) 796226

DIRECTIONS

From A30 roundabout, signed to St. Ives.

OPENING HOURS

April 1st to Sept. 30th, Mon to Sat, 11am-7pm, Sun & Bank holidays, 11am-5pm. Oct. 1st to March 31st, Tue to Sun 11am-5pm (closed Mon). The garden closes at 5pm or at dusk, whichever is earlier.

DISABLED ACCESS

Limited access.

ACTIVITIES/FACILITIES

Under the auspices of The Tate Gallery, this small museum celebrates the work of Dame Barbara Hepworth through a gallery, archives, workshops, sculpture garden and bookshop. Admission in the high season may be restricted to present overcrowding.

> IT IS ADVISABLE, ESPECIALLY IN THE SEPTEMBER TO MAY LOW SEASON, TO RING ATTRACTIONS TO CONFIRM OPENING ARRANGEMENTS BEFORE MAKING A LONG JOURNEY.

21 THE CRYPT

ADDRESS & TELEPHONE
24 Foundry Square, Hayle. (01736) 756666

DIRECTIONS
Located 2 mins from the train station in Hayle.

OPENING HOURS
Easter -Oct, 10am last admission 4.30pm.

DISABLED ACCESS
No

ACTIVITIES/FACILITIES
Museum of mysteries and legends with a bloodcurdling collection of sights and sounds. Chance to meet Sweeny Todd the demon barber of Fleet Street, Burke and Hare the body snatchers, Vlad the Impaler and Elizabeth Batharoi the countess who bathed in blood!

22 PARADISE PARK

ADDRESS & TELEPHONE
Hayle, Nr. St. Ives. TR27 4HY. (01736) 757407 (info. line). (01736) 753365 (other enquiries)

DIRECTIONS
Follow tourist signs from A30 Hayle, near St. Ives.

OPENING HOURS
Open all year from 10am. Last entrance Winter 4pm, Summer 6pm.

DISABLED ACCESS
Yes, access to shop, cafe and park. Disabled toilets.

ACTIVITIES/FACILITIES
Outstanding collection of rare birds, home of the World Parrot Trust, Cornish Otter Sanctuary and Eagles of Paradise falconry display. Noted for its conservation work. Childrens play equipment, events and feeding times. Shop, cafe and licensed pub on site.

23 JEEPERS KARTS

ADDRESS & TELEPHONE
Chenhalls Road, St. Erth, Hayle. (01736) 754960

DIRECTIONS
On the B3302 Hayle-Helston road.

OPENING HOURS
Easter to end Sept., every day from 10am.

DISABLED ACCESS
Spectating access available.

ACTIVITIES/FACILITIES
Karting centre with beginners tuition and spectators welcome. Helmets supplied. Refreshments. **Dog Access:** On leads.

24 COUNTRY SKITTLES

ADDRESS & TELEPHONE
Townshend, Hayle. (01736) 850209

DIRECTIONS
Hayle-Helston road (B3302). From Hayle direction, take Townshend road just past the Smugglers Inn and drive exactly one mile. From Helston direction, turn left at Leedstown crossroads, go to Townshend, turn right and drive three quarters of a mile.

OPENING HOURS
Mid Sept to mid June, Mon to Fri, 6pm-11pm, Sat, 2pm-11pm, Sun, 11am-11pm. Mid Jun to mid Sept, Mon to Sat, 2pm-11pm. Sun, 11am-11pm. Summer opening may extend according to weather. No babies/children after 7.30pm on Sats.

DISABLED ACCESS
Gentle slope to entrance. Toilet facilities.

ACTIVITIES/FACILITIES
Fully automated and computerised 9 pin bowling centre with laser clay pigeon and target rifle shooting plus about 60 additional games, 40 of which are free within entrance fee. Licensed bar, bar meals and refreshments. **Dog Access:** Guide dogs only.

25 GODOLPHIN HOUSE

ADDRESS & TELEPHONE
Godolphin House, Breage, Helston. TR13 9RE (01736) 762409

DIRECTIONS
On the B3302 Helston to Hayle road.

OPENING HOURS
May and June, Thurs, 2pm-5pm. July and Sept, Tues and Thurs, 2pm-5pm. Aug, Tues, 2pm-5pm, Thurs, 10am-1pm, 2pm-5pm. Bank Hol Mons (exc. Christmas) 2pm-5pm. Open all year for groups by arrangement.

DISABLED ACCESS
Very limited for wheelchairs, on request can drive to the front door.

ACTIVITIES/FACILITIES
15th Century house with displays of horse drawn vehicles, reproduction maps, prints and documents as well as arms and armour. Old roses and herbs for sale. Teas in aid of charity on all open days.
Dog Access: Only guide dogs in house and garden.

Kerrier Tourist Office

26 STITHIANS LAKE

ADDRESS & TELEPHONE
Nr. Redruth. (01209) 860301

DIRECTIONS
Take B3297 from A393 in Redruth. Turn left at Four Lanes towards Stithians. Entrance adjacent to the Golden Lion Pub.

OPENING HOURS
9.30am-5.30pm (weekends only in Winter). For waterski club, ring for details.

DISABLED ACCESS
Yes, phone for more details.

ACTIVITIES/FACILITIES
Major watersports centre with windsurfing, sailing and canoeing. Natural trout fishery (permits available from the watersports centre). 2 bird hides run by Cornwall Birdwatching and Preservation Society. **Dog Access:** Yes though dogs must be kept on leads and out of picnic and play areas.

27 ROWE BOWL BOWLING CENTRE

ADDRESS & TELEPHONE
Trevithick Road, Camborne. TR14 8LQ. (01209) 711971

DIRECTIONS
Turn off at Camborne West on the A30 and proceed towards Camborne. Rowe Bowl is the first left past the roundabout.

OPENING HOURS
7 days a week, 11am-11pm.

DISABLED ACCESS
Yes.

ACTIVITIES/FACILITIES
9 lanes of ten pin and 6 lanes of nine pin bowling. Family room, amusements, pool tables and bar.

28 CAMBORNE KARTING

ADDRESS & TELEPHONE
Old Teagle Works, Pendarves Street, Tuckingmill, Camborne. TR14 8RE (01209) 711993.

DIRECTIONS
Leave A30 at Pool/Camborne turn off, turn right at traffic lights and continue for 400 yds, centre on left next to Torex Hire.

OPENING HOURS
Easter to Oct., daily, 10am-10pm. Evenings only in winter if enough bookings.

DISABLED ACCESS
Access available by ramp.

ACTIVITIES/FACILITIES
Indoor Go-kart race track. Race meetings can be arranged by appointment. Light snacks.

29 CORNISH ENGINES

ADDRESS & TELEPHONE
Pool, Redruth. (01209) 216657

DIRECTIONS
At Pool 2 miles west of Redruth on either side of the A3047.

OPENING HOURS
1 April to 31 October, daily, 11am-5.00pm.

DISABLED ACCESS
To shop only.

Andrew Besley/ National Trust

ACTIVITIES/FACILITIES
2 Cornish beam engines preserved in their houses and administered by the Trevithick Trust. The 30 inch Whim Engine at Mitchell's Shaft can be seen in action with the fly wheel and drum turning as the beam rises and falls. The 90 inch pumping engine at Taylor's Shaft is the largest left in Cornwall and was still working as late as 1954. Shop also. Refreshments can be obtained at the cafe in the nearby Safeway Superstore. **Dog Access:** Guide dogs only.

- **MUSEUMS & ART GALLERIES**
- **HISTORIC BUILDINGS & GARDENS**
- **LEISURE, WILDLIFE & THEME PARKS**
- **OTHER**

30 ST. AGNES LEISURE PARK

ADDRESS & TELEPHONE
St. Agnes. (01872) 552793

DIRECTIONS
Situated on the B3277 off the A30, on the right before the entrance to St. Agnes village.

OPENING HOURS
April to June, daily, 10am-6pm. July and Aug, daily, 10am-7pm. Sept to Oct, daily, 10am-6pm.

DISABLED ACCESS
Yes.

ACTIVITIES/FACILITIES
Fairyland, Cornwall in Miniature, Dinosaur World, Haunted House, Super X Simulator, Grand Animated Circus, ball pond, bouncy maze and aqua blaster. Cafe and gift shop, fully accessible for disabled persons and pushchairs.
Dog Access: Yes, on a lead.

31 CORNISH GLIDING AND FLYING CLUB

ADDRESS & TELEPHONE
Trevellas Airfield, St. Georges Hill, Perranporth. TR6 0EB. (01872) 572124

DIRECTIONS
Signed to Perranporth from A30. Through Perranporth on St. Agnes road (B3285) at top of St. Georges Hill.

OPENING HOURS
May to Sept, every day, 9am-dusk. Oct to April, weekends and Wednesdays, 9am-dusk (weather permitting).

DISABLED ACCESS
With notice we do fly some disabled people.

ACTIVITIES/FACILITIES
Gliding club and holiday courses based at Trevellas Airfield, a wartime R.A.F. station on the north Cornish Coast. Launching by winch or aero tow, trial flights also.

32 A.T.V. MOTORSPORT CENTRE

ADDRESS & TELEPHONE
Blackwater, Nr. Truro. TR4 8HJ. (01872) 560753

DIRECTIONS
From A30 Chiverton Cross roundabout, turn off for Blackwater, turn right by Red Lion Pub and left at crossroads.

OPENING HOURS
March to Oct, 10am-7pm. Nov to March, 10am-4pm (midweek requires 24hr. booking notice).

DISABLED ACCESS
Yes.

ACTIVITIES/FACILITIES
3 circuits for quad racers with spectator bridge and cafe. 50cc. machines (6-10yrs.), 80cc. (11-13yrs.), 125cc (14-16yrs.), and 200cc. (16yrs.+).
Dog Access: On leads.

TO CONFIRM THE LOCATION OF INDIVIDUAL ATTRACTIONS, USE THE MAP ON PAGE 111

MATCH THE ATTRACTION NUMBER AGAINST THE RELEVANT COLOURED SQUARE.

33 FLAMBARDS VILLAGE THEME PARK

ADDRESS & TELEPHONE
Culdrose Manor, Helston.
TR13 0GA.
(01326) 564093 (info. line).

DIRECTIONS
On Helston/Lizard
A3083 road.

OPENING HOURS
Easter to Oct from 10am,
every day. Last
admission 4.30pm.

DISABLED ACCESS
90% wheelchair accessible.

ACTIVITIES/FACILITIES   Large theme park including Flambards
Victorian Village, Britain in the Blitz exhibition, Aeropark
collection, Cornwall's Exploratorium, Grand Canyon Log Flume,
prize winning gardens, Pirate F.M. parrot show, 3D cinema,
amusements and rides for the whole family, including the Hornet
Rollercoaster, Britains most southerly coaster, 412 metres of
family fun.   **Dog Access:** No dogs in park but shaded parking for
cars containing dogs, dog walking area, water.

34 HELSTON GOLF & LEISURE

ADDRESS & TELEPHONE   Wendron, Nr. Helston. TR13 0LX.
(01326) 572518

DIRECTIONS   1 mile north of Helston on B3297.

OPENING HOURS   All year, daily, 7am-dusk.

DISABLED ACCESS   Limited access due to nature of activity.

ACTIVITIES/FACILITIES   Short course golf (18 hole, Par 3),
duration of play under 2 hours, course distance 2000 yards, length
of holes 70-170 yards. Challenging approach course, ideal for
beginners and fun golfers alike. Good greens, sand traps and
natural hazards. Golf for all ages and playable all year round. Also
crazy golf, boule and short tennis. Coffee lounge. All facilities are
pay as you play with no entrance fee.   **Dog Access:** Guide dogs only.

35 POLDARK MINE

ADDRESS & TELEPHONE
Wendron, Helston.
(01326) 573173/563166
(info. line).

DIRECTIONS
On B3297, near Helston.

OPENING HOURS
End March to end Oct,
daily, 10am-5.30pm (last
admission 4pm).

DISABLED ACCESS
Limited access therefore free admission.

ACTIVITIES/FACILITIES   Early 18th century tin mine
incorporating heritage display and museum as well as Poldark
Village and Ross and Demelza's residence. Award winning gardens
and indoor and outdoor amusements and rides. Restaurant, cafe
and gift shops.
Dog Access: On leads.

36 GOONHILLY EARTH SATELLITE STATION

ADDRESS & TELEPHONE
Goonhilly Downs,
Helston. TR12 6LQ.
(01326) 221333

DIRECTIONS
Situated on the B3293
Helston/St. Keverne road.

OPENING HOURS
Easter to last Fri in Oct,
daily, 10am-6pm (last
entry 4.30pm). During
Aug, open until 7.30pm
on Tues/Wed/Thur (last
entry 6pm).

DISABLED ACCESS
Yes.

ACTIVITIES/FACILITIES
Guided bus tour around the complex. Superb visitor centre with
audio visual show, hi-tec interactive displays, licensed cafe and
kids adventure playground. The tour includes a 'Fly on the wall'
experience in the operational control centre of the station allowing
visitors to see B.T.'s global communications centre at work.
Dog Access: Only to car park where there are special shaded
parking areas for cars with dogs.

37 NATIONAL SEAL SANCTUARY

ADDRESS & TELEPHONE
Gweek, Nr.Helston. TR12
6UG. (01326) 221361

DIRECTIONS
Follow signs from B3291
south of Helston.

OPENING HOURS
Daily from 9am, not Xmas.

DISABLED ACCESS
All facilities suitable for disabled. Information sheet available
from reception upon request.

ACTIVITIES/FACILITIES   The largest seal sanctuary in Europe,
rescuing and returning to the wild around 30 grey seals every
year. Spacious outdoor pools and well equipped seal hospital.
Underwater observatory and childrens farm. Woodland walk,
childrens play area, cafe and gift shop.
Dog Access: Well behaved dogs admitted if kept on a lead.

38 GLENDURGAN GARDEN

ADDRESS & TELEPHONE
Mawnan Smith,
Falmouth. TR11 5JZ.
(01326) 250906

DIRECTIONS
Half a mile south west
of Mawnan Smith.

OPENING HOURS
1 Mar to 31 Oct, Tues -
Sat (closed Good Fri but
open Bank Hol Mons),
10.30am-5.30pm. Last admission 4.30pm.

David Hastilow/National Trust

DISABLED ACCESS   No.

ACTIVITIES/FACILITIES   Set in a wooded valley rich in trees and
exotic plants, Glendurgan is noted as one of the great subtropical
gardens of the South West. At the foot of the garden on the
Helford Estuary is the waterside hamlet of Durgan. Children love
the 'Giants Stride' and the great laurel maze dating from 1833.
Dog Access: Guide dogs only.

39 TREBAH

ADDRESS & TELEPHONE
Trebah Garden, Mawnan Smith, Falmouth. TR11 5JZ. (01326) 250448

DIRECTIONS
Signed from Treliever Cross roundabout on A39 near Falmouth.

OPENING HOURS
Daily, 10.00am-5pm (last admission). Garden closes 6.30pm.

DISABLED ACCESS
Yes.

ACTIVITIES/FACILITIES
25 acre sub tropical garden. All year round colour; water gardens with waterfalls and Koi Carp, glades of 100 year old Tree Ferns and 18 feet high giant Gunneva (rhubarb). Rolling canopy of Rhododendrons over 2 acre valley of blue and white Hydrangeas leading down to a private beach open to visitors. Childrens play areas and trails, coffee shop seating 65 and garden and plant shops. **Dog Access:** Yes, on leads.

40 PENJERRICK GARDENS

ADDRESS & TELEPHONE Budock Water, Nr. Falmouth. TR11 5ED. (01326) 250074 or (01872) 870105.

DIRECTIONS Leave A39 Falmouth by-pass, follow signs to Mabe and Mawnan. A mile from Argal Reservoir, Penjerrick Garden is marked to the left and situated opposite Penmorvah Manor Hotel.

OPENING HOURS Mar to Sept, Sun, Wed and Fri, 1.30pm-4.30pm.

DISABLED ACCESS No.

ACTIVITIES/FACILITIES 15 acre gardens with Rhododendrons, Camelias, Tree Ferns and Wilder Aquatic woodland garden over bridge. Guided tours possible on request.
Dog Access: Welcome on leads.

41 FALMOUTH FERRY/ CRUISE SERVICES

ADDRESS & TELEPHONE Prince of Wales Pier, Falmouth (01326) 313201

DIRECTIONS Prince of Wales Pier is opposite Burger King and next to Superdrug in Falmouth town centre.

OPENING HOURS **Cruises:** Mar-Oct, daily. **Ferry:** April-Oct, half hourly Mon-Sat. Sun hourly. Oct-April, winter service only.

DISABLED ACCESS Yes.

ACTIVITIES/FACILITIES **Cruises:** Passenger cruising boats with daily excursions to River Fal, Helford River and Frenchman's Creek. Covered boats with bar, refreshments and toilets. **Ferry:** 25 minute cruise each way between Falmouth and St Mawes. Regular sailings allow time ashore in St. Mawes.

42 FALMOUTH MARITIME MUSEUM

ADDRESS & TELEPHONE 2, Bell's Court, Market St., Falmouth TR11 2AZ. (01326) 316745

DIRECTIONS Market St, Falmouth, opp. Marks & Spencer.

OPENING HOURS Easter to October, Mon. to Sat., 10am-4pm. November to Easter, Mon. to Sat., 10am-3pm.

DISABLED ACCESS No.

ACTIVITIES/FACILITIES Models, displays, artefacts and illustrations of Cornwall's maritime heritage. Book/gift shop.

43 PRINCESS PAVILION & GYLLYNGDUNE GARDENS

ADDRESS & TELEPHONE
Melvill Rd, Falmouth. TR11 4AR. (01326) 311277, (01326) 211222 (box office).

DIRECTIONS
Falmouth, close to Gyllyngvase beach.

OPENING HOURS
Open all year, for show see phone number above.

DISABLED ACCESS Yes plus facilities.

ACTIVITIES/FACILITIES Theatrical and musical shows throughout the year plus many events held within the hall and gardens. Licensed bar and cafe. **Dog Access:** Yes but on a lead.

44 FALMOUTH PITCH & PUTT

ADDRESS & TELEPHONE Swanpool Road, Goldenbank, Falmouth. TR11 5BH. (01326) 317311

DIRECTIONS Half a mile past Swanpool Beach.

OPENING HOURS Mar to Sept, daily, 9am-dusk.

DISABLED ACCESS Yes with wide doors and help usually at hand.

ACTIVITIES/FACILITIES 12 hole course, crazy golf, boules, Childrens bumper cars, rides and play area. Cafe and tea gardens. Free admission with activities individually charged.
Dog Access: Welcome on front lawn on leads.

45 PENDENNIS CASTLE

ADDRESS & TELEPHONE Falmouth. TR11 4LP. (01326) 316594

DIRECTIONS A39 to Falmouth, follow signs to Castle Drive and Pendennis Headland.

OPENING HOURS April to Sept, daily, 10am-6pm. Oct to March, daily, 10am-4pm.

DISABLED ACCESS To grounds and part of castle keep.

ACTIVITIES/FACILITIES Tudor castle built by Henry VIII with excellent views over Carrick Roads. Sight and sound Tudor gun deck display as well as military display, coffee shop and gift shop. Suitable for picnics. Events during summer (ring above number to confirm). **Dog Access:** Only in certain areas.

English Heritage

46 WORLD IN MINIATURE

ADDRESS & TELEPHONE
Goonhavern,
nr. Perranporth.
(01872) 572828

DIRECTIONS
Situated on the B3285
off the A30 and A3075
in Goonhavern.

OPENING HOURS
Apr to Oct, daily, 10am-
6pm (last admission 4pm). July and Aug, daily 10am-7pm (last
admission 5pm).

DISABLED ACCESS   Yes.

ACTIVITIES/FACILITIES   World in miniature model village,
adventure dome, Tombstone Wild West town, bouncy maze, ball
pond and the Orbitors, a dodgem based ride suitable for all ages.
Childrens rides and amusements. Cafe and gift shop, fully
accessible for disabled and pushchairs.
Dog Access: Yes, on a lead.

47 CALLESTOCK CIDER FARM

ADDRESS & TELEPHONE
Penhallow, Truro. TR4
9LW. (01872) 573356

DIRECTIONS
Signed off the A3075
Newquay road at
Penhallow.

OPENING HOURS
Easter to Oct, Mon-Sat,
9am-6pm (8pm and Suns 10 -6pm in July/Aug). Nov to mid Dec,
Feb and March, Mon to Fri, 10am-5pm.

DISABLED ACCESS   Yes though cobbled courtyard so help
always at hand.

ACTIVITIES/FACILITIES   Cornish cider farm where range of
ciders, wines and jams are made; all processes are available to
view according to season. Though admission to the farm is free,
there is a small charge to visit the cider museum demonstrating
traditional methods and associated trades of coopers and
blacksmiths. Tractor rides around the farmyard and orchards as
well as farm animals and free tastings of produce.

48 ROYAL CORNWALL MUSEUM

ADDRESS & TELEPHONE
River St., Truro. TR1 2SJ.
(01872) 72205

DIRECTIONS
Take A390 into Truro,
turn down past the B.R.
station in the direction
of the town centre.

OPENING HOURS
All year, Mon to Sat
(except Bank Holidays),
10am-5pm.

DISABLED ACCESS   Ramp to main entrance. Level access to
café. Lift. Toilets for disabled use.

ACTIVITIES/FACILITIES   Museum of Cornish archaeology and
history with important collections of minerals, fine and decorative
art, costume and natural history. Café and gift/book shop.
Dog Access: Guide dogs welcome.

49 ENTERPRISE BOATS PLEASURE TRIPS

ADDRESS & TELEPHONE   66 Trefusis Road, Flushing, Falmouth.
TR11 5TY. (01326) 374241/313234

DIRECTIONS   On dual carriageway by-pass at Truro
(near Tesco).

OPENING HOURS   During season, 9am-3.30pm.

DISABLED ACCESS   No.

ACTIVITIES/FACILITIES   Pleasure boat trips on the River Fal
aboard the 130 seat Enterprise Boats. Regular sailings during
season from Malpas/Truro to Falmouth and vice versa.
Dog Access: Welcome on leads.

50 TRURO BOWL

ADDRESS & TELEPHONE   1 and 2 Oak Way, Moresk, Truro.
(01872) 222333

DIRECTIONS   Situated behind 'Hardy Carpets' in St.
Clement Street.

OPENING HOURS   Every day except Christmas Day,
11am-11pm.

DISABLED ACCESS   Yes.

ACTIVITIES/FACILITIES   Bowling centre, riverside grill
restaurant and Land's End Bar.

**TO CONFIRM THE LOCATION OF INDIVIDUAL
ATTRACTIONS, USE THE MAP ON PAGE 111**

**MATCH THE ATTRACTION NUMBER AGAINST
THE RELEVANT COLOURED SQUARE.**

IT IS ADVISABLE, ESPECIALLY IN THE SEPTEMBER
TO MAY LOW SEASON, TO RING ATTRACTIONS
TO CONFIRM OPENING ARRANGEMENTS BEFORE
MAKING A LONG JOURNEY.

MUSEUMS & ART GALLERIES

HISTORIC BUILDINGS & GARDENS

LEISURE, WILDLIFE & THEME PARKS

OTHER

51 TRELISSICK GARDEN

ADDRESS & TELEPHONE
Feock, Truro. TR3 6QL. (01872) 862090. (01872) 865808 (Recorded Information line). (01872) 863486 (Restaurant). (01872) 864084 (Gallery).

DIRECTIONS
4 miles south of Truro, the gardens are sited on both sides of the B3289 above King Harry Ferry.

OPENING HOURS
1 March to 31 October, Mon-Sat, 10.30am-5.30pm, (closes 5.00pm in March & October). Nov & Dec, Mon-Sat 10.30-4pm, Sun 12.30-4pm (shop, restaurant and gallery only).

DISABLED ACCESS
Wheelchair access and availability.

ACTIVITIES/FACILITIES
A garden which offers both peace and tranquillity and splendid panoramic views across Carrick Roads and Falmouth Harbour. Trelissick has been planted with an abundance of those tender shrubs so characteristic of Cornish gardens: magnolias, camellias and rhododendrons with many rare species. Fine woodlands encircle the gardens through which a varied circular walk can be enjoyed all the year round. The house is not open. Art and Craft Gallery, shop and restaurant.
Dog Access: Dogs on leads in the park only.

Tony Kent/National Trust

52 PROBUS GARDENS

ADDRESS & TELEPHONE
Probus, Nr. Truro. TR2 4HQ. (01726) 882597

DIRECTIONS
On eastern boundary of Probus village on A390 between Truro and St. Austell.

OPENING HOURS
April 2nd-Oct 2nd, daily, 10am-5pm. Oct 3rd-April 1st, Mon-Fri, 10am-4pm.

DISABLED ACCESS
Wheelchair access and toilets.

ACTIVITIES/FACILITIES
Seven and a half acre garden explaining many aspects of gardening with displays of annuals, herbaceous perennials, shrubs, trees, conifers and hedges. Layouts for fruit, vegetables and general garden designs. Best season from June to Sept. Cafe.

Ailsa Allaby/Probus Gardens

53 TREWITHEN GARDENS

ADDRESS & TELEPHONE
Trewithen, Grampound Road, Truro TR2 4DD. (01726) 882763/4

DIRECTIONS
On A390 between Probus and Grampound.

OPENING HOURS
Gardens: March to Sept, Mon to Sat, 10am-4.30pm (Sundays in April/May).
House: April to July, Mon and Tues only, 2pm-4pm. Nursery: all year, Mon to Fri, 9am-4.30pm.

DISABLED ACCESS
Generally good throughout garden.

ACTIVITIES/FACILITIES
Covering some thirty acres, the gardens contain a large collection of Camellias, Magnolias and Rhododendrons as well as many other trees and shrubs. Woodland gardens are surrounded by traditional landscaped parkland, there is also a video presentation of the house and gardens. Childrens playground and tea shop.
Dog Access: On leads please.

54 VERYAN VINEYARD

ADDRESS & TELEPHONE
Tregenna, Portloe, nr. Truro. TR2 5PS. (01872) 501404

DIRECTIONS
Veryan Vineyard, Tregenna, is just off the coast road between Portloe and Portholland and is approx. 2 miles from Veryan village. Veryan is signed from the A3078 St. Mawes road, reached from the A390 Truro-St. Austell road near Probus.

OPENING HOURS
Easter to end of Sept, Mon-Sat, 2pm-6pm.

DISABLED ACCESS
Regret difficult.

ACTIVITIES/FACILITIES
Vineyard and winery located on the south facing slope of a sheltered valley on the Roseland Peninsula. Free tastings of ciders as well as a picnic area in the grounds. Though admission to the vineyard is free, guided tours (including wine tasting) are available Easter to end of September on Wednesdays at 3pm for which a small charge is made.
Dog Access: Well behaved dogs on a lead only please.

55 ST. MAWES CASTLE

ADDRESS & TELEPHONE
St. Mawes. TR2 3AA. (01326) 270526

DIRECTIONS
In St Mawes on A3078.

OPENING HOURS
April to Sept, daily, 10am-6pm. Oct, daily, 10am-4pm. Nov to March, Wed to Sun, 10am-4pm.

DISABLED ACCESS
No.

English Heritage

ACTIVITIES/FACILITIES
Built by Henry VIII to guard the Carrick Roads anchorage. Its three circular bastians were formidable defences but today stand in a sub-tropical garden. Toilets and shop. Suitable for picnics.

56 AUTOMOBILIA

ADDRESS & TELEPHONE
The Old Mill, St. Stephen, St. Austell. PL26 7RX. (01726) 823092

DIRECTIONS
On A3058 Newquay to St. Austell road, Newquay side of St. Stephen.

OPENING HOURS
April, May, Oct, 10am-4pm. June to Sept, 10am-6pm (last admission 5pm). Closed Saturdays early and late season.

DISABLED ACCESS To all but one floor with admission free to wheelchair users.

ACTIVITIES/FACILITIES Cornwall's Motor Museum with an exhibition of over 50 vehicles covering period 1904-1960's. Audio visual display and permanent auto jumble as well as gift/model shop and cafe.
Dog Access: Yes within the museum through not in the cafe.

57 BEN'S PLAYWORLD

ADDRESS & TELEPHONE
Stadium Retail Park, St. Austell. (01726) 815553

DIRECTIONS
Just off the main A390 in St. Austell, next to the Stadium Retail Park.

OPENING HOURS
Daily, 10am-7pm.

DISABLED ACCESS
Please ring for details.

ACTIVITIES/FACILITIES Massive children's adventure centre featuring Mega Slides, Giant Tubes, Ball Ponds, Death Slides, Aerial Runways, Mystical Wizards, Bouncers and much more. Free car parking, indoor pram park and baby changing facilities. Party rooms and Sunset Boulevard cafe. Adults and children under 2 admitted free.

58 ST. AUSTELL BREWERY VISITOR CENTRE

ADDRESS & TELEPHONE
63 Trevarthian Rd, St. Austell. PL25 4BY. (01726) 66022

DIRECTIONS
Signed from the A391 or follow B.R. signs as the brewery is situated behind the station.

OPENING HOURS
Mon to Fri, 9.30am-4.30pm.

DISABLED ACCESS Unsuitable.

ACTIVITIES/FACILITIES Visitor centre and gift shop (licensed). Guided tours of the working brewery by appointment only (number above). Beer sampling included in admission charges for adults. Unsuitable for children under 8 years.

59 CORNWALL COLISEUM

ADDRESS & TELEPHONE Carlyon Bay, St. Austell. (01726) 814004

DIRECTIONS Signed within St. Austell.

OPENING HOURS **Season:** 8am-1am. **Low season:** 9am-5.30pm.

DISABLED ACCESS Parking and toilet facilities provided.

ACTIVITIES/FACILITIES Cornwall's largest live entertainment centre located on its own blue flag sandy beach with nightclub, function rooms and family evenings. Restaurant, naturist beach, Olympic size swimming pool and seasonal watersports facilities. There is a car parking charge in the season.

60 KID'S KINGDOM

ADDRESS & TELEPHONE
Albert Road, St Austell PL25 4TZ. (01726) 77377

DIRECTIONS
Follow brown tourist signs from A390 St Austell by-pass.

OPENING HOURS
Easter-Sept, daily, 10am-7pm. Sept to Easter, Tues-Sun, 10am-6pm.

DISABLED ACCESS Yes.

ACTIVITIES/FACILITIES Children's indoor adventure play centre with demon drops, monster hut maze, go karts, ball pool, rope bridge and much more. Baby care room, souvenir shop and water hole refreshment centre. Free admission for adults, child admission charge entitles a stay as like long as you like.

61 OZZELL BOWL

ADDRESS & TELEPHONE Priory Car Park, Priory Road, St. Austell. (01726) 77766

DIRECTIONS Adjacent to Priory Car Park in central St. Austell.

OPENING HOURS Everyday, 11am-11pm.

DISABLED ACCESS Yes plus toilets.

ACTIVITIES/FACILITIES 8 lane bowling centre with restaurant, fast food facilities and licensed bar.

62 WHEAL MARTYN CHINA CLAY HERITAGE CENTRE

ADDRESS & TELEPHONE
Carthew, St. Austell. PL26 8XG. (01726) 850362

DIRECTIONS
From the A391 from St. Austell, take the B3274 at Stenalees.

OPENING HOURS
Apr to Oct, daily, 10am-6pm.

DISABLED ACCESS Limited access therefore free admission for wheelchairs.

ACTIVITIES/FACILITIES China clay industry museum including audio visual display, historic trail through 19th century clay works with working water wheels. Nature trail, childrens play area and adventure trail. Coffee shop and gift shop.
Dog Access: Welcome on leads.

63 CHARLESTOWN SHIPWRECK & HERITAGE CENTRE

ADDRESS & TELEPHONE
Quay Road, Charlestown PL25 3NJ. (01726) 69897

DIRECTIONS
Signed from the Mount Charles roundabout on the A390 Truro to St. Austell road.

OPENING HOURS
Mar 1st to Oct 31st, daily, 10am-5pm (later in high season).

DISABLED ACCESS Yes, including disabled toilets.

ACTIVITIES/FACILITIES A favourite location of film directors, Charlestown was developed in the eighteenth century as a working port, primarily for use within the china clay industry. Modern day activities include the Scarborough lifeboat, old china clay tunnels, audio visual theatre, 1st and 2nd World War exhibits, diving exhibition and largest shipwreck artefact collection in the British Isles. Restaurant and refreshments.
Dog Access: Well behaved and on leads.

64 LOST GARDENS OF HELIGAN

ADDRESS & TELEPHONE
Pentewan, St Austell. PL26 6EN. (01726) 844157

DIRECTIONS
From the A390 St. Austell Road, take the B3273 to Mevagissey. Pass through Pentewan, at top of steep hill follow sign by turning right and continue for half a mile following signs.

OPENING HOURS Daily throughout the year, 10am-6pm (last admission 4.30pm).

DISABLED ACCESS Yes to large areas of the gardens. Toilets.

ACTIVITIES/FACILITIES The award winning "Lost Gardens of Heligan" is thought to be the largest garden restoration project in Europe. 57 acres of gardens lost for 70 years are being rediscovered and restored as a working Victorian garden. Containing a crystal grotto, an Italian garden, summerhouse, rockery and four walled gardens, one containing a fully restored pineapple pit. 22 acre sub tropical garden with fine specimen trees including large collection of palms, bamboos and tree ferns. Tea room and covered picnic area, gift shop and plant sales, toilets. **Dog Access:** Welcome on leads.

65 POLMASSICK VINEYARD

ADDRESS & TELEPHONE
Polmassick, St. Ewe. PL26 6HA. (01726) 842239

DIRECTIONS
From A390 at Hewaswater (between St. Austell and Truro), take B3287 signed Tregony/St. Mawes. After 2 miles, take left signed Polmassick. At Polmassick cross roads, take right turn to vineyard.

OPENING HOURS Last weekend May to last weekend Sept, Tues-Sun and Bank Holidays, 11am-5pm.

DISABLED ACCESS Good access to vinery and wine garden. Access to vineyard limited.

ACTIVITIES/FACILITIES Estate produced white and rose, dry and medium wines by bottle or glass in flowery all weather gardens. Refreshments as well as vineyard tour (small charge for vineyard walk only).
Dog Access: Welcome on leads.

66 MEVAGISSEY MUSEUM

ADDRESS & TELEPHONE East Quay, Mevagissey. (01726) 843568

DIRECTIONS Mevagissey is signed from St. Austell.

OPENING HOURS Easter until end of Sept, Mon-Fri, 11am-5pm (Aug 6pm). Sat 11am-4pm, Sunday 2pm-4pm.

DISABLED ACCESS Ground floor only.

ACTIVITIES/FACILITIES Display of local articles, boat models and photographs of Mevagissey over the last 100 years.
Dog Access: On lead only.

67 WORLD OF MODEL RAILWAYS

ADDRESS & TELEPHONE Meadow St, Mevagissey. (01726) 842457

DIRECTIONS Located in the centre of Mevagissey.

OPENING HOURS Easter, then Spring Bank Holiday to October from 11am-5pm (last entry 4.30pm). In October, afternoons only.

DISABLED ACCESS Yes, wide enough for wheelchair, but sorry no W.C.

ACTIVITIES/FACILITIES Model railway exhibition with over 2000 models. Model railway layout and shop.

68 MEVAGISSEY HARBOUR AQUARIUM

ADDRESS & TELEPHONE South Quay, Mevagissey Harbour. (01726) 843305

DIRECTIONS Take B3273 to Mevagissey from St. Austell roundabout A390.

OPENING HOURS April to Sept, every day, 10am-5pm.

DISABLED ACCESS Yes.

ACTIVITIES/FACILITIES Exhibition of the many species of fish found in Cornish waters. As a registered charity, all proceeds go towards Mevagissey harbour maintenance and improvement.

MUSEUMS & ART GALLERIES

HISTORIC BUILDINGS & GARDENS

LEISURE, WILDLIFE & THEME PARKS

OTHER

69 HOLYWELL BAY FUN PARK

ADDRESS & TELEPHONE
Holywell Bay, Newquay. TR8 5PW. (01637) 830095

DIRECTIONS
Take A3075 Newquay to Perranporth road and follow signs to Cubert and Holywell.

OPENING HOURS
Mid April to Sept 30th, every day, 10.30am-5pm (Aug 10.30 am -6.30pm). Times can vary in off season.

DISABLED ACCESS Yes.

ACTIVITIES/FACILITIES Action orientated family fun rides requiring skill and judgement including Battle Boats, Skidpan and Go-Karts on a figure of eight track. Childrens indoor adventure play area, crazy golf, massive maze and much more. Family cafe serving snacks and meals throughout the day. There is no admission charge to the park as activities are pay as you play.

70 NEWQUAY SEA LIFE CENTRE

ADDRESS & TELEPHONE
Towan Promenade, Newquay. TR7 1DU. (01637) 872822

DIRECTIONS
Seafront location overlooking Towan Beach in Newquay.

OPENING HOURS
Every day (except Christmas), from 10am.

DISABLED ACCESS Full access including toilets & lift.

ACTIVITIES/FACILITIES Opened only in June 1994, the centre has more than 30 displays providing close encounters with many different types of sea creature ranging from shrimps, starfish and sharks, to conger eels, rays and octopus. 'Walk through' tunnel creates the illusion of a walk on the sea bed. Gift shop and coffee shop.
Dog Access: Guide dogs only.

71 NEWQUAY ANIMAL WORLD

ADDRESS & TELEPHONE
Trenance Leisure Park, Newquay. TR7 2LZ. (01637) 873342

DIRECTIONS
East Newquay, follow signs.

OPENING HOURS
All year, 9.30am-6pm (not Christmas).

DISABLED ACCESS Yes.

ACTIVITIES/FACILITIES Cornwall's only zoo, set within 8 acres of landscaped gardens, over 300 animals including Black Lemurs, Monkeys, Lions and Reptiles. Tarzan Trail, Dragon Maze and Activity Play Area for children. Cafe, barbecue and gift shop.

72 TUNNELS THROUGH TIME

ADDRESS & TELEPHONE
St. Michaels Road, Newquay. (01637) 873379

DIRECTIONS
Below Mount Wise and above Newquays pedestrian precinct.

OPENING HOURS
Easter to Oct, Sun-Fri from 10am. Every day from mid July to end of Aug. As last admission times vary, ring the above number to confirm.

DISABLED ACCESS Please ring first for advice, not easily accessible, stairs inside and out - but not impossible when exhibition is quiet.

ACTIVITIES/FACILITIES This attraction cleverly recreates with life size figures and sound and lighting effects, Cornish stories and legends. Included in the splendid mix of fact and fiction are Giant Bolster, King Arthur and his trusted magician; pirates, wreckers, an honest smuggler and more. Beware the Dungeon of Despair - not for the faint hearted. Enjoy the tranquillity of Lyoness and a mermaid's fishy tale. Stocks and pillory available - tomatoes too! Souvenir shop also.
Dog Access: Please ring first for advice, well behaved dogs welcome when exhibition is quiet.

73 THE FUN FACTORY

ADDRESS & TELEPHONE
1 St. Georges Road, Newquay. TR7 1HZ. (01637) 877555

DIRECTIONS
Clearly signed from A392.

OPENING HOURS
July to Aug (school holidays), 10am-8pm. Sept to June, 10am-6pm.

DISABLED ACCESS By arrangement.

ACTIVITIES/FACILITIES The Fun Factory is an adventure play centre for 2-12 year old children, housed in a tastefully converted old stone warehouse near Newquay town centre. Attractions include a softplay area, adventure play equipment, inflatable bouncer, large ball pool, grand prix circuit and, for children over 6, the new "Temple of Doom" terror trail. Coffee shop, ice cream parlour and baby care room. Admission charged for children, adults free.

74 TRENANCE HERITAGE COTTAGES

ADDRESS & TELEPHONE
Trenance, Newquay. (01637) 873922/875859

DIRECTIONS
Just a short distance from the Trenance boating lake on the southern edge of Newquay (close to Animal/Water Worlds).

OPENING HOURS March until October, daily from 10am.

DISABLED ACCESS Partial access to ground floor only.

ACTIVITIES/FACILITIES The cottages are grade II listed buildings built around 1702 and originally a row of four dwellings. A reconstruction allows the visitor to step back in time to view the way of life in Cornwall during the 1900s. Modest admission charge, children under 12 free with a paying adult. Art gallery and craft shop.

75 LAPPA VALLEY STEAM RAILWAY & PARK

ADDRESS & TELEPHONE
Benny Halt, St. Newlyn East, Newquay. TR8 5HZ. (01872) 510317

DIRECTIONS
From A3075, 2.5 miles south of Newquay, follow signs for St. Newlyn East.

OPENING HOURS
Easter to Oct. On season, 10am-6pm. Off season, 10.30am-5pm.

DISABLED ACCESS Yes (wheelchairs must be folded for carrying on the train).

ACTIVITIES/FACILITIES 2 mile return trip on 15" guage steam train with historic mine engine house, educational film, boating lakes, crazy golf, miniature train rides, brick path maze, nature walks, gypsy caravan and play/picnic areas. Other facilities include cafe, gift shop, remote control boats, bumper cars and bikes. Leisure facilities are at the far end of the railway, it is therefore advisable to phone to confirm railway timetable.

76 TRERICE

ADDRESS & TELEPHONE Newquay. TR8 4PG. (01637) 875404

DIRECTIONS 3 miles south east of Newquay via A392 and A3058 (turn right at Kestle Mill).

OPENING HOURS 1 Apr to 31 Oct, daily except Tues & Sat, 11am-5.30pm. Closes 5pm in Oct. Open daily late July to early Sept. Last admission 30 mins before closing.

DISABLED ACCESS Wheelchair access and availability.

ACTIVITIES/FACILITIES Trerice is an architectural gem - a small Elizabethan manor house, built before the Armada in 1571. Behind the symmetrical gabled façade are ornate fireplaces, elaborate plaster ceilings and a collection of English furniture of the highest quality. The summer flowering garden is unusual in content and layout and there is an orchard planted with old varieties of fruit trees. A small museum traces the history of the lawn mower. **Dog Access:** Guide dogs only.

David Hastilow/National Trust

77 DAIRYLAND FARM WORLD

ADDRESS & TELEPHONE
Summercourt, Newquay. TR8 5AA. (01872) 510246

DIRECTIONS
On the A3058 between Summercourt and Newquay. Summercourt (southbound) or Mitchell (northbound), turnings off A30.

OPENING HOURS Apr-Oct, daily, 10.30am-5.00pm. School hols 10.00am-5.00pm, July 24 to Aug 31, Mon-Thurs, open to 7.00pm.

DISABLED ACCESS All areas have access by ramp where there are steps, wide doors, toilet and viewing gallery for milking - wheelchair loan.

ACTIVITIES/FACILITIES Farm park, heritage centre, playground, nature trail and milking parlour. Daily events include pony rides, tractor rides, bottle feeding, pat-a-pet, and milking. Many animals to feed and pet including goats, lambs, pigs, donkeys, rabbits, guinea pigs, chipmunks and chinchillas. Gift shop, tea stop and stable nosebag. New for 1995, Rally Karts, woodcraft workshop and Westcountry Brass Rubbing Centre. Homemade Dairyland Ice Cream and clotted cream.
Dog Access: Car park only, shaded car port and drinkers provided.

78 SPRINGFIELDS PONY CENTRE & FUN PARK

ADDRESS & TELEPHONE St. Columb Major. (01637) 881224.

DIRECTIONS From A39 roundabout at St. Columb or follow 'Airport' signs from A30.

OPENING HOURS One week before Easter to Sept, daily, 9.30am-5.30pm (Oct 10am-3.30pm).

DISABLED ACCESS Access to all parts.

ACTIVITIES/FACILITIES Pony riding, tractor rides, carriage rides and rowing boats. Bottle feeding of lambs, calves and goats several times daily. Hands on experience of all the animals plus birds, rabbits and kittens. 10,000 sq. ft. all weather covered area housing gardens and play areas. Cafe seating 200 with hot and cold meals and full range of drinks. Ice cream bar. Baby changing room.
Dog Access: Shaded area for dogs - not allowed in the park.

79 CORNWALL KARTING

ADDRESS & TELEPHONE
Retallack, Winnard's Perch, St. Columb. (01637) 881530.

DIRECTIONS
Signed from the Winnard's Perch roundabout on the A39 near Wadebridge.

OPENING HOURS
Daily, 10am-10pm.

DISABLED ACCESS
Access and toilets.

ACTIVITIES/FACILITIES
Indoor karting centre with full helmets, suits and safety marshals. 2500 square foot first floor spectator area with video games, pool table, children's Grand Prix circuit and views of the main race track. Burger bar refreshments. Free parking and spectating.

80 SPIRIT OF THE WEST

ADDRESS & TELEPHONE Retallack Park, Winnard's Perch, Near St. Columb. TR9 6DE (01637) 881160

DIRECTIONS Signed from the Winnard's Perch roundabout on the A39 near St. Columb.

OPENING HOURS **Spirit of the West:** Easter-end of Sept., from 10.30am (closed Sats). **Fishery:** Open all year, daily from 8.30pm. Gates close for both at 6pm.

DISABLED ACCESS Yes plus toilets also.

ACTIVITIES/FACILITIES American theme park featuring Silver City, the original 1880's frontier town. American Cowboy and Indian museums as well as rifle and pistol shooting gallery, "pan for gold" mining camp and pony/horse rides. Eating house and restaurant and western and souvenir stores. The park includes the Retallack Waters Coarse Fishery.
Dog Access: No but shaded area available for parking.

81 PRIDEAUX PLACE

ADDRESS & TELEPHONE
Padstow. PL28 8RP.
(01841) 532411

DIRECTIONS
Follow brown tourist
signs from A389
Padstow ring road.

OPENING HOURS
Easter to mid October,
Sun to Thurs incl, 1.30-
5pm. Bank Holidays, 11am-5pm.

DISABLED ACCESS
Access to ground floor rooms in house
and tea room.

ACTIVITIES/FACILITIES
Elizabethan mansion, home of the
Prideaux family since 1588. Filled with treasures from Royal
pictures to Armada loot and the oldest cast iron cannon in
Britain. Extensive grounds and deer park with views over the
Camel Estuary. Formal garden, 9th century Celtic cross, terrace tea
room and grotto.
Dog Access: Welcome on leads.

82 PADSTOW SHIPWRECK MUSEUM

ADDRESS & TELEPHONE
South Quay, Padstow.
(01841) 532663

DIRECTIONS
Adjacent to Old Station
car park.

OPENING HOURS
April to Oct, daily, 10am-
5pm.

DISABLED ACCESS
Yes.

ACTIVITIES/FACILITIES
Shipwreck artefacts dating from the
17th century to the present day from around the coast of Great
Britain and other parts of the world.
Dog Access: Yes providing it is not too busy (for the dog's sake).

83 SHIRES ADVENTURE PARK

ADDRESS & TELEPHONE
Trelow Farm, Wadebridge. PL27 7RA.
(01841) 540276

DIRECTIONS
Signed from A39 Wadebridge to St.
Columb Major road.

OPENING HOURS
Mid April to end of Oct, daily,
10am-5pm. Closed Sats in Oct.

DISABLED ACCESS
Yes.

ACTIVITIES/FACILITIES
Shire Horse Centre including daily
parades in the fully seated indoor arena. Owl sanctuary and Old
Mac Donalds Barn of small animals including pygmy goats, rabbits
and vietnamese pot bellied pigs. Adventure World, Death Slide, 3D
maze, Fantasy Jungle as well as a museum, cart rides and lakeside
walks. Craft shop, gift shop and restaurant.

84 MELLINGEY MILL WILLOW CRAFT CENTRE

ADDRESS & TELEPHONE
Mellingey, St. Issey, Wadebridge.
PL27 7QU. (01841) 540604

DIRECTIONS
2.5 miles from A39, quarter mile off
A389, follow brown tourist signs.

OPENING HOURS
Easter to Oct, 10am-5pm. Oct to Easter,
10.30am-4.30pm (basket shop only).

DISABLED ACCESS
75% of the Mill is accessible to
wheelchairs.

ACTIVITIES/FACILITIES
Set in the tranquil surroundings of a
wooded valley, the craft centre has a basket showroom/shop,
basket workshop, information gallery, craft/gift shop, tearoom and
terrace by the waterwheel. Nature trail through willow beds and
woodland as well as lakeside walks and picnic area. Photographic
exhibition. Admission charge refunded on basket sale over £10.
Dog Access: Yes except nature trail.

85 TRENOUTH FARM RARE BREEDS CENTRE

ADDRESS & TELEPHONE
Trenouth, St. Ervan,
Wadebridge. PL27 7SG.
(01841) 540606

DIRECTIONS
Signed from A39 St.
Columb-Wadebridge road.

OPENING HOURS
Easter-Sept, 10am-5pm.

DISABLED ACCESS
Free admission due to limited access in some areas and
cafe/toilets inaccessible.

ACTIVITIES/FACILITIES
Traditional farm with friendly animals
including rare breeds such as Iron Age pigs crossed with wild
boar as well as White Park cattle, believed to be the oldest breed
of British cattle. Opportunities to mingle with, feed and touch the
animals including Pygmy goats, Sika and Fallow deer, donkeys
and Shetland ponies. Trout ponds, conservation area, peacocks,
barn owls and kestrels, as well as tea shop and gift shop.
Dog Access: Dogs welcome on leads. Kennels available.

86 PORTEATH BEE CENTRE

ADDRESS & TELEPHONE
St. Minver, Wadebridge.
PL27 6RA. (01208) 862192

DIRECTIONS
Follow brown tourist signs
from Wadebridge (B3314).

OPENING HOURS
Easter to Oct, daily, 9am-
7pm. Winter (shop only),
daily, 10am-5pm.

DISABLED ACCESS
To shop and toilets only.

ACTIVITIES/FACILITIES
Living bee exhibition
behind glass. See the
honey bees working and
storing honey in their
natural habitat as well as
continuous descriptive videos. Craft shop including honey
products (ice cream, cosmetics etc.) as well as beeswax candles
and polishes etc. Coffee shop and picnic area.
Dog Access: Yes but not in the shop.

87 LONG CROSS VICTORIAN GARDENS

ADDRESS & TELEPHONE
Long Cross, Trelights, Nr. Port Isaac. PL29 3TF. (01208) 880243

DIRECTIONS
Marked off the B3314 Wadebridge-Camelford road.

OPENING HOURS
Daily, 10.30am-dusk.

DISABLED ACCESS
Yes.

ACTIVITIES/FACILITIES The only major public garden so close to the sea on the North Cornwall Coast. This restored Victorian Garden includes a maze, "secret gardens", water granite features, pets corner and childrens adventure play area. Plants for sale. Refreshments/meals and drinks also available in the Freehouse Tavern.

88 CORNWALL DONKEY & PONY SANCTUARY

ADDRESS & TELEPHONE Lower Maidenland, St. Kew, Nr. Bodmin. PL30 3HA. (01208) 841710

DIRECTIONS Signed from St. Kew Highway on A39 (between Wadebridge and Camelford).

OPENING HOURS Sunday before Easter to Oct, every day, 10am-5pm.

DISABLED ACCESS Yes.

ACTIVITIES/FACILITIES Free admission to bike hire, farm kitchen shop, gift shop and coffee shop. By becoming a "friend" of the sanctuary (charged for), visitors can visit the sanctuary free until the following March to see the donkeys, feed the baby animals and use the children's play area, adventure swamp and the 'Eeyore Club'. Donkey cart rides for children also.

89 DELABOLE SLATE QUARRY

ADDRESS & TELEPHONE
Pengelly Road, Delabole. PL33 9AZ. (01840) 212242

DIRECTIONS
Follow signs for Pengelly in Delabole.

OPENING HOURS
Mon to Fri, 8am-4.30pm.

DISABLED ACCESS
Showroom and viewing platform only.

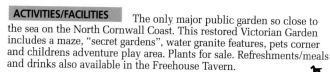

ACTIVITIES/FACILITIES Primarily a working quarry, hence limited tourist facilities. However, viewing platform of quarry (500ft deep) and showroom with souvenir gifts. Tours of quarry and production available by appointment (introduced in 1995). Free admission to viewing platform, small charge for tours. **Dog Access:** Car park and viewing platform only.

90 DELABOLE WIND FARM

ADDRESS & TELEPHONE
Delabole, North Cornwall, PL33 9BZ. (01840) 213377

DIRECTIONS
North of Delabole on the B3314 to Camelford.

OPENING HOURS
Easter until October, daily, 10am-5pm.

DISABLED ACCESS
Yes but sorry no toilets.

ACTIVITIES/FACILITIES
10 turbine wind farm established in 1991 and now producing enough power for 3,000 households. The adjacent visitor and information centre deals with all forms of renewable energy through the use of display boards, working models, video and photographs. Guided visits by appointment throughout the year.

91 NORTH CORNWALL MUSEUM & GALLERY

ADDRESS & TELEPHONE
The Clease, Camelford. PL32 9PL. (01840) 212954

DIRECTIONS
Enter Camelford on the A39, follow signs to tourist information centre (which is in the museum). Free car park opposite.

OPENING HOURS
April to Sept, Mon to Sat, 10am-5pm.

DISABLED ACCESS
Ground floor of museum only. Door not wide enough for electric wheelchairs.

ACTIVITIES/FACILITIES Museum shows aspects of life in North Cornwall from fifty to a hundred years ago. Gallery has monthly changing exhibitions of arts and crafts. **Dog Access:** Guide dogs only.

92 BRITISH CYCLING MUSEUM

ADDRESS & TELEPHONE
The Old Station, Camelford. (01840) 212811

DIRECTIONS
1 mile north of Camelford on the Boscastle road.

OPENING HOURS
Open all year, Sun-Thurs, 10am-5pm.

DISABLED ACCESS Yes

ACTIVITIES/FACILITIES Britain's foremost collection of cycling history with over 300 cycles on display dating from 1818. 300 enamel advertising signs and posters with 900 cycling medals, fobs and club badges. Housed within an idealistic setting of an old Victorian railway station. **Dog Access:** Guide dogs only.

93 RESTORMEL CASTLE

ADDRESS & TELEPHONE Nr. Lostwithiel. (01208) 872687

DIRECTIONS 1½ miles north of Lostwithiel off A390.

OPENING HOURS April to Sept, daily, 10am-6pm. Oct, daily, 10am-4pm.

DISABLED ACCESS No.

ACTIVITIES/FACILITIES A fortified hilltop since the time of the Norman Conquest, Restormel is one of the best preserved Motte-and-Bailey castles in Cornwall. Huge circular keep and walk around the battlements. Seasonal shop, toilets. Events during summer (ring above number). Suitable for picnics.
Dog Access: Allowed on leads.

English Heritage

94 DUKE OF CORNWALL'S LIGHT INFANTRY MUSEUM

ADDRESS & TELEPHONE The Keep, Bodmin. PL31 1EG. (01208) 72810

DIRECTIONS From Parish Church in Bodmin on the A389, take the B3268 to Lostwithiel. The museum is behind a prominent War Memorial 1½ mile up this road.

OPENING HOURS Mon to Fri, 9am-5pm. Open Sundays & Bank Hols but please ring for details.

DISABLED ACCESS The museum has stairs, no lifts but there is usually someone on hand to help.

ACTIVITIES/FACILITIES History of the Duke of Cornwall's Light Infantry and local militia and volunteer forces of Cornwall dating from 1702. Illustrated by artefacts, pictures and uniforms. Collection of medals and infantry small arms. Comprehensive military reference library may be used on request.
Dog Access: Guide dogs only.

IT IS ADVISABLE, ESPECIALLY IN THE SEPTEMBER TO MAY LOW SEASON, TO RING ATTRACTIONS TO CONFIRM OPENING ARRANGEMENTS BEFORE MAKING A LONG JOURNEY.

> ■ MUSEUMS & ART GALLERIES
> ■ HISTORIC BUILDINGS & GARDENS
> ■ LEISURE, WILDLIFE & THEME PARKS
> ■ OTHER

95 CAMEL VALLEY WINE

ADDRESS & TELEPHONE Little Denby Vineyard, Nanstallon, Bodmin. PL30 5LG. (01208) 77959

DIRECTIONS From A389 Bodmin to Wadebridge road, take the Nanstallon road 2 miles from Bodmin. After 1 mile, turn right at vineyard sign.

OPENING HOURS May to Sept, Mon to Fri, 2pm-5pm & Wed 5pm-6.30pm.

DISABLED ACCESS Access not good but assistance given.

ACTIVITIES/FACILITIES Cornish wine sales, tastings and vineyard tours. Admission to vineyard free but charge made for vineyard tours. Easily visited while using the Camel Trail. **Dog Access:** Not in winery.

96 BODMIN & WENFORD RAILWAY

ADDRESS & TELEPHONE General Station, Bodmin. PL31 1AQ. (01208) 73666

DIRECTIONS Follow signs for Bodmin then take B3268, station ¼ mile from town centre.

OPENING HOURS Easter to Oct and Christmas/New Year, 10am-5.30pm. Trains run to timetable.

DISABLED ACCESS Yes.

ACTIVITIES/FACILITIES 3.5 branch railway linking Bodmin Town to B.R. Mainline Station at Bodmin Parkway. Train usually steam hauled with diesel on Saturdays. Access on foot from steam railway stations to Cardinham Woods and Lanhydrock House and Park. Free parking, buffet and gift shop at Bodmin General Station. 🐕

97 BODMIN JAIL

ADDRESS & TELEPHONE Berrycoombe Road, Bodmin. (01208) 76292

DIRECTIONS Follow signs within Bodmin.

OPENING HOURS All year, Mon to Fri, 10am-6pm, Sat 11-6pm, Sun 10am-6pm. In winter may close early.

DISABLED ACCESS No.

ACTIVITIES/FACILITIES The former county prison now houses an exhibition detailing its history as well as a chance to visit the dungeons. Coffee shop and gift shop. 🐕

98 LANHYDROCK

ADDRESS & TELEPHONE Bodmin. PL30 5AD. (01208) 73320

DIRECTIONS 2⅕ miles south east of Bodmin. Follow signs from either A38 Bodmin-Liskeard, or B3268 Bodmin-Lostwithiel roads.

OPENING HOURS 1 April to 31 Oct daily except Mon when the house only is closed (garden, shop and restaurant remain open), but open Bank Hol Mons, 11am-5.30pm. Closes at 5pm in Oct.

DISABLED ACCESS Wheelchair access and availability.

ACTIVITIES/FACILITIES The finest house in Cornwall, superbly set in wooded parkland of 450 acres and encircled by a garden of rare shrubs and trees, lovely in all seasons. Come in good time to view the 49 rooms ranging from the richly furnished main rooms reflecting Victorian comfort to maids' bedrooms, the great kitchen and the newly-opened Nursery Wing. First built in the 17th century and largely rebuilt after a fire in 1881, the principal rooms all have beautifully worked plaster ceilings, including that of the Long Gallery magnificently illustrating Old Testament scenes. Through the crenellated gatehouse (1651) an idyllic walk down to the River Fowey at Respryn Bridge and back through the woods should not be missed.
Dog Access: On leads in the park only.

Simon Bache/National Trust

99 PENCARROW HOUSE & GARDENS

ADDRESS & TELEPHONE Washaway, Bodmin. PL30 3AG. (01208) 841369

DIRECTIONS Signed off the A389, north of Bodmin.

Barry Aughton

OPENING HOURS Easter to Oct 15th, Sun-Thurs, 1.30pm-5pm. Bank Holiday Mondays and June 1st-Sep 10th from 11am.

DISABLED ACCESS Access to all ground floor rooms, tea rooms, toilets and craft centre and majority of the garden.

ACTIVITIES/FACILITIES Georgian house and grade 2 listed gardens still owned and lived in by the Molesworth-St. Aubyn family. Large collection of pictures, furniture and porcelain with marked walks through 50 acres of formal and woodland gardens. Victorian rockery, Italian and American gardens with over 600 different Rhododendrons. Internationally recognised specimen conifer collection. Lake and Ice House. Craft centre, childrens play areas and tea rooms. Children and dogs are welcome free in the grounds.
Dog Access: In grounds only. Able to be off a lead away from the house.

100 FERNLEYS

ADDRESS & TELEPHONE Bolventor, Bodmin Moor. PL14 6PZ. (01208) 821469

DIRECTIONS Follow the road signs to the park from the A30 on Bodmin Moor.

OPENING HOURS Easter until end of Sept, daily from 10.30am-5pm (last admission 4pm).

DISABLED ACCESS Limited access.

ACTIVITIES/FACILITIES Moorland setting on the north shore of Colliford Lake Reservoir, the park contains rare breeds of birds, cattle, poultry and sheep. Some animal pens can be entered, with other animals observed from covered walkways. The 50 acre park has a further 20,000 sq feet of attractions undercover including Ball Pool, Volcano Drop and an indoor activity course and museum. Cafeteria, shop and picnic areas as well as a lakeside walk.
Dog Access: Welcome but must be kept on short leads.

101 POTTER'S MUSEUM OF CURIOSITY

ADDRESS & TELEPHONE Jamaica Inn Courtyard, Bolventor, Nr.Launceston. PL15 7TS. (01566) 86838

DIRECTIONS Situated just off A30, 9 miles west of Launceston, 8 miles east of Bodmin, signed 'Jamaica Inn Museums, Bolventor'.

OPENING HOURS **Museum:** All year except Christmas and January. Low season 11am-4pm. Mid season 10am-5pm. High season 10am-8pm. **Inn:** All year, normal hours.

DISABLED ACCESS Wheelchair access to ground floor of museum including newly opened extension.

ACTIVITIES/FACILITIES Museum, founded in 1861, containing fascinating lifetimes' work of Victorian taxidermist/naturalist Walter Potter. 'Kitten's Wedding', 'Death of Poor Cock Robin' and many more plus numerous unusual curiosities collected from all over the world. Adjacent to Jamaica Inn, made famous by the late Daphne du Marier, built in 1547. Two giftshops and a childrens' play area. Admission charged for Museum, free admission to Inn.
Dog Access: No dogs allowed in the museum.

102 SIBLYBACK LAKE

ADDRESS & TELEPHONE St. Cleer, Liskeard. (01579) 346522

DIRECTIONS Signed from A38 at Liskeard & Bodmin.

OPENING HOURS All year, 9.30am-5.30pm. (weekends only in winter).

DISABLED ACCESS Yes, phone for more information.

ACTIVITIES/FACILITIES Major watersports centre with windsurfing, sailing and canoeing instruction. There are a number of walks including the 1.5 mile round reservoir walk and surfaced path to the dam. Childrens play areas and tea/gift shop. **Dog Access:** Yes though dogs must be kept on leads and out of picnic and play areas.

103 FOWEY RIVER STEAMERS

ADDRESS & TELEPHONE
Town Quay, Fowey. (01726) 833192.

DIRECTIONS
Central Fowey.

OPENING HOURS
Throughout the year but advisable to ring prior in low season.

DISABLED ACCESS
Yes and never been beaten yet!!

ACTIVITIES/FACILITIES
Cruise the beautiful River Fowey aboard the Gallant, a 12 seater Edwardian steam launch rebuilt and equipped with a new engine and boiler in 1988. The 45 minute trip explores Daphne du Maurier country with a full commentary provided. The first cruise leaves at 11am. Seats may be booked in advance by phoning the above number before 9am or after 6pm.

104 LAND OF LEGEND & MODEL VILLAGE

ADDRESS & TELEPHONE
The Old Forge, Mill Hill, Polperro, Pl13 2RP. (01503) 272378.

DIRECTIONS
Central Polperro.

OPENING HOURS
Apr 1st - Oct 31st, daily from 10am. Closes 10pm mid July to Sept, otherwise 6pm.

DISABLED ACCESS
Sorry, no.

ACTIVITIES/FACILITIES
Seven different stories of legends and superstitions from Cornish folklore as well as the chance to meet Merlin the Wizard. OO guage model railway and Polperro model village. Children under 8 free with paying adult.

105 POLPERRO HERITAGE MUSEUM

ADDRESS & TELEPHONE
Polperro Harbour. (01503) 272423.

DIRECTIONS
Reached via The Warren on the eastern side of Polperro Harbour.

OPENING HOURS
Easter til end of Oct., daily, 10am-6pm.

DISABLED ACCESS
Hoped for. Ring for current status.

ACTIVITIES/FACILITIES
Situated in the old pilchard factory overlooking the harbour, the museum houses a remarkable collection of exhibits and 19th century photographs as well as many items of memorabilia dating from the 18th century when both smuggling and fishing thrived in Polperro. Modest admission charges used for the upkeep of Polperro Harbour.

106 I-SPY GLASS BOTTOM BOAT

ADDRESS & TELEPHONE
Banjo Pier, East Looe. Day (01503) 263011. Eve (01503) 262380

DIRECTIONS
From A387, proceed through East Looe Town to seafront.

OPENING HOURS
All year, weather dependant.

DISABLED ACCESS
Limited access.

ACTIVITIES/FACILITIES
Trips of approx. 1 hour on boat with glass bottom viewing panels. Everyone can look under water at the same time. **Dog Access:** Any size dog depending on how many people are on the boat.

107 OLD GUILDHALL MUSEUM

ADDRESS & TELEPHONE
Higher Market St., East Looe. (01503) 263709 (East Looe Town Trust).

DIRECTIONS
Park in Looe car park, proceed on foot.

OPENING HOURS
Easter then Spring Bank Holiday to 30th Sept, 12 noon-4pm (not Sat)

DISABLED ACCESS
Ground floor access only by request.

ACTIVITIES/FACILITIES
Former fifteenth century guildhall converted into a 2 floor museum in 1972, exhibits include a collection of Punch and Judy puppets, model ships and smuggling aids, watercolours and photographs of Looe, stocks, local mineral specimens, pilchard press and pilchard industry exhibits, china and porcelain as well as an early 1900's ambulance. **Dog Access:** Guide dogs only.

108 MONKEY SANCTUARY

ADDRESS & TELEPHONE
Looe. PL13 1NZ. (01503) 262532

DIRECTIONS
From Liskeard or Plymouth, take A38 to Trerulefoot roundabout (near Tideford), follow signs for Looe. Signed on B3253 at No Mans Land between East Looe and Hessenford.

OPENING HOURS
Easter to end of Sept, Sun to Thurs, 10.30 am-5pm. Closed Fridays and Saturdays (except Easter).

DISABLED ACCESS
Limited. Slopes and special toilet.

ACTIVITIES/FACILITIES
Sanctuary with 23 Woolly monkeys in residence. Three generations of monkeys, all born in Cornwall, who have free range between heated indoor rooms and surrounding trees. Talks given throughout the day. Cafe in free car park. Conservation garden and childrens play area. **Dog Access:** No. May be left in shaded part of car park.

109 PORFELL ANIMAL LAND

ADDRESS & TELEPHONE
Trecangate, Nr. Lanreath, Liskeard. PL14 4RE. (01503) 220211

DIRECTIONS
From A390 at East Taphouse, turn onto B3359 and follow brown tourist signs.

OPENING HOURS
Easter to end of Oct, daily, 10am-6pm.

DISABLED ACCESS
Yes.

ACTIVITIES/FACILITIES
15 acre family attraction where you can meet zebra, deer, wallabies, goats, ducks, chickens, leopard cats and "Bert" the capybara. Beautiful woodland walk, ponds. Peacock tea room and gifts.

110 LANREATH FOLK AND FARM MUSEUM

ADDRESS & TELEPHONE
Lanreath, Nr. Looe. PL13 2NX.

DIRECTIONS
Take the B3359 to Looe from the A390 at Middle Taphouse.

OPENING HOURS
Good Fri to May 31st, 11am-5pm. June to Sept, 10am-6pm. Oct, 11am-5pm.

DISABLED ACCESS
Yes.

ACTIVITIES/FACILITIES
Countryside museum with dairy and barn equipment housed in the Lanreath Tithe Barn. Range of farm implements including steam roller and stationary engines. Free play phone system for children. Bric a Brac, books and crafts for sale. Cafe and pub next door.

111 MAGNIFICENT MUSIC MACHINES

ADDRESS & TELEPHONE
St. Keyne Station, Nr. Liskeard. PL14 4SH. (01579) 343108

DIRECTIONS
Follow the B3254 from Looe or Liskeard town centre and turn off at the brown "Magnificent Music Machines" signs. By train, hourly services to St. Keyne Station from Looe or Liskeard, for 'Music on a Branch Line'.

OPENING HOURS
Good Fri for 10 days incl. April, Suns & Thurs. May- Oct, daily, 10.30am-5pm.

DISABLED ACCESS
Yes.

ACTIVITIES/FACILITIES
Exhibition of performing music machines including fair organs, orchestrions, player pianos and the Mighty Wurlitzer Theatre Pipe Organ. Picnic area by the river.

112 CARNGLAZE SLATE CAVERNS

ADDRESS & TELEPHONE
St. Neot, Liskeard. PL14 6PG. (01579) 320251

DIRECTIONS
Follow brown tourist signs from A38 between Liskeard and Bodmin.

OPENING HOURS
Easter to Sept., 10.30am-5pm, last admission 4pm. Closed on Sats. Parties during Winter by prior appointment only.

DISABLED ACCESS
Unsuitable for disabled.

ACTIVITIES/FACILITIES
Underground slate cavern and subterranean lake with full guided tours. Strategically placed lighting ensures a tremendous spectacle. Gift shop.

113 DOBWALLS FAMILY ADVENTURE PARK

ADDRESS & TELEPHONE
Dobwalls, Nr. Liskeard. PL14 6HD. (0800) 521812

DIRECTIONS
North of A38 at Dobwalls.

OPENING HOURS
April to Sept, every day, 10.30am-5pm (longer hours in peak season). Oct, weekends and Devon/Cornwall half terms only, 10.30am-5pm (last entry 3.30pm). During the Winter months, the Krazee Kavern and Mr. Blobby Mania will be open at weekends 11am-5pm. During Summer Mr. Blobby will be at Dobwalls on selected dates (ring for details).

DISABLED ACCESS
Yes, facilities for disabled people, free loan of wheelchairs (if available).

ACTIVITIES/FACILITIES
Extensive miniature railway complex including tunnels, ridges, gradients and forest routes. Large adventure playgrounds, radio controlled boats and trucks, shooting gallery and aqua blasters. Edwardian countryside wildlife art exhibition, tearoom, coffee shop and souvenir shops. Krazee Kavern, a vast underground play experience as well as Mr. Blobby Mania, Skydome and Cornish craft centre.
Dog Access: Dogs on leads please provided they keep on paths and off playgrounds.

114 LOOE VALLEY LINE

ADDRESS & TELEPHONE
From Liskeard or Looe railway stations. Enquiry line (0345) 484950

DIRECTIONS
Park and ride from Liskeard railway station.

OPENING HOURS
Mon. to Sat, all year round. Sundays between mid July and mid Sept. Check timetable for services.

DISABLED ACCESS
Ring (0345) 484950 to arrange ramps to be provided (48 hrs notice please).

ACTIVITIES/FACILITIES
The historic Looe Valley Line runs through the 8 miles of unspoilt countryside of the East Looe River valley between Liskeard and Looe. The railway was originally built in the 19th century to transport copper ore and granite but now provides half hour train rides to Looe through a steepsided valley. The service provides an ideal way to visit Looe with the shops and harbour just a short walk from the station. Timetables can be found at both stations as well as the excellent South East Cornwall Discovery Centre (01503) 262777. **Dogs:** Yes, up to 2 per person.

115 QUAD & KART CENTRE

ADDRESS & TELEPHONE
Menheniot Station, Liskeard.
PL14 3PT. (01579) 347229

DIRECTIONS
On A38 between Saltash &
Liskeard.

OPENING HOURS
Easter to Oct, daily, 10am-6pm.
Oct to Easter, Sat/Sun 11am-4pm and weekdays by appointment.

DISABLED ACCESS Facilities for the disabled.

ACTIVITIES/FACILITIES Quads, Kiddie Quads, Karts, Scorpions
and electric cars, childrens play area and cafe. Free admission
with activities individually charged. **Dog Access:** Strictly on leads.

116 STERTS ARTS AND ENVIRONMENTAL CENTRE

ADDRESS & TELEPHONE Upton Cross, Liskeard. PL14 5AZ.
(01579) 362382

DIRECTIONS 6 miles from A38 Liskeard on B3254.

OPENING HOURS Summer season: Mon to Sat, 9am-11pm
(if event on). Off season: Tues to Fri, 10.30am-4.30pm.

DISABLED ACCESS Access to Theatre and main buildings.

ACTIVITIES/FACILITIES Open air theatre, art gallery, craft shop
and coffee shop. Some indoor productions held during off season.
Free admission to site. **Dog Access:** Guide dogs only.

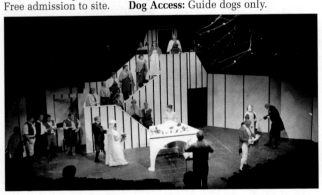

117 LYNHER VALLEY DAIRY -THE CHEESE FARM

ADDRESS & TELEPHONE
Netherton, Upton Cross,
Liskeard. PL14 5BD.
(01579) 362244

DIRECTIONS
From A30, take B3257
between Launceston and
Jamaica Inn. Through
Coads Green, after
approx. 1 mile turn right
at crossroads. Continue through Rilla Mill with sign to Cheese Farm
on the right.

OPENING HOURS Easter to Oct, Mon-Sat, 10am-4.30pm.

DISABLED ACCESS Wheelchair access with a little help.

ACTIVITIES/FACILITIES Working farm and home of the famous
Cornish Yarg Cheese. Guided tour of milking parlour, pasteurisation
and cheese rooms where Cornish Yarg is made. Cheese tasting, coffee
shop, gift shop and picnic area. Small families of animals including
wild boar. Nature trail and conservation area. Audio-visual
presentation. Free admission with tour of cheese processes charged
for. It is advisable to wear footwear suitable for a farmyard visit.
Dog Access: On leads. Not allowed in the coffee shop.

118 TAMAR VALLEY DONKEY PARK

ADDRESS & TELEPHONE St. Anns Chapel, Gunnislake.
PL18 9HW. (01822) 834072

DIRECTIONS Just off A390 Callington to Tavistock
road at St. Anns Chapel.

OPENING HOURS Easter to Oct, daily, 10am-5.30pm.
Weekends Nov, Feb, March. Daily during Dec until 24th.

DISABLED ACCESS Yes.

ACTIVITIES/FACILITIES Donkey rides and donkey cart rides,
free range tame cuddly animals, adventure playground, toddlers
playground, picnic area, cafe and gift shop. A free donkey ride for
each child. **Dog Access:** Welcome on a lead.

Murray King/Tamar Valley Donkey Park

119 COTEHELE

ADDRESS & TELEPHONE St. Dominick, Saltash. PL12 6TA.
(01579) 51346, (01579) 51222 information line.

DIRECTIONS On the west bank of the Tamar, 1 mile
west of Calstock by footpath (6 miles by road), 4 miles from
Gunnislake (turn at St. Ann's Chapel).

OPENING HOURS 1 April to 31 Oct. House, mill,
restaurant 11am-5.30pm, (closes 5pm in Oct) daily except Friday
(but open Good Friday). Shop, tea room on quay and garden daily,
11am-5.30pm, (closes 5pm in Oct).

DISABLED ACCESS Wheelchair acccess and available.

ACTIVITIES/FACILITIES Home to the Edgcumbe family for
nearly 600 years, the house has evolved from its early origins
though retains a medieval atmosphere. Terraced garden with
pools and a dovecote, a working watermill and adjoining
ciderpress as well as contemporary furnishings and objets d'art.
The Victorian river quay with the last Tamar sailing barge,
"Shamrock", moored alongside, harks back to a busier time on
this waterway. Restaurants, shop and gallery.
Dog Access: Guide dogs welcome. Others on leads in woods only.

Andrew Besley/National Trust

120 TAMAR CANOE EXPEDITION

ADDRESS & TELEPHONE
Tinnel, Landulph, Saltash. PL12 6QG. (01579) 351113

DIRECTIONS
Phone above number to confirm starting point:- **Barnside:** Drive to Gunnislake Village on the A390 Callington to Tavistock road. Opposite the Cornish Inn, in the middle of the village, turn off into Calstock Road. Continue for 1.4 miles, turn left at the road junction. **Halton Quay:** Take A388 Saltash to Callington road. Turn off half a mile north of St. Mellion, following road signs to Quay.

OPENING HOURS
Easter to Sept, meeting times change daily due to tide.

DISABLED ACCESS
Welcome with prior notification please.

ACTIVITIES/FACILITIES
Family canoeing expeditions in double or single kayaks along 7 mile stretch of Tamar with the tide; no white water. Inspected and licenced for safety.
Dog Access: Obedient dogs can acompany you in your canoe.

121 ANTONY HOUSE & GARDEN

ADDRESS & TELEPHONE
Torpoint. PL11 2QA. (01752) 812191

DIRECTIONS
5 miles west of Plymouth via Torpoint car ferry. 2 miles north west of Torpoint, north of A374. 16 miles south east of Liskeard, 15 miles east of Looe.

OPENING HOURS
1st April to 31st October, Tues, Wed, Thurs and Bank Holiday Mondays, plus Sundays in June, July and August, 1.30 pm-5.30pm (tea room opens 12.30 pm). Last admission 4.45 pm.

DISABLED ACCESS
No.

ACTIVITIES/FACILITIES
Early 18th century mansion set in parkland and fine gardens overlooking the River Lynher. Antony House has been the home to the Cornish family of Carew for almost six centuries and the house contains a wealth of paintings, tapestries, furniture and embroideries. Fine walks in the parkland and woodland garden. Shop and tea room.
Dog Access: Guide dogs only.

Peter Cade/National Trust

122 MARY NEWMAN'S COTTAGE

ADDRESS & TELEPHONE
Culver Road, Saltash. (01579) 347993

DIRECTIONS
1/4 mile from Saltash town centre near waterside.

OPENING HOURS
May to Sept, Thurs, 12 noon-4pm, Sat, 11am-4pm. Easter 4 days and Bank Holidays also.

DISABLED ACCESS
No.

ACTIVITIES/FACILITIES
Legend has it that this was the childhood home of Mary Newman, first wife of Sir Francis Drake and Mayoress of Plymouth during Elizabethan times. A small, medieval 15th century cottage, furnished by the Victoria and Albert Museum with garden overlooking Tamar bridges. Saltash in bloom award 1993. Cornish buildings group award 1984.

123 TAMAR CRUISING & CREMYLL FERRY

ADDRESS & TELEPHONE
Cremyll Quay, Cremyll, Torpoint. (01752) 822105

DIRECTIONS
Barbican, Plymouth.

OPENING HOURS
Ferry all year round. Cruises April to October.

DISABLED ACCESS
Yes.

ACTIVITIES/FACILITIES
1. Cremyll Ferry (passengers only) from Mount Edgcumbe, Cornwall to Plymouth (Stonehouse). **2.** Cruises including 1 hour cruise of dockyard and warships, 4 hour cruise up the River Tamar past Saltash to Calstock (1 hour landing). **3.** Barbecue and disco cruise during the evenings in the summer season. The Plymouth Sound I and II Boats are covered with bar, buffet and toilet facilities. Commentary. All cruises depart from Mayflower Steps, Barbican, Plymouth.

124 MOUNT EDGCUMBE HOUSE

ADDRESS & TELEPHONE
Cremyll, Torpoint. PL10 1HZ. (01752) 822236

DIRECTIONS
From A374 to B3247 via Millbrook.

OPENING HOURS
April to Oct, Wed to Sun, 11am-5pm.

DISABLED ACCESS
Toilets and wheelchairs at Cremyll shop and house. Limited access to some areas.

ACTIVITIES/FACILITIES
Historic home of the Earls of Mt. Edgcumbe. Family paintings and furniture. Earl's garden with ancient trees, shell seat and summer houses. Shop.
Dog Access: On leads in formal gardens and sheep fields.

125 LAUNCESTON CASTLE

ADDRESS & TELEPHONE
Launceston. PL15 7DR.
(01566) 772365

DIRECTIONS
From A30 at Launceston.

OPENING HOURS
Apr-Sept, daily, 10am-6pm.
Oct, daily, 10am 4pm.

DISABLED ACCESS
Limited to outer bailey.

English Heritage

ACTIVITIES/FACILITIES
The shell keep and tower survive of this medieval castle which controlled the main route to Cornwall. Suitable for picnics. English Heritage maintained.
Dog Access: On leads.

126 LAUNCESTON STEAM RAILWAY

ADDRESS & TELEPHONE
The Old Gasworks,
St. Thomas Rd,
Launceston. PL15 8DA.
(01566) 775665

DIRECTIONS
Car park is on the Newport Industrial Estate, just off the Bude-Holsworthy road, half a mile from Launceston town centre.

OPENING HOURS
Whitsun to end of Sept, daily except Sat, 10.30am-4.30pm. Low season, Sun and Tues only.

DISABLED ACCESS
Yes.

ACTIVITIES/FACILITIES
Steam railway through the Kensey Valley from Launceston to New Mills (2.5 miles) using Victorian locomotives. The line provides access to country walks and to the Launceston Town Trail. Museum, workshop tours, gift shop and buffet/restaurant. Though admission is free, train tickets are charged for and are valid for unlimited travel on the date of issue.

127 TRETHORNE LEISURE FARM

ADDRESS & TELEPHONE
Kennards House,
Launceston. PL15 8QE.
(01566) 86324

DIRECTIONS
3 miles south of Launceston, turn right off the A30, proceed up A395 for 300 yards before turning right.

OPENING HOURS
All year, Mon-Sat, 10am-6pm.

DISABLED ACCESS
Yes.

ACTIVITIES/FACILITIES
25,000 sq. ft. under cover. Horse and pony rides, bottle fed lambs, miniature pony walking and cow milking as well as falconry (Mon, Wed, Thurs, Fri). Leisure facilities including ball pools, fun castles, trampolines, demon slide, toddlers indoor play area, 9 hole pay and play golf course and floodlit golf driving range. Licensed restaurant and gift shop. All inclusive price with no hidden extras.

128 TREDIDON TRAILS

ADDRESS & TELEPHONE
St. Thomas, Near Launceston, PL15 8SJ.
(01566) 86463

DIRECTIONS
Signed from the A395 between Kennards House junction on the A30 and Pipers Pool.

OPENING HOURS
Easter-end of Oct, daily, 10am-5.30pm.

DISABLED ACCESS
No

ACTIVITIES/FACILITIES
Environment World, an undercover display detailing conservation and alternative energy and technologies. Themed treasure hunt trail as well as Hickory Farmyard where you can meet rabbits, pigs, sheep, goats and many other animals. Woodland and countryside trails, children's adventure play area, tea-room, craft and gift shop. **Dog Access:** No though shaded area in car park.

129 TAMAR OTTER SANCTUARY

ADDRESS & TELEPHONE
North Petherwin, Nr. Launceston. PL15 8LW.

DIRECTIONS
5 miles north west of Launceston, off the B3254 road to Bude.

OPENING HOURS
April (or Good Friday if earlier) to October, 10.30am-6pm (or sunset if earlier).

DISABLED ACCESS
Yes.

ACTIVITIES/FACILITIES
The only place in the West Country breeding British otters and reintroducing young otters into the wild every year as part of the Otter Trust's re-introduction programme. 3 species of deer, 2 lakes with a large collection of water fowl, peacocks and wallabies as well as a woodland walk. Tea room and gift shop. **Dog Access:** Car park only.

130 COLD NORTHCOTT WIND FARM

ADDRESS & TELEPHONE
St Clether. (01566) 86276

DIRECTIONS
A395 between Launceston & Camelford.

OPENING HOURS
April till end of Oct, daily from 10am. Last admission 4.30pm.

DISABLED ACCESS
Yes

ACTIVITIES/FACILITIES
Exhibition centre in the middle of a 22 turbine wind farm that produces electricity for 5,500 homes. Photographic exhibition, models and information on wind energy. Windmill tea-room, craft and gift shop and guided walks (on Tuesday afternoons only). **Dog Access:** Outside only.

131 MOORLAND FLYING CLUB

ADDRESS & TELEPHONE
Davidstow Aerodrome, Camelford. PL32 9YF. (01840) 261517

DIRECTIONS
Take Altarnun turn off A39, 2 miles Bude side of Camelford.

OPENING HOURS
All year, 9am-4pm (weather permitting).

DISABLED ACCESS
Yes.

ACTIVITIES/FACILITIES
Flying lessons and club.

132 TINTAGEL OLD POST OFFICE

ADDRESS & TELEPHONE
Tintagel. PL34 0DB.
(01840) 770024

DIRECTIONS
In the centre of Tintagel.

OPENING HOURS
1st April to 31 Oct daily,
11am-5.30pm. Closes
5pm in Oct.

DISABLED ACCESS
No.

J Hicks/National Trust

ACTIVITIES/FACILITIES One of the most characterful buildings in Cornwall, and a house of great antiquity, this small 14th centry manor is full of charm and interest. Tumble-roofed and weathered by the centuries, it is restored in the fashion of the Post Office it was for nearly 50 years.

133 KING ARTHUR'S GREAT HALLS

ADDRESS & TELEPHONE
Fore St., Tintagel. PL34
0DA. (01840) 770526

DIRECTIONS
In the centre of Tintagel.

OPENING HOURS
Open all year, 10.00am-
5pm (later in high
season). Winter, 11am-
5pm (please ring to
check times).

DISABLED ACCESS Yes.

ACTIVITIES/FACILITIES The Halls tell the story of King Arthur and The Knights of the Round Table with narration by Robert Powell as well as laser lights and music. The granite throne and sword in the stone are endorsed by the Pre-Raphaelite paintings, and 72 stained glass windows depict the deeds of the Knights and their Coats of Arms. Large shop selling Arthurian/Celtic Pre-Raphaelite products.

134 TINTAGEL CASTLE

ADDRESS & TELEPHONE
Tintagel. (01840) 770328

DIRECTIONS
Off A39 at Camelford,
on Tintagel Head half
mile from village.

OPENING HOURS
Apr to Sept, daily, 10am-
6pm. Nov to Mar, daily,
10am-6pm (or dusk if
earlier).

English Heritage

DISABLED ACCESS
None, due to coastal terrain.

ACTIVITIES/FACILITIES Famous ruins of medieval castle and Celtic settlement probably dating from the Dark Ages. With a cliff top location, this English Heritage maintained castle has long been associated with King Arthur; Merlin's Sea Cave is located below the Castle. Small exhibition and shop on site. Toilets. Parking in village.
Dog Access: Allowed on leads.

135 THE CRYSTAL CAVE

ADDRESS & TELEPHONE The Bridge, Boscastle. (01840) 250248

DIRECTIONS Take Boscastle turning from A39 at Camelford. Located in centre of Boscastle.

OPENING HOURS April/May/Oct, 11am-5pm. June/July /Sept, 10.30am-6pm. August, 10.30am-8pm.

DISABLED ACCESS Yes.

ACTIVITIES/FACILITIES Exhibition of Holography and Illusion suitable for all ages plus gift shop for related items.
Dog Access: Usually OK.

136 BUDE-STRATTON MUSEUM

ADDRESS & TELEPHONE The Castle, Bude. EX23 8LG. (01288) 353576

DIRECTIONS On entering Bude, take first left at the first roundabout. Museum is beside the canal next to the Wharf car park.

OPENING HOURS Easter to Sept, every day, 11am-5pm (last admission 4.45 pm).

DISABLED ACCESS Yes.

ACTIVITIES/FACILITIES The story of Bude canal told through photos, models and audio visual presentation as well as artefacts of sailing and shipwrecks seen along this part of the coast. Museum shop and adjacent cafe.
Dog Access: Guide dogs only.

137 UPPER TAMAR LAKE

ADDRESS & TELEPHONE Nr. Kilkhampton, Bude. (01288) 321262

DIRECTIONS Follow brown tourist signs from A39 at Kilkhampton.

OPENING HOURS April to Oct., 9.30 am-5.30pm.

DISABLED ACCESS Yes, phone (01288) 321712 for more information.

ACTIVITIES/FACILITIES Watersports centre including sailing, windsurfing and canoeing instruction. Children's play area and gift shop/tea room.

138 PIXIELAND FUN PARK

ADDRESS & TELEPHONE
West St., Kilkhampton,
Nr. Bude. EX23 9QW.
(01288) 321225

DIRECTIONS
Short distance off A39
Bude-Bideford road in
Kilkhampton.
Tourist signed.

OPENING HOURS
Easter to Sept, Sun to Friday, 11am-5pm (high season, 10am-6pm). Mid Nov to Easter, weekends, 12-4.30pm.

DISABLED ACCESS Yes, but some steep slopes.

ACTIVITIES/FACILITIES 2 seater supa karts, bumper boats, ball pools, supa bouncy , train rides, paddle boats, racing cars, pony rides, crazy golf, play rooms, trampolines and lots more! Many activities under cover. Cafe, shop, toilets and picnic areas.
Dog Access: Allowed on a lead.

SPORTS & LEISURE

BLUE LAGOON LEISURE

Address & Tel. No Cliff Road, Newquay. TR7 2NE. (01637) 850741/2
Directions In the centre of Newquay, opposite railway station.
Details Fun pool, 10 pin bowling, laser warriors, bar & cafe.
Opening Hours On season, 10am-1am. Off season, 11am-1am.

BODMIN LEISURE CENTRE

Address & Tel. No Walker Lines Industrial Estate, Normandy Way, Bodmin PL31 1EU. (01208) 72210
Directions From A30, take roundabout signed to Walker Lines Industrial Estate, follow signs.
Details 25m swimming pool, squash courts, multi gym and solarium.
Opening Hours **Pool:** Mon-Thurs, 7.30am-10pm. Fri, 7.30am-6.30pm. Weekends, 9am-6pm. **Other activities:** 9am-10pm.

CAMELFORD SPORTS CENTRE

Address & Tel. No Dark Lane, Camelford. PL32 9UE. (01840) 213188
Directions From Camelford (A39), take B3266 road signed Boscastle. The centre is at the 'Sportsmans' junction.
Details Newly designed 20 metre swimming pool as well as weights room and sports hall. All kinds of activities offered - contact the centre for details of the timetable.
Opening Hours Term time, Mon-Fri, 2.30pm-10.30pm, weekends, 9am-6pm. Holidays, Mon-Fri, 9am-11pm, weekends, 9am-6pm.

CARN BREA LEISURE CENTRE

Address & Tel. No Station Road, Pool. (01209) 714766
Directions Signed from the Redruth/Pool exit on the A30.
Details Cornwall's largest leisure centre with 3 swimming pools including a waterslide and parents and babies pool. Space Bowl and all weather athletics track. Double sized sports hall catering for all team games, badminton and squash etc. Health suite, restaurant and bar.
Opening Hours Phone to confirm as each activity differs.

THE CORNWALL INDOOR TENNIS & SPORTS CENTRE

Address & Tel. No Lostwithiel Road, Bodmin. (01208) 75715
Directions A30 to Bodmin. Follow signs towards Lostwithiel, the centre is 1.5 miles out of Bodmin.
Details Indoor and outdoor tennis as well as fitness studio, health suite (jacuzzi, sauna, steam room and solarium), as well as football, hockey, childrens soft play and trampolining. Licensed bar.
Opening Hours Weekdays, 10am-10.30pm. Weekends 10am-6pm.

HELSTON SPORTS CENTRE

Address & Tel. No Church Hill, Helston. TR13 8HR. (01326) 563320
Directions Follow the A3083 towards Redruth. Leave Helston on B3297 and follow signs to Helston Sports Centre.
Details Swimming pool, squash courts, fitness centre and outdoor tennis courts. Full sports hall facilities. Vending area.
Opening Hours Term time, Mon-Fri, 12-1.30 pm, 3.30pm-8.30pm (except Thurs evening). Holidays, Mon 11am-8.30pm, Tues-Fri 10.30am-8.30pm (except Thurs eve. when its 9.30pm in Aug.). Weekends, 10am-5.30pm.

JUBILEE BATHING POOL

Address & Tel. No Battery Rd, The Promenade, Penzance. (01736) 69224
Directions From Penzance Harbour follow signs towards Newlyn, the Pool is on the left after leaving the harbour area.
Details The largest surviving seaside lido in the country, holding a million gallons of clean treated seawater, the vast Grade II listed Art-Deco structure was built in 1935 to commemorate the Silver Jubilee of King George V. Suntrap terraces and unrivalled views over Mount's Bay. Children may use inflatables under lifeguard supervision. Light refreshments. Car park opposite.
Opening Hours End of May to early September, daily 11.00am-7.00pm (Last admissions 6.30pm).

LUX PARK LEISURE CENTRE

Address & Tel. No Coldstyle Road, Liskeard. PL14 3HZ. (01579) 342544
Directions Signed from central Liskeard with brown tourist signs.
Details Sports hall, bowls hall, squash courts, fitness and health suite, creche. Large restaurant, leisure pool and 40 metre flume.
Opening Hours All year, daily.

NEWQUAY WATERWORLD

Address & Tel. No Trenance Leisure Park, Newquay. (01637) 875982
Directions East Newquay, follow signs.
Details 25 metre pool, animal slide, 60 metre water flume and fun pool. Weight training room and aerobic studio with viewing gallery and cafe.
Opening Hours Summer, Mon/Wed/Thurs 10am-8pm, Tues/Fri 10am-10pm, weekends, 10am-5pm. Winter as per timetable.

POLKYTH LEISURE CENTRE

Address & Tel. No Carlyon Road, St. Austell. PL25 4DB. (01726) 61585
Directions Head for main roundabouts on outskirts of town, signed from all directions to leisure centre.
Details 25m x 11m main swimming pool with teaching pool, diving pool and hydrotherapy pool. Other activities include Badminton, Volleyball, Squash, Tennis and Basketball. Fitness suite and sauna, cafeteria and bar.
Opening Hours Mon to Fri, 9am-10pm. Weekends and public holidays, 9am-5pm.

SHIPS AND CASTLES LEISURE POOL

Address & Tel. No The Hornworks, Castle Drive, Pendennis Headland, Falmouth. (01326) 212129
Directions From Falmouth town centre, follow the signs for Castle Drive and Pendennis Castle.
Details Leisure pool with wave machine, 70 metre flume, fast flow river, fountains, geysers, bubble pools, jacuzzis, solariums and fitness suite/weight training facilities. Restaurant and creche.
Opening Hours Open all year, Mon to Fri, 8am-9.30pm, Sat, 8.30am-5pm, Sun, 9am-5pm.

WADEBRIDGE SPORTS CENTRE

Address & Tel. No Bodieve road, Wadebridge PL27 6BU (01208) 814980
Directions A39 to large roundabout. Follow signs into town, signed from 1st small roundabout.
Details 25m swimming pool and learner pool, solarium, weights room, glass back squash court, climbing wall and cafe.
Opening Hours Mon to Fri, 7am-10.30pm. Weekend, 9am-6pm.

FISHING

ARGAL AND COLLEGE RESERVIORS

Address & Tel. No Nr Penryn. (01326) 372544

Directions Follow brown tourist signs from A39 Truro/Falmouth road or A394 Helston - Falmouth road.

Details College Water is a coarse fishery including Pike, whilst Argal is a rainbow trout fishery. Permits available form the self service barn at Argal.

Opening Hours All year dawn to dusk. Fly fishing season open March to October.

BOSCATHNOE RESERVOIR

Address & Tel. No Nr. Penzance. (01837) 871565

Directions Follow A30 to Penzance, turning off for Madron on B3312. Turn left at school crossroads.

Details Coarse fishing. Permit availability on above number.

Opening Hours All year.

BUSSOW RESERVOIR

Address & Tel. No Nr. St. Ives. (01837) 871565

Directions Signed from B3311 south west of St. Ives.

Details Coarse fishery. Permit availability on above number.

Opening Hours All year.

COLLIFORD LAKE

Address & Tel. No Near Bolventor, Bodmin Moor. (01837) 871565

Directions Signposted from A30, west of Bolventor.

Details Just south of Jamaica Inn and close to Dozmary Pool, Colliford Lake offers a tranquil 900 acre area of water set in sweeping moorland. The lake offers traditional fly fishing for natural brown trout and has become Cornwall's premier brown trout fishery. Permit available from self service kiosk on site.

Opening Hours All year.

CRAFTHOLE RESERVOIR

Address & Tel. No Nr. Torpoint.

Directions Accessed via footpath entrance behind public house in Crafthole from the B3247.

Details Coarse fishery.

Opening Hours All year.

PORTH RESERVOIR

Address & Tel. No Nr. Newquay. (01837) 871565

Directions Signposted from A3059 on Newquay to St. Columb Major road.

Details Coarse fishery. Permits available from self service kiosk on site.

Opening Hours Open all year.

SIBLYBACK LAKE

Address & Tel. No St. Cleer, Liskeard. (01579) 346522

Directions Follow brown tourist signs from A38 at Liskeard and Bodmin.

Details Trout fishery with fishing permits available from self service kiosk on site.

Opening Hours 9.30am-5.30pm. (weekends only in winter).

STITHIANS LAKE

Address & Tel. No Nr. Redruth. (01209) 860301

Directions Take B3297 from A393 in Redruth. Turn left at Four Lanes towards Stithians. Entrance adjacent to the Golden Lion Pub.

Details Natural trout fishery (permits available from the watersports centre).

Opening Hours All year, 9.30am-5.30pm (weekends only in Winter). For waterski club, ring for details.

LOWER TAMAR LAKE

Address & Tel. No Nr. Kilkhampton, Bude. (01837) 871565

Directions Follow brown tourist signs from A39 at Kilkhampton.

Details The lake is an important area for over wintering wildfowl and has some relaxing walks along waymarked footpaths.

Opening Hours All year.

UPPER TAMAR LAKE

Address & Tel. No Nr. Kilkhampton, Bude. (01288) 321262

Directions Follow brown tourist signs from A39 at Kilkhampton.

Details Watersports centre including sailing, windsurfing and canoeing instruction. Game and coarse fishing. Permits available from self service kiosk on site. Walks in the area as well as childrens play area and gift shop/tea room.

Opening Hours April to Oct, 9.30am-5.30pm.

GOLF IN CORNWALL

All courses 18 holes unless otherwise stated.

BOWOOD GOLF CLUB
Address & Tel. No Bowood Park, Lanteglos, PL32 9RT. (01840) 213017
Directions Turn off the main A39 south of Camelford at the village of Valley Truckle.
Details Set in 230 acres of rolling hills and woodland. Practice area and driving range nets. Yardage: Men (6692), Ladies (5700). Par 72

BUDE AND NORTH CORNWALL GOLF CLUB
Address & Tel. No Burn View, Bude. EX23 8DA. (01288) 352006
Directions From A39, follow signs to Bude. Golf club at top of town on the one way system.
Details A seaside links course with practice areas and putting green. Clubhouse and restaurant.

CAPE CORNWALL GOLF AND COUNTRY CLUB
Address & Tel. No Cape Cornwall, St. Just, Penzance. TR19 7NL. (01736) 788611
Directions A30 to Penzance, follow signs to St. Just (7 miles), turn left in St. Just following golf club signs.
Details Headland course (first and last in Britain) of 5600 yds. (Par 70). Indoor heated swimming pool and refreshments.

CARLYON BAY HOTEL GOLF COURSE
Address & Tel. No Carlyon Bay, St. Austell, PL25 3RD. (01726) 814250
Directions Follow signs in St. Austell for Cornwall Coliseum. Golf course on left hand side.
Details Outward 9 holes adjoin cliff top, return holes via treelined parkland. Golf club membership required. Yardage: Men (6505), Ladies (5806). Par 72

CARVYNICK GOLF AND COUNTRY CLUB
Address & Tel. No Summercourt, Nr. Newquay. TR8 5AF. (01872) 510716
Directions From the A30, take exit for Summercourt and Carvynick is on the Newquay road approx. half a mile from the traffic lights.
Details 9 hole Par 3 course of 2492 yards. No handicap needed.

CHINA FLEET COUNTRY CLUB
Address & Tel. No Saltash, PL12 6LT. (01752) 848668
Directions Take New Rd from Saltash end of Tamar Bridge tunnel. Signed after a right turn near a pedestrian crossing.
Details Tranquil setting near the River Tamar. Handicap certificate required. Extensive leisure facilities including swimming pool, restaurant and bars. Yardage: Men (6551), Ladies (5160). Par 72

FALMOUTH GOLF CLUB
Address & Tel. No Swanpool Road, Falmouth. TR11 5BQ. (01326) 311262
Directions Quarter of a mile west of Swanpool Beach, Falmouth, on the road to Maenporth Beach.
Details 18 hole (5680 yards, Par 70) half downland, half woodland course with magnificent views over Falmouth Bay. Practice ground and putting greens. Refreshment facilities.

HELSTON GOLF AND LEISURE
Address & Tel. No Near Wendron, Helston, TR13 0LX. (01326) 572518
Directions 1 mile north of Helston on B3297 Redruth road.
Details 18 hole Short Golf course of 2000 yards (Par 3). Leisure and refreshment facilities.

HOLYWELL BAY GOLF CLUB
Address & Tel. No Holywell Bay, Newquay. TR8 5PW. (01637) 830095
Directions From Newquay take A3075 towards Perranporth. Turn right to Cubert/Holywell. Through Cubert village, 1 mile on right hand side adjacent to Holywell Bay Leisure Park.
Details Par 3 links course with excellent coastal views. No handicap/membership required. 18 hole pitch and putt. Golf club house and licensed bar.

KILLIOW PARK GOLF CLUB
Address & Tel. No Killiow, Kea, Truro, TR3 6AG. (01872) 261055
Directions Signed from A39 Truro-Falmouth rd at Playing Place.
Details Parkland course near Truro. Floodlit driving range, bar. Yardage: Men (3829), Ladies (3739). Par 62

LANHYDROCK GOLF CLUB
Address & Tel. No Lostwithiel Road, Bodmin. (01208) 73600
Directions 1 mile south of Bodmin on the B3268 via A30/A38.
Details Parkland course of 6412 yards (71 Par), in mature setting.

LAUNCESTON GOLF CLUB
Address & Tel. No St. Stephens, Launceston, PL15 8HF. (01566) 773442
Directions 1 mile from Launceston on B3254 at St. Stephens.
Details Parkland course, handicap certificate required. Yardage: Men (6407), Ladies (5739). Par 70

LOOE GOLF CLUB
Address & Tel. No Bin Down, Looe. PL13 1PX. (01503) 240239
Directions By the village of Bin Down on B3253, off the A387.
Details Downland/parkland course of 5,940 yards (Par 70) with superb views, designed by Harry Vardon. Refreshment facilities.

LOSTWITHIEL GOLF AND COUNTRY CLUB
Address & Tel. No Lower Polscoe, Lostwithiel. PL22 0HQ. (01208) 873822
Directions Off A390 between Liskeard and Lostwithiel.
Details 18 hole undulating parkland course. Floodlit undercover driving range and sports facilities. Handicap required (men 28, ladies 36). Yardage: Men (5882), Ladies (5517). Par 72.

MERLIN GOLF CLUB AND DRIVING RANGE
Address & Tel. No Mawgan Porth, Newquay. TR8 4AD. (01814) 540222
Directions Located on the Mawgan Porth to St. Eval road north of Newquay.
Details 9 hole (Par 32) hilltop and valley course with easy walking and seaviews across Mawgan Porth. Driving range.

MULLION GOLF CLUB
Address & Tel. No Cury, Helston. TR12 7BP. (01326) 240685
Directions Leave Helston on the A3083 past Culdrose Naval Air Station. Right turn signed 3 miles.
Details Cliff top links of 6022 yards (Par 69). Handicap certificate required. Restaurant and refreshments.

NEWQUAY GOLF CLUB
Address & Tel. No Tower Road, Newquay. TR7 1LT. (01637) 874354
Directions 800 yards from Newquay town Centre.

Details	6,140 yards links type course. Tennis and restaurant also available.

PENWITH PITCH AND PUTT

Address & Tel. No	Chenhalls Road, St. Erth, Hayle. (01736) 754343
Directions	On the B3302 Hayle-Helston road.
Details	18 hole course with clubs and balls supplied. 18 hole putting green as well as a children's play area, tea garden, pool table, storm shelters and golf shop.

PERRANPORTH GOLF CLUB

Address & Tel. No	Budnic Hill, Perranporth. TR6 0AB. (01872) 572317
Directions	On B3285, off A3075 at Perranporth.
Details	Links course designed by James Braid overlooking Perran Bay. Handicap certificates required at weekends only. Restaurant and refreshments.

PORTHPEAN GOLF CLUB

Address & Tel. No	Porthpean, St. Austell, PL26 6AY. (01726) 64613
Directions	Follow signs for Porthpean from A390 in St. Austell.
Details	9 hole course with views over St. Austell Bay (extending to 18 holes in future). Floodlit driving range and licensed clubhouse. Yardage: Men (3266), Ladies (3011). Par 36

PRAA SANDS GOLF

Address & Tel. No	Praa Sands Golf Club, Germoe Cross Roads, Penzance. TR20 9TQ. (01736) 763445
Directions	Situated on main A394 Helston to Penzance road.
Details	9 x 2 hole Par 62 (4104 yds.) undulating course with sea views. Refreshment facilities.

RADNOR GOLF CLUB

Address & Tel. No	Radnor Road, Redruth. (01209) 211059
Directions	Signed on old Redruth by-pass (A3047) at Treleigh and the crossroads at North Country.
Details	Covered, floodlit driving range with 9 hole Par 3 golf course with various hazards. Indoor ski training (booked in advance). Bar, snooker.

ST. AUSTELL GOLF CLUB

Address & Tel. No	Tregongeeves, St. Austell. PL26 7DS. (01726) 74756
Directions	1 mile west of St. Austell on A390 St. Austell-Truro rd.
Details	Parkland course of 6089 yards. Handicap certificates required.

ST. ENODOC GOLF CLUB

Address & Tel. No	Rock, Wadebridge. PL27 6LB. (01208) 862402
Directions	From Wadebridge take route signed to Rock. Proceed through village until you see the River Camel on your left, golf club is on the right.
Details	Championship course (handicap certificate required) of 6243 yards (men) and 5683 yards (ladies), Par 69. Holywell course of 4134 yards (men) and 4074 yards (ladies), Par 63. Views of Camel Estuary throughout.

ST. ERTH GOLF DRIVING RANGE

Address & Tel. No	Chenhalls Road, St. Erth, Near Hayle. TR27 6HJ (01736) 757600
Directions	From southern end of the A30 Hayle by-pass, turn off to Hayle. In half a mile turn right to St. Erth, golf range a further half a mile on the left.
Details	Covered bays, outdoor bays, grass lies, bunkers and putting etc. Light refreshments and childrens play area. Opposite 18 hole short course.

ST. KEW GOLF CLUB

Address & Tel. No	St. Kew Highway, Bodmin, PL30 3EF. (01208) 841500
Directions	Just off the main A39, 2 miles from Wadebridge towards Camelford.
Details	Parkland 9 hole course with 18 separate tees. Views to Camel Estuary. Clubhouse and covered driving range. Yardage: Men (4543), Ladies (4333). Par 64

ST. MELLION GOLF AND COUNTRY CLUB

Address & Tel. No	Saltash. PL12 6SD. (01579) 50101/51182
Directions	From A38 at Carkeel, turn right on the A388 Saltash to Callington road. St. Mellion is approximately 4 miles from the Carkeel roundabout.
Details	Two 18 hole parkland/downland golf courses including championship designed Jack Nicklaus Course. Handicap certificate required. Restaurants, bars and sports facilities.

SAFFRON PARK GOLF DRIVING RANGE

Address & Tel. No	Saffron Park, Padstow Road, Roche, St. Austell. PL26 8NL. (01726) 890007
Directions	On the B3274 just off the A30 at cross roads to Padstow/Roche.
Details	8 bay undercover floodlit driving range and bunker practice.

TEHIDY PARK GOLF CLUB

Address & Tel. No	Camborne. TR14 0HH. (01209) 842914
Directions	From A30 Redruth-Camborne by-pass, follow signs to Portreath. Golf club signed.
Details	Parkland course of 6241 yards (Par72). Handicap certificate required. Bar and refreshments.

TORPOINT GOLF CENTRE

Address & Tel. No	Trevol Business Park, Torpoint. PL11 2TB. (01752) 816616
Directions	Brown tourist signs from A374.
Details	20 bay, all weather floodlit golf driving range, sand bunker playing to the range and a 9 hole putting green. Refreshment facilities.

TRETHORNE GOLF CLUB

Address & Tel. No	Kennards Hse, Launceston, PL15 8QE. (01566) 86324
Directions	Follow signs for Trethorne Leisure Park from the Kennards House junction on the A30.
Details	Parkland 9 hole course. Yardage: Men (3169), Ladies (2725). Par 72

WHITSAND BAY HOTEL GOLF AND COUNTRY CLUB

Address & Tel. No	Portwrinkle, Torpoint, PL11 3BU. (01503) 230276
Directions	Just off the A374 between Trerulefoot roundabout and Torpoint.
Details	Cliff top golf course with fine sea views. Yardage: Men (5898), Ladies (5698). Par 69

China Fleet Country Club.

RIDING IN CORNWALL

The following riding establishments have been issued with a license and approved by the individual District Councils:

PENWITH *Penzance and the far west of Cornwall*

OLD MILL STABLES	Lelant Downs, Hayle. (01736) 753045
PENHALWYN TREKKING CENTRE	Halsetown. (01736) 796461
TREGURTHA DOWNS	Marazion. (01736) 711422

KERRIER *Camborne/Redruth, Falmouth and the Lizard Peninsula*

STRAWBERRY GARDENS RIDING STABLES	Reskadinnick, Camborne. (01209) 713661
WHEAL BULLER RIDING SCHOOL	Redruth. (01209) 211852
TRANNACK FARM HOUSE RIDING SCHOOL	Sithney, Helston. (01326) 561281
NANFAN FARM	Cury, Helston. (01326) 240413
BOSVATHICK FARM	Constantine, Falmouth. (01326) 340367

CARRICK *Truro, St. Agnes, Perranporth and Roseland Peninsula*

TREVORNICK FARM STABLES	Cubert, Nr. Newquay. (01637) 830531
CHIVERTON RIDING STABLES	Silverwell, Truro. (01872) 560471
THE MANOR RIDING CENTRE	Veryan, Truro. (01872) 501574
FOXHOLE FARM RIDING STABLES	Chacewater, Truro. (01209) 820162
TRENISSICK STABLES	Cubert, Newquay. (01637) 830413
GOONBELL RIDING STABLES	St. Agnes. (01872) 552063
POLGODA RIDING SCHOOL	Goonhavern. (01637) 873586 *evenings only*
REEN MANOR RIDING STABLES	Reen, Perranporth. (01872) 573064
PERRAN SANDS TREKKING CENTRE	Perranporth. (01872) 573884

RESTORMEL *Newquay, St. Austell*

BLACKACRE RIDING STABLES	Blackacre, St. Columb. (01637) 880628
TRILL FARM	Par, St. Austell. (01726) 812071
BOSKELL RIDING CENTRE	Trethowel, St. Austell. (01726) 73049
TREMBLEATH FARM	St. Columb Major.
POWDERHAM RIDING CENTRE	Lanlivery. (01208) 872277
KILLIEWORGIE RIDING CENTRE	Blackcross, Newquay. (01637) 880570
TRENANCE STABLES	Trenance Lane, Newquay. (01637) 872699

NORTH CORNWALL *Bude, Camelford, Boscastle & Tintagel*

ST. LEONARDS EQUITATION CENTRE	Polson, Launceston. (01566) 775543
DENBY STABLES	Nanstallon, Bodmin. (01208) 72013
TREDOLE FARM	Trevalga, Boscastle. (01840) 250495
MAER LANE STABLES	Bude. (01288) 354141
TREVILLET PARC FARM	Trevillet, Tintagel. (01840) 770662
DUCHY HOME FARM	Stoke Climsland, Callington.
EFFORD FARM	Bude.
NINE TORS RIDING CENTRE	Launceston.
MIDDLE BARTON	Cardinham, Bodmin.
TRESALLYN FARM	St. Merryn, Padstow.
GOOSEHAM BARTON	Morwenstow, Bude. (01288) 331204
LAKEFIELD CARAVAN PARK	Lower Pendavey, Camelford. (01840) 213279
RICK PARK FARM	Kilkhampton, Bude.
THE PADDOCK	Edmonton, Wadebridge. (01208) 812832
ELM PARK EQUESTRIAN CENTRE	Boyton, Launceston. (01566) 785353
TIMBERDOWN RIDING CENTRE	Lidwell, Callington. (01579) 370577
ST. BREOCK DOWNS FARM STABLES	St. Breock, Wadebridge.
BENBOLE FARM	St. Kew Highway, Bodmin. (01208) 841281
HALLAGENA FARM	St. Breward, Bodmin. (01208) 850439
TALL TREES RIDING CENTRE	Davidstow, Nr. Camelford. (01840) 261249
WOODA CARAVAN PARK	Poughill, Bude. (01288) 352069

CARADON *South east Cornwall including Looe and Polperro*

LITTLE HADLEY	St. Veep, Lostwithiel. (01208) 873521
GOOSEFORD FARM	St. Mellion, Saltash.
VENTON VANES RIDING CENTRE	Morval, Looe. (01503) 240325
LOWER TOKENBURY	Upton Cross, Liskeard.
TM INTERNATIONAL SCHOOL OF HORSEMANSHIP	Liskeard. (01579) 62895
LANSALLOS BARTON	Lansallos, Looe.
TREWORGY COTTAGES	Duloe.

OPINION PAGE

Cornwall Explored will only remain Cornwall's best selling guide by continuing to improve and listening to its customers. For this reason, I would really appreciate you spending a few minutes to give your views on Cornwall Explored. All replies will receive an exclusive Cornwall Explored car sticker (only available direct from the publishers) as well as automatic entry to our free draw. First prize is £100 with 10 runner up prizes of delicious Cornish Clotted Cream, direct by post. Thank you for your help,
Mark Norton,
Director, Norton Publishing Limited.

Exclusive CORNWALL EXPLORED CAR STICKER FREE!

1 *Did you purchase Cornwall Explored:*   In Cornwall ☐   Outside Cornwall ☐   By Post ☐

2 *If purchased in Cornwall, were you aware of Cornwall Explored as a result of:*

Saw it in a newsagent, bookshop, attraction or similar outlet ☐   Radio advertising ☐
Saw it in a place of holiday accommodation ☐   Leaflet advertising ☐
Friends/relatives recommendation ☐   Other reason (please state) ....

3 *Overall view of Cornwall Explored:* Excellent ☐ Good ☐ Satisfactory ☐ Poor ☐ Very Poor ☐

4 *How would you rate the following aspects of Cornwall Explored:*

	Excellent	Good	Satisfactory	Poor	Very Poor
Value for money	☐	☐	☐	☐	☐
Breadth of subjects covered	☐	☐	☐	☐	☐
Detail of subjects covered	☐	☐	☐	☐	☐
Overall design	☐	☐	☐	☐	☐
Photographs	☐	☐	☐	☐	☐
Detail of directions	☐	☐	☐	☐	☐
Maps	☐	☐	☐	☐	☐

Sections:

	Excellent	Good	Satisfactory	Poor	Very Poor
Gazetteer	☐	☐	☐	☐	☐
Cornish Life	☐	☐	☐	☐	☐
Beaches	☐	☐	☐	☐	☐
Pubs	☐	☐	☐	☐	☐
Walking Areas & Viewpoints	☐	☐	☐	☐	☐
It's Free!	☐	☐	☐	☐	☐
Attractions	☐	☐	☐	☐	☐

5 *Any other general comments on Cornwall Explored* (likes/dislikes etc)
....

6 *Have you used any of the discount vouchers:* ATTRACTIONS: Yes ☐ No ☐   PUBS: Yes ☐ No ☐

IF A VISITOR TO CORNWALL:

7 *How many times have you been to Cornwall before?* Never ☐   1-5 ☐   6+ ☐

8 *Was your visit:* Main holiday ☐   Second holiday ☐   Weekend Break ☐   Visiting friends/relatives ☐

9 *Month(s) of visit* ....
Main resort of residence ....

10 *Will you be coming to Cornwall next year?*   Yes ☐   No ☐   Hopefully ☐   Unlikely ☐

11 *Most favourite thing about Cornwall*...
Least favourite thing about Cornwall...

Name ....
Address ....
....Postcode...................................

Please send completed opinion page to **Norton Publishing Limited, PO Box 12, Perranporth, Cornwall, TR6 0YE.**
A draw will be made on December 1st each year with winners by post.
The judge's decision is final and no correspondence will be entered into.

GAZETTEER

Altarnun . . . 6
Blisland . . . 6
Bodmin . . . 6
Bodmin Moor . . . 6
Boscastle . . . 6
Botallack . . . 7
Breage . . . 7
Bude . . . 7
Cadgwith . . . 7
Callington . . . 7
Calstock . . . 8
Camborne . . . 8
Camelford . . . 8
Cape Cornwall . . . 8
Cardinham . . . 9
Cawsand . . . 9
Kingsand . . . 9
Charlestown . . . 9
Coverack . . . 9
Crackington Haven . . . 9
Crantock . . . 9
Delabole . . . 10
Devoran . . . 10
Duloe . . . 10
Falmouth . . . 10
Flushing . . . 10
Fowey . . . 10
Gerrans Bay . . . 11
Godrevy . . . 11
Golant . . . 11
Grampound . . . 11
Gunnislake . . . 12
Gunwalloe . . . 12
Gweek . . . 12
Gwennap . . . 12
Hayle . . . 12
Helford . . . 12
Helston . . . 13
Kilkhampton . . . 13
Kynance Cove . . . 13
Lamorna . . . 13
Land's End . . . 14
Lanlivery . . . 14
Launceston . . . 14
Lelant . . . 14
Lerryn . . . 14
Liskeard . . . 14
Lizard . . . 14
Looe . . . 15
Lostwithiel . . . 15
Madron . . . 15
Marazion . . . 15
Mevagissey . . . 15
Minions . . . 16
Morwenstow . . . 16
Mousehole . . . 16
Mullion . . . 16
Mylor . . . 16
Newlyn . . . 17
Newquay . . . 17
Padstow . . . 17
Par . . . 18
Pendeen . . . 18
Penryn . . . 18
Pentewan . . . 18
Penzance . . . 18
Perranporth . . . 19
Polperro . . . 19
Polzeath . . . 19
Porthcurno . . . 19
Porthleven . . . 19
Port Isaac . . . 20
Portloe . . . 20
Portreath . . . 20
Probus . . . 20
Prussia Cove . . . 20
Redruth . . . 20
Roche . . . 21
Saltash . . . 21
Sennen . . . 21
St Agnes . . . 21
St Austell . . . 22
St Buryan . . . 22
St Cleer . . . 22
St Clement . . . 22
St Columb Major . . . 22
St Ewe . . . 23
St Germans . . . 23
St Ives . . . 23
St Just-in-Penwith . . . 23
St Just-in-Roseland . . . 23
St Keverne . . . 24
St Mawes . . . 24
St Neot . . . 24
Tintagel . . . 24
Tregony . . . 24
Tresillian . . . 24
Truro . . . 25
Veryan . . . 25
Wadebridge . . . 25
Zennor . . . 25

BEACHES

Bossiney Cove . . . 31
Cadgwith . . . 42
Carbis Bay . . . 38
Carlyon Bay . . . 46
Carne . . . 44
Castle . . . 43
Cawsand . . . 49
Chapel Porth . . . 36
Constantine Bay . . . 32
Coverack . . . 42
Crackington Haven . . . 30
Crantock . . . 35
Crooklets . . . 30
Daymer Bay . . . 32
Downderry . . . 48
Duckpool . . . 30
East Looe . . . 48
Fistral . . . 34
Godrevy . . . 36
Gorran Haven . . . 45
Great Western . . . 34
Gunwalloe Church Cove . . . 41
Gwithian Towans . . . 37
Gyllyngvase . . . 43
Hannafore . . . 48
Harbour Cove, Padstow . . . 32
Harbour, Newquay . . . 34
Harbour, St Ives . . . 38
Harlyn Bay . . . 32
Hayle Towans . . . 37
Hemmick . . . 45
Holywell Bay . . . 36
Kennack Sands . . . 42
Kenneggy Sands . . . 40
Kingsand . . . 49
Kynance Cove . . . 42
Lamorna . . . 39
Lansallos . . . 47
Lantic Bay . . . 46
Long Rock . . . 40
Lusty Glaze . . . 34
Maenporth . . . 42
Marazion . . . 40
Mawgan Porth . . . 33
Millendreath . . . 48
Mullion Cove . . . 42
Newlyn . . . 40
Northcott Mouth . . . 30
Par Sands . . . 46
Pendower . . . 44
Pentewan . . . 46
Penzance . . . 40
Perranporth . . . 36
Perranuthnoe . . . 40
Poldhu Cove . . . 41
Polkerris . . . 46
Polridmouth Cove . . . 46
Polurrian Cove . . . 41
Polzeath . . . 32
Portgaverne . . . 31
Porth . . . 34
Porth (Polly) Joke . . . 35
Porthallow . . . 42
Porthchapel . . . 38
Porthcothan Bay . . . 33
Porthcurnick . . . 44
Porthcurno . . . 39
Portheras Cove . . . 38
Porthgwarra . . . 38
Porthgwidden . . . 38
Porthleven . . . 40
Porthluney . . . 44
Porthmeor . . . 38
Porthminster . . . 38
Portholland . . . 44
Porthoustock . . . 42
Porthpean . . . 46
Porthtowan . . . 36
Portreath . . . 36
Portwrinkle . . . 48
Praa Sands . . . 40
Prussia Cove . . . 40
Readymoney Cove . . . 46
Rock . . . 32
Sandy Mouth . . . 30
Seaton . . . 48
St Georges Well . . . 32
St Mawes . . . 44
Summerleaze . . . 30
Swanpool . . . 43
Talland Bay . . . 47
Tolcarne . . . 34
Towan, Newquay . . . 34
Towan, Roseland . . . 44
Trebarwith Strand . . . 31
Trevaunance Cove . . . 36
Trevone Bay . . . 32
Treyarnon Bay . . . 33
Vault . . . 45
Watergate Bay . . . 34
Whitesand Bay . . . 38
Whitsand Bay . . . 48
Widemouth Sand . . . 30

WALKING AREAS & VIEWPOINTS

Map . . . 58

Argal/College Reservoirs . . . 69
Bedruthan Steps . . . 76
Black Head . . . 75
Boscastle . . . 81
Brea Hill . . . 77
Bude Canal . . . 82
Camel Trail . . . 77
Cape Cornwall . . . 59
Cardinham Woods . . . 79
Carn Brea . . . 69
Chapel Carn Brea . . . 60
Chapel Porth . . . 69
Cligga Head . . . 72
Compass Point . . . 83
Coombe Valley . . . 83
Coverack . . . 67
Crackington Haven . . . 81
Cudden Point . . . 63
Daymer Bay . . . 77
Deerpark Wood . . . 80
Dodman Point . . . 75
Fowey . . . 78
Frenchman's Creek . . . 68
Godrevy Point . . . 63
Golitha Falls . . . 80
Gribbin Head . . . 77
Gunwalloe Church Cove . . . 65
Hall Walk . . . 78
Helford . . . 68
Holywell . . . 73
Idless Woods . . . 72
Jericho Valley . . . 70
Kelsey Head . . . 73
Killigerran Head . . . 72
Kilminorth Woods . . . 79
Kit Hill . . . 82
Kynance Cove . . . 66
Lamorna Cove . . . 61
Land's End . . . 59
Landewednack . . . 67
Lerryn . . . 78
Lizard Point . . . 66
Loe Pool . . . 65
Logan Rock . . . 60
Looe . . . 79
Marconi Monument . . . 65
Mawnan Church . . . 68
Morwenstow . . . 83
Mullion Cove . . . 66
Nare Head . . . 74
Newquay . . . 74
Park Head . . . 76
Pedn-men-an-mere . . . 59
Pencarrow Head . . . 78
Pentire Point . . . 76
Pentire Point East . . . 74
Pentire Point West . . . 73

Penzance Promenade 61
Perranporth 72
Poldhu Cove 65
Polperro 79
Portloe 75
Prussia Cove 63
Ralph's Cupboard 64
Rame Head 82
Reskajeage Downs 64
Rinsey Head 63
Rocky Valley 80
Rosemullion Head 68
Rumps 76
Sancreed Beacon 60
Sennen 59
St Agnes Beacon. 70
St Anthony Head 71
St Ives 62
St Mawes 71
St Michaels Mount 61
St Piran's Oratory 73
Tehidy Woods 64
Towan Head 74
Treen 60
Trefusis Point 70
Trelissick 71
Trelowarren 67
Trencrom Hill 62
Trevose Head 76
Valency Valley. 81
Zennor Head 61

IT'S FREE!

Map 90
Bedruthan Steps. 97
Bodmin Museum 98
Bonsai Nursery. 97
Boscastle Visitors Centre 100
Candle Shop. 98
Carn Euny. 91
Castle Drive and Pendennis Head . . 95
Castle-an-Dinas. 97
Cheesewring. 100
Church of St Nonna 101
Cornish Gold Centre 93
Coronation Boating Lake 93
Crowns Engine House 91
CSM Geological Museum 93
Devil's Frying Pan. 94
Drift Reservoir 91
Duloe Stone Circle. 99
Dupath Holy Well. 101
Falmouth Art Gallery 95
Gwennap Pit. 93
Halliggye Fougou 94
Hawker's Hut 101
Hell's Mouth. 92
Helston Folk Museum 93
Huer's Hut 96
Hurlers Stone Circles 100
Images Of Cornwall 96
John Betjeman Centre 98
Kennack Pottery. 94
Kernewek Pottery Factory Shop . . 96
Kernow Mill 100
King Doniert's Stones 99

Lakeside Gallery. 101
Lamorna Pottery. 92
Lanyon Quoit 91
Lawrence House Museum 101
Leach Studio Pottery 92
Lizard Lighthouse. 94
Men Scryfa 91
Men-an-Tol 91
Merry Maidens 92
Mid Cornwall Galleries 97
Mineral Tramways Discovery Centre 92
Minions Heritage Centre 100
Mount Edgcumbe Country Park . . 101
Newlyn Art Gallery. 92
Newquay Pearl 97
Old Forge 100
Pendeen Gem &
Jewellery Workshop. 91
Perranzabuloe Folk Museum 96
Presingoll Barns 95
RNAS Culdrose Viewing Area 94
Roche Rock 97
Screech Owl Sanctuary 97
South East Cornwall
Discovery Centre 99
St Agnes Museum. 95
St Breock Gallery 98
St Catherines Castle 98
St Cleer Well. 99
St Enodoc Church 98
St Juliot's Church 101
St Just-in-Roseland Church 95
St Neot Pottery. 99
St Petroc's Church 98
St Senara Church 92
Tamar Glass 101
Tescan Sheepskin. 93
Trenance Boating Lake 96
Trethevy Quoit. 99
Trevaunance Cove Craft Workshops 96
Truro Cathedral 95

ATTRACTIONS

Map. 111

Antony House 133
ATV Motorsport Centre 117
Automobilia 122
Barbara Hepworth Museum 115
Ben's Playworld 122
Bodmin and Wenford Railway 128
Bodmin Jail. 128
British Cycling Museum 127
British International 114
Bude-Stratton Museum 135
Callestock Cider Farm 120
Camborne Karting 117
Camel Valley Wine 128
Carnglaze Slate Caverns 131
Charlestown Shipwreck
and Heritage Centre. 123
Chysauster 113
Cold Northcott Wind Farm 134
Cornish Engines 117
Cornish Gliding and Flying Club . . 117
Cornwall Coliseum 122
Cornwall Donkey &
Pony Sanctuary. 127

Cornwall Karting 125
Cotehele. 132
Country Skittles 116
Crypt 116
Crystal Cave 135
Dairyland 125
Delabole Slate Quarry 127
Delabole Wind Farm 127
Dobwalls Family Adventure Park . . 131
Duke of Cornwall's
Light Infantry Museum. 128
Enterprise Boats. 120
Falmouth Ferry/Cruise Services. . . 119
Falmouth Maritime Museum 119
Falmouth Pitch and Putt 119
Fernleys 129
Flambards. 118
Fowey River Steamers 130
Fun Factory 124
Geevor Tin Mine 112
Glendurgan Garden 118
Godolphin House 116
Goonhilly Earth Satellite Station . . 118
Helston Golf & Leisure 118
Holywell Bay Fun Park. 124
I-Spy Glass Bottom Boat 130
Isles of Scilly Steamship Co 114
Jeepers Karts 116
Kid's Kingdom 122
King Arthur's Great Halls 135
Land of Legend and Model Village. 130
Land's End 112
Land's End Aerodrome 112
Lanhydrock. 129
Lanreath Folk and Farm Museum . 131
Lappa Valley Steam Railway. 125
Launceston Castle 134
Launceston Steam Railway 134
Levant Beam Engine 113
Long Cross Victorian Gardens 127
Looe Valley Line 131
Lost Gardens of Heligan. 123
Lynher Valley Dairy 132
Magnificent Music Machines 131
Mary Newman's Cottage 133
Mellingey Mill Willow Craft Centre 126
Mevagissey Harbour Aquarium . . . 123
Mevagissey Museum 123
Minack Theatre 112
Monkey Sanctuary 130
Moorland Flying Club 134
Mount Edgcumbe House 133
National Seal Sanctuary 118
Newquay Animal World 124
Newquay Sea Life Centre 124
North Cornwall Museum & Gallery 127
Old Guildhall Museum 130
Ozzell Bowl 122
Padstow Shipwreck Museum 126
Paradise Park. 116
Pencarrow 129
Pendeen Lighthouse 113
Pendennis Castle 119
Penjerrick Gardens 119
Penlee House Art Gallery
& Museum 114
Pilchard Works 113
Pixieland Fun Park 135

Poldark Mine 118
Polmassick Vineyard 123
Polperro Heritage Museum 130
Porfell Animal Land 131
Porteath Bee Centre 126
Porthcurno Museum 112
Potters Museum of Curiosity 129
Prideaux Place 126
Princess Pavilion 119
Probus Gardens 121
Quad & Kart Centre 132
Restormel Castle 128
Rowe Bowl 117
Royal Cornwall Museum. 120
Shires Adventure Park 126
Siblyback Lake 129
Spirit of the West 125
Springfields Pony Centre
and Fun Park 125
St Agnes Leisure Park. 117
St Austell Brewery Visitor Centre. . 122
St Ives Aquasports 115
St Ives Museum 115
St Mawes Castle 121
St Michael's Mount 114
Sterts Arts & Environmental Centre 132
Stithians Lake 116
Tamar Canoe Expedition 133
Tamar Cruising 133
Tamar Otter Sanctuary. 134
Tamar Valley Donkey Park 132
Tate Gallery 115
Tintagel Castle 135
Tintagel Old Post Office 135
Trebah Garden 119
Tredidon Trails. 134
Trelissick Garden 121
Trenance Heritage Cottages. 124
Trengwainton 115
Trenouth Farm Rare Breeds Centre 126
Trerice 125
Trethorne Leisure Farm. 134
Trewithen Gardens 121
Trinity House Lighthouse Centre 114
Truro Bowl. 120
Tunnels Through Time 124
Upper Tamar lake 135
Veryan Vineyard 121
Wayside Folk Museum 113
Wheal Martyn China
Clay Heritage Centre 122
World in Miniature 120
World of Model Railways 123

CORNISH LIFE

A Director's Paradise 106,107
Ancient Cornwall*. 88
Classic Cornish Fishing Villages . . . 89
Cornish Engine Houses. 104,105
Cornish Lifeboat Stations 86
Cornwall Air Ambulance 87
Literary Cornwall 102,103
National Trust In Cornwall 50,51
Powerhouse Hayle 54
Sardina Pilchardus 27
Tate St Ives 28,29

144